THE MOSAICS READER

KIM FLACHMANN
California State University, Bakersfield

Prentice Hall
Boston   Columbus   Indianapolis   New York   San Francisco   Upper Saddle River
Amsterdam   Cape Town   Dubai   London   Madrid   Milan   Munich   Paris   Montréal   Toronto
Delhi   Mexico City   São Paulo   Sydney   Hong Kong   Seoul   Singapore   Taipei   Tokyo

Senior Acquisitions Editor: *Matthew Wright*
Editorial Assistant: *Samantha Neary*
Managing Editor: *Linda Mihatov Behrens*
Associate Managing Editor: *Bayani Mendoza de Leon*
Manufacturing Buyer: *Mary Ann Gloriande*
Marketing Director: *Megan Galvin*
Marketing Manager: *Tom DeMarco*
Media Editor: *Stefanie Liebman*

Senior Supplements Editor: *Donna Campion*
Art Director: *Anne Bonanno Nieglos*
Image Permission Coordinator: *Lee Scher*
Text Permission Specialist: *Wesley Hall*
Project Coordination, Text Design, and Electronic Page Makeup: *Integra*
Cover Designer: *Ximena Tamvakopoulos*
Cover Image: *mihau/iStockphoto*

Library of Congress Cataloging-in-Publication Data

Flachmann, Kim.
  The Mosaics reader / Kim Flachmann.—1st ed.
    p. cm.
  Includes bibliographical references and index.
  ISBN 978-0-205-82302-4 (alk. paper)
  1. College readers.   2. English language—Rhetoric—Problems, exercises, etc.
  3. Report writing—Problems, exercises, etc.   4. Critical thinking—Problems, exercises, etc.   I. Title.
  PE1417.F495 2011
  808'.0427—dc22

                         2010047321

1 2 3 4 5 6 7 8 9 10—CRS—14 13 12 11

Prentice Hall
is an imprint of

www.pearsonhighered.com

ISBN-13: 978-0-205-82302-4
ISBN-10:   0-205-82302-5

CONTENTS

PREFACE

Experience tells us that students have the best chance of succeeding in college if they learn how to respond productively to the varying academic demands made on them throughout the curriculum. One extremely important part of this process is being able to analyze ideas and think critically about issues in many different subjects. *The Mosaics Reader* is the fourth in a series of four books that focus on critical reading and writing. It presents all the readings from the series in one book so you can focus on them exclusively or pair them with another book of your choice. Printed here with the same apparatus as in their original *Mosaics* books, they move the students from literal to analytical thinking, reading, and writing.

OVERALL GOAL

Ultimately, each book in the *Mosaics* series portrays writing as a way of thinking and processing information. One by one, these books encourage students to discover how the "mosaics" of their own reading and writing processes work together to form a coherent whole. By demonstrating the interrelationship among thinking, reading, and writing on progressively more difficult levels, these books promise to help prepare students for success in college throughout the curriculum.

THE *MOSAICS* SERIES

Each of the three original books of the *Mosaics* series has a different emphasis: *Reading and Writing Sentences, Reading and Writing Paragraphs,* and *Reading and Writing Essays.* As the titles imply, the first book highlights sentence structure and grammar, the second paragraph development, and the third the composition of essays. The fourth book, *The Mosaics Reader,* includes all the reading selections from *Mosaics: Reading and Writing Paragraphs* and *Mosaics: Reading and Writing Essays* in one publication.

This entire series is based on the following fundamental assumptions:

- Students build confidence in their ability to read and write by reading and writing.
- Students learn best from discovery and experimentation rather than from instruction and abstract discussions.
- Students profit from studying both professional and student writing.
- Students need to discover their personal reading and writing processes.
- Students learn both individually and collaboratively.
- Students benefit most from assignments that actually integrate reading and writing.
- Students learn how to revise by following clear guidelines.
- Students learn grammar and usage rules by editing their own writing.
- Students must be able to transfer their writing skills to all their college courses.
- Students must think critically/analytically to succeed in college.

UNIQUE FEATURES OF THIS BOOK

Several other unique and exciting features define this book.

It teaches and demonstrates the reading-writing connection:

- It introduces and demonstrates reading as a process.
- It integrates reading and writing throughout the text.
- It examines rhetorical modes as patterns of thought.
- It features culturally diverse reading selections that are of high interest to students.
- It moves students systematically from personal to academic writing.
- It helps students discover their own reading and writing processes.

This book teaches a different reading strategy in every chapter:

<u>Chapter</u>	<u>Strategy</u>
Description	Making Personal Associations
Narration	Thinking Aloud
Illustration	Chunking
Process Analysis	Graphing the Ideas
Comparison/Contrast	Peer Teaching

- Division/Classification
- Definition
- Cause/Effect
- Argument

Summarizing
Reacting Critically
Making Connections
Recognizing Facts and Opinions
Reading with the Author/
Against the Author

The series provides three comprehensive Instructor's Resource Manuals:

Especially designed by the author, the IRMs for the first three books in the series provide explanations of key rhetorical theories; ideas for the first day of class; sample syllabi; additional practices, activities, quizzes, and teaching tips for each chapter; grading rubrics for each rhetorical mode; and a list of sources for further reading. These manuals also feature detailed information on how instructors can fully integrate MyWritingLab into their curriculum.

HOW THIS BOOK WORKS

The Mosaics Reader teaches students how to read and write critically through three coordinated elements in this book:

Introduction: Reading Critically introduces the reading process and explains the reading strategies featured in each chapter.

The Reader moves from personal to more academic writing, offering four professional essays for each of the following rhetorical modes—describing, narrating, illustrating, analyzing a process, comparing and contrasting, dividing and classifying, defining, analyzing causes and effects—and six for arguing. Within each chapter, students learn how to read an essay by practicing a different reading strategy. The professional writing samples in each chapter let students actually see the features of an essay at work in different reading selections. Each professional essay is preceded by prereading activities and then followed by 10 questions that move students from literal to analytical understanding as they consider the essay's content, purpose, audience, and structure. A Writing Workshop, offering 10 writing prompts as well as guidelines for revising and editing, concludes each chapter.

The appendixes will help students keep track of their progress with the various skills they are learning in this text. References to these appendixes are interspersed throughout the book so students know when to use them in each chapter:

- Appendix 1: Critical Thinking Log
- Appendix 2: Revising and Editing Peer Evaluation Forms

- Appendix 3: Error Log
- Appendix 4: Spelling Log

ACKNOWLEDGMENTS

I want to acknowledge the support, encouragement, and sound advice of several people who have helped me through the development of the *Mosaics* series. First, Pearson Higher Education has provided guidance and inspiration for this project through the enduring wisdom of Craig Campanella, previous senior acquisitions editor of developmental English, and Matt Wright, current senior acquisitions editor; the foresight and prudence of Joe Opiela, editor-in-chief; the special creative inspiration of Thomas DeMarco, senior marketing manager; the unparalleled support of Jessica Kupetz, assistant editor; the exceptional organizational skills of Bayani Mendoza de Leon, production manager; the care and wisdom of Debbie Meyer, production editor; the hard work and patience of Wesley Hall, permissions editor; the flawless organization of Samantha Neary, editorial assistant for developmental English; the brilliant leadership of Roth Wilkofsky, President of Humanities and Social Sciences.

I want to give very special thanks to Cheryl Smith, my constant source of inspiration in her role as consultant and adviser for the duration of the entire Mosaics series and the motivation behind this particular book.

I am also grateful to Cheryl Smith, Rebecca Hewett, Valerie Turner, and Li'l Pearl for their discipline and hard work, past and present, on the *Instructor's Resource Manuals* for each of the books in the series.

INTRODUCTION: Reading Critically

Reading critically is the source of all successful college work. But only after much practice that includes time and reflection will your mind be engaged so you can read critically and be productive students and citizens in a very fast-moving world. Reading critically will affect every aspect of your life in and out of college in a positive way—especially your writing ability.

This chapter demonstrates various activities readers use as they read. As you work through the chapter, you will see how Travis Morehouse uses each strategy on a paragraph and then have a chance to try out the technique yourself. Consider keeping your responses to these activities in a journal you can refer to throughout the course.

PREPARING TO READ

Activities that take place before you actually start reading are labeled **pre-reading** or **preparing to read.** More specifically, prereading consists of the following tasks:

- Survey and analyze the title
- Find out what you can about the author
- Focus your attention on the subject of the reading selection

Title: Micanopy

Travis learned that the paragraph he was assigned is from an essay entitled "Micanopy." Travis doesn't know what that word means, so he looks it up and discovers it is not in the dictionary. Then he looks on the Internet and finds out it is the name of a small town (population about 600) in northern Florida, just south of Jacksonville. So Travis is expecting the author to be characterizing some aspects of the town.

Author: Bailey White

Travis then learns that the author's name is Bailey White, but he doesn't even know if this is a male or a female. So he does a Google search for the name and finds the following biography:

> White was born in 1950 in Thomasville, Georgia. White still lives in the same house in which she grew up, on one of the large tracts of virgin longleaf pine woods. Her father, Robb White, was a fiction writer and later a television and movie script writer. Her mother, Rosalie White, was a farmer, and worked for many years as the executive director of the local Red Cross Chapter. She has one brother, who is a carpenter and boat builder, and one sister, who is a bureaucrat. White graduated from Florida State University in 1973, and has taken a break from teaching first grade to pursue writing full-time.
>
> White is the author of *Sleeping at the Starlite Motel, Mama Makes Up Her Mind,* and *Quite a Year for Plums.* Her commentaries can be heard on NPR's award-winning newsmagazine *All Things Considered.*
>
> *Source:* http://www.npr.org/templates/story/story.php?storyid=2101366

Focusing Your Attention

In this book, a set of questions is furnished to help you focus your attention on the material you are about to read. Without this book, you should try to generate your own questions (about the author, about the subject matter, about the title) so that you start your reading actively rather than passively.

Here are some questions to focus your attention on the Bailey White paragraph. Writing your thoughts to these questions in a journal is the most beneficial approach to this exercise. Travis recorded his personal reactions to these questions before he started reading the essay.

1. What sights, sounds, smells, tastes, and textures are you aware of on a daily basis? Do these sensory signals have any special meaning for you?

2. In the paragraph you are about to read, the writer describes one of her favorite places so vividly it feels as if we are there. What are some of your favorite places? What details do you remember about these places?

READING

As you approach a reading task, you should plan to **read** it three times if you want to understand it critically. To get to the deeper levels of meaning, you need to work through literal and interpretive comprehension first.

As you read, you are making meaning out of a text that someone else has written. You must work in partnership with the author and his or her words to make sense of the material. Usually this does not happen in one reading. In like manner, when someone reads your writing, he or she must work with your words on the page to figure out what you are saying and what your words are implying.

Expanding Your Vocabulary

The first task you should undertake in your reading is to get the gist of the selection and look up vocabulary words you don't understand. In this book, difficult vocabulary words are identified and defined for you. You should keep this list handy and add other words to it as you read.

If you actually want to increase your vocabulary and take these words with you into your own speaking and writing, you should highlight the words, compose your own lists, create index cards—interact with the text in some way that will make the words your own. In this text, a specific task is suggested in each vocabulary section so you can try a few different activities and then choose those that work best for you.

Here is a list of difficult words you need to know for the first reading of "Micanopy." Circle those that are new for you and start a vocabulary log of your own in your journal.

Micanopy: small town in northern Florida
wisteria: a climbing plant with blue, pink, or white flowers
stealthily: quietly

Using a Reading Strategy

As you work through the material in Part II, you will be prompted to use a reading strategy with each reading assignment. Here are the ten reading strategies we introduce in this book:

Making Personal Associations   We all naturally make personal associations with our reading. However, one person's associations are usually quite different from those of someone else. Recording the associations you make with a reading selection lets you "own" the ideas. It allows you to connect the author's ideas to your own experiences. To perform this strategy, make notes in the margin that relate some of your specific memories to the details in the reading. Be prepared to explain the connection between your notes and the facts in the selection.

Travis's Personal Associations   Travis read the following paragraph by Bailey White. He was fascinated by the level of detail in this small paragraph and jotted a couple notes to himself in the margins as he read.

Wow! She must really like this place!

But the reason <u>I drive the two hundred miles year after year</u> is the bookstore. The building is tall, a beautiful pink brick. The sign says,

O. Brisky
Books
Old Used Rare
Bought and Sold
<u>Out of Print Search Service</u>

Name of town?

Even before you go inside, <u>you can smell the old, used, and rare books</u>. On sunny days, Mr. Brisky arranges a collection of books on a table on the sidewalk. There are books in the windows and stacks of books on the floor just inside the entrance. From an open back door the misty green light of (Micanopy) shines into the dust. <u>Tendrils of wisteria</u> have crept in through the doorway and are stealthily making their way toward the religion and philosophy section.

I can always smell old books.

What is this— plants?

Your Personal Associations   Read Bailey White's paragraph, and add your own notes to Travis's comments in the margins.

Thinking Aloud   As we read and interpret an author's words, we absorb them on a literal level, add to them any implications the author suggests, think about how the ideas relate to one another, and keep the process going until the entire reading selection makes sense. These focused thoughts are what help us process the author's writing. On another level, however, we may stray from the essay in a wide variety of ways—thinking about chores we need to do, calls we forgot to return, and plans we are looking forward to on the weekend. These random ideas are only loosely related to the reading. As you might suspect, focused reading is more productive than random reading, but you can teach yourself to apply your stray ideas to a better understanding of the material. To do this strategy, stop and "think aloud" about what is on your mind as you read. Point out confusing passages, connections you make, specific questions you have, related information you know, and personal experiences you associate with the text. In this way, you can hear what your mind does (both focused and randomly) as you read.

Travis's Think Aloud   Travis read Bailey White's paragraph and recorded his thoughts in brackets as accurately as possible so we could see how his mind worked as he read this passage.

But the reason I drive the two hundred miles year after year [*I don't think I drive that much for any reason all year long*] is the bookstore. [*Really? What could be so great about a bookstore? Sounds like more school work to me.*] The building is tall, a beautiful pink brick. [*Oh wow! That was the color of the brick on the boardwalk at Pismo Beach. What a great weekend! And the. . . .*] The sign says,

O. Brisky
Books
Old Used Rare
Bought and Sold
Out of Print Search Service [*This could be useful*]

Even before you go inside, you can smell the old, used, and rare books. [*I feel like I'm in this bookstore. It makes me think of my Grandma's house.*] On sunny days, Mr. Brisky arranges a collection of books on a table on the sidewalk [*a boardwalk of books!*]. There are books in the windows and stacks of books on the floor just inside the entrance. From an open back door the misty green light of Micanopy [*I'd love to go to Florida—maybe to see/smell this bookstore*] shines into the dust [*makes me think of a puddle of water*]. Tendrils of wisteria have crept in through the doorway and are stealthily making their way [*like invaders—Twilight Zone stuff*] toward the religion and philosophy section.

Your Think Aloud   Read Bailey White's essay, and put your own thoughts in brackets as you read.

Chunking   Reading critically means looking closely at the selection to discover what its purpose is and how it is structured to make its point. To understand how a reading selection works, circle the main idea. Then draw horizontal lines throughout the selection to separate the various topics that support the main idea. These lines may or may not coincide with paragraph breaks in an essay. Finally, in the margins, label the topics of each "chunk." Be prepared to explain the divisions you made.

Travis's Chunking   Travis marked the following chunks in the White paragraph and labeled them in the margin.

Entrance   But the reason I drive the two hundred miles year after year is the bookstore. The building is tall, a beautiful pink brick. The sign says,

O. Brisky
Books
Old Used Rare
Bought and Sold
Out of Print Search Service

Smell   Even before you go inside, you can smell the old, used, and rare books./On sunny days, Mr. Brisky arranges
Sight   a collection of books on a table on the sidewalk. There are books in the windows and stacks of books on the floor just inside the entrance. From an open back door the misty green light of Micanopy shines into the dust./Tendrils of
Crawling   wisteria have crept in through the doorway and are stealth-
plants   ily making their way toward the religion and philosophy section.

Your Chunking   Divide and label the chunks you see in Bailey White's paragraph.

Graphing the Ideas   To understand their reading material and see how it works, students often find that making drawings of its ideas and details is much more effective than outlining. Graphic organizers, or concept maps, let you literally "draw" the relationship of ideas to one another. Figuring out what framework to use for this exercise is part of the process. You can make up a drawing of your own or do a Web search for "graphic organizers" to see some different options. Be prepared to explain your drawing.

Travis's Graphic   Travis created the following framework for the White paragraph.

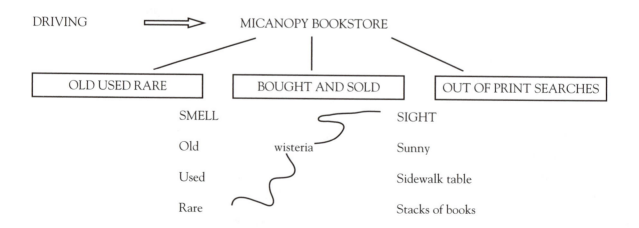

Your Graphic   Draw your own picture of the structure of White's paragraph.

Peer Teaching   Teaching something to your peers is an excellent way to test your understanding. To practice this technique, the class must first divide a reading selection into parts. The class members should then form groups representing each of these sections and choose one of the topics/sections. After identifying the main ideas, the details, and their relationships to one another, each group should teach its section to the rest of the class.

Travis's Peer Teaching   Travis chooses the following section to teach with his group.

> On sunny days, Mr. Brisky arranges a collection of books on a table on the sidewalk. There are books in the windows and stacks of books on the floor just inside the entrance. From an open back door the misty green light of Micanopy shines into the dust.

The group first asks the class to think about a bookstore they have visited. Then they ask the class members to list the sights they can remember from that bookstore. Finally, Travis and his group ask the class to list the sights that White talks about in this portion of her paragraph.

Your Peer Teaching   Form a group, and teach another portion of the paragraph to the rest of your class.

Summarizing   As you read more difficult selections, the ability to summarize is essential. A summary features the main ideas of a selection in a coherent paragraph. First, identify the main ideas in your reading; then fold them into a paragraph with logical transitions so your sentences flow from one to another. After you write your summary, draft three questions for discussion.

Travis's Summary   Travis wrote the following summary of the White paragraph.

> Bailey White drives 200 miles every year to her favorite bookstore in Micanopy, Florida, that buys and sells old and used books. The store smells of old books that are stacked on the sidewalk and all over the floors and windowsills. Crawling among the books is wisteria.

Your Summary   Write your own summary of White's paragraph.

Reacting Critically   Forming your own opinions and coming up with meaningful ideas in response to your reading are very important parts of the reading process that you need to learn how to produce. As you read a selection, record your notes on a separate piece of paper. First, draw a vertical line down the center of your paper. Then, as you read, write the author's main ideas on the left and your reactions to those ideas on the right side of the page. Be prepared to explain the connection between your notes and the material in the reading.

Travis's Critical Reactions   Here are Travis's critical notes on the paragraph by Bailey White.

White's Main Ideas	My Reactions
White drove 200 miles to this bookstore.	That's a long way to drive to a bookstore.
The bookstore was in Micanopy.	I found out Micanopy is in Florida.
The bookstore smelled like old books.	That's a distinctive smell that anyone can recognize.
Books were stacked everywhere.	I can tell the character of the bookstore and the bookstore owner from this detail.
A wisteria plant was crawling around the bookstore.	This living plant is a nice contrast to the nonliving books in the bookstore.

Your Critical Reactions   Create your own list of main ideas from the paragraph, and add your critical reactions to them.

Making Connections   Separating causes from effects is an important part of understanding a cause/effect paragraph. After a first reading of a cause/effect paragraph, divide a sheet of paper into two parts with a vertical line. Then as you read the selection for a second time, record the causes in the left column and the results on the right. Draw lines from each cause to its related effect (if applicable). Be prepared to explain the connection between your lists and the details in the essay.

Travis's Connections   Travis generated the following lists using this strategy.

First List	Related Ideas
Smell of books	old, used, rare
Stacks of books	on floor, on windowsills, on sidewalk, at entrance
Sights	pink brick, green light, books, dust, wisteria
Living things	wisteria plant

Your Connections   Generate your own lists from White's paragraph.

Recognizing Facts and Opinions Reading an argument critically calls for very high-level skills. You need to understand your reading on a literal level, know the difference between opinions and facts, and come up with your own thoughts on the topic by challenging the author's ideas. To do this, highlight facts in one color and the author's opinions in another color. This activity works very well with the next strategy.

Travis's Highlighting Travis highlighted the facts in White's paragraph in light yellow and the author's opinions in dark green.

But the reason I drive the two hundred miles year after year is the bookstore. **X**
The building is tall, a beautiful pink brick. The sign says,

> O. Brisky
> Books
> Old Used Rare
> Bought and Sold
> Out of Print Search Service

Even before you go inside, you can smell the old, used, and rare books. On sunny days, Mr. Brisky arranges a collection of books on a table on the sidewalk. There are books in the windows and stacks of books on the floor just inside the entrance. From an open back door the misty green light of Micanopy shines into the dust. Tendrils of wisteria have crept in through the doorway and are stealthily making their way toward the religion and philosophy section.

Your Highlighting Do you disagree with any of Travis's highlighting? Explain your answer.

Reading with the Author/Against the Author* This approach is a very advanced form of reading. It asks you to consciously figure out which ideas you agree with and which you disagree with. By doing this, you force yourself to form your own reactions and opinions. From the previous highlighting exercise, put an X by any facts or opinions that you do not agree with or that you want to question in some way. Then record your own thoughts and opinions on a separate sheet of paper. Be prepared to explain any marks you made on the paragraph.

*This strategy is most effective with an argument rather than a description, like White's paragraph.

Travis's Response

I put an X by the bookstore because, as much as I love to read, I can't imagine driving 200 miles to a bookstore. There would have to be something very special about the store. I can imagine the sights and smells, but gas prices now would discourage me from that trip.

Your Response   Write your own response to your highlighting.

Practice 1: Now that you have been introduced to several prereading strategies, which is your favorite? Why do you like it best?

Practice 2: Using two reading strategies on one reading assignment is often a good idea. What is your second favorite reading strategy? Why do you like this strategy?

FIRST REREADING

Your **first rereading** should now focus on raising your level of thinking, which means trying to reach a deeper understanding of the words and sentences in the paragraph or essay. Looking again at the reading material with an inquiring mind is the heart of this stage.

This book provides questions on increasingly more difficult levels to help you accomplish this goal. But without this assistance, you need to ask your own questions as you read. Focusing on questions that wonder "why" or "how" something happened will move you to these higher levels.

Travis's First Rereading   As Travis read White's essay a second time, he saw several details he had not seen earlier. He made more notes on the essay and then answered the following questions provided in the text. His answers appear after each question.

Thinking Critically About Content

1. How do you know that White really enjoyed visiting Brisky's bookstore?
   Driving "two hundred miles year after year" shows the reader that she really appreciates this bookstore.

2. How can plants invade the bookstore?
   It seems that the wisteria in particular has "crept through the doorway" and is now literally growing into different areas of the store.

3. What details from the paragraph work together to make the bookstore real for you?
   I can see the stacks of books all over this store—on a table on the sidewalk, in the windows, on the floor. Those details remind me of a bookstore I visited long ago on a family trip with my parents in Cedar City, Utah.

Thinking Critically About Purpose and Audience

4. What do you think White's purpose is in this paragraph?

    I think White is trying to share her love of this bookstore with us so we see it the same way she does.

5. What type of audience do you think would most understand and appreciate this paragraph?

    Anyone can appreciate this paragraph, but it might be especially appealing to people who like books and bookstores.

6. Why do you think White included the entire bookstore sign in her paragraph?

    Reading the sign word for word makes us feel like we are really there with the author. It also slows us down, like we are entering the bookstore.

Thinking Critically About Paragraphs

7. What is the paragraph's main idea?

    The main idea is that White loves to visit this particular bookstore.

8. Does White give you enough examples to understand her feelings about this bookstore? Explain your answer.

    Yes she does. Of the five senses, she covers sight, smell, and touch, so readers can feel as if they are appreciating the bookstore with her.

9. Does the paragraph move smoothly from one sentence to the next? If so, how does the author accomplish this?

    The paragraph moves very smoothly because of transitions White uses to connect her sentences.

10. Think of a favorite place of yours. What purpose does this place serve for you?

    I have a favorite place high above the city that I retreat to when I need to think clearly and solve problems.

Your First Rereading   Read the excerpt from "Micanopy" a second time, and take more notes about assumptions and relationships between ideas, writing them in the margins as you read. Then, in your journal, generate two "why" or "how" questions about ideas in this paragraph. Exchange questions with a classmate, and answer each other's questions in your journal.

SECOND REREADING

This **final reading** is the real test of your understanding. It has the potential to raise your grades in all subjects if you complete it for each of your reading assignments. It involves understanding the author's ideas as you also form your own opinions and analyze your thoughts.

To accomplish this reading, you should ask more questions that go beyond the words on the page and then answer them in writing. You should also bring your own opinions to the surface. Write them down as they occur to you. Finally, analyze your thoughts so that you end with some form of self-evaluation.

Travis's Second Rereading   Travis took the following notes in his journal as he read White's essay for the third time. He asked himself some questions, answered those questions as best he could, recorded his opinions as they occurred to him, and analyzed his thoughts along the way.

I really liked Bailey White's description of the bookstore. The first sentence shows how much she likes this place. She gives so many examples about why she drives two hundred miles just to go to this bookstore. I don't really have a place that I would drive that far to see. I wish I did! I wouldn't say a bookstore or library is my favorite place. I get too bored looking at so many books, but I do like feeling alone in such a big place. I guess my favorite place would just be out of the house. Far, far away where no one can find me. I love to be by myself, even though most of my friends don't understand this.

Your Second Rereading   Take notes in your journal as you read White's essay for the third time. Ask yourself more "how" and "why" questions, answer those questions, record your opinions, and analyze your thoughts as they occur.

Description: From Reading to Writing

This chapter includes four reading selections followed by several writing assignments. It then offers guidance in peer evaluation and reflection, ending with suggestions about how to lead your instructor through your writing in ways that will benefit both of you.

Reading Description

Here are four essays that demonstrate good description. In the excerpt from *The Joy Luck Club* by Amy Tan, entitled "Magpies," a young girl observes the sights, sounds, smells, textures, and tastes she encounters when she arrives at her new home. The second selection, an essay called "Longing to Die of Old Age" by Alice Walker, considers the right of human beings to die a natural death. The third essay, "El Hoyo" by Mario Suarez, describes a small town near Tucson and its citizens, and "Dwellings" by Linda Hogan focuses on the habitats of different animals. As you read, notice how the writers pull you into each experience through sensory details.

MAGPIES
by Amy Tan

Focusing Your Attention

1. Think of a place you are very familiar with: your room, your home, your school, your place of employment, a garden, a restaurant. Then make a list of the sights, sounds, textures, smells, and tastes that come to mind as you think of that place.

2. In the excerpt you are about to read, a young girl recounts the many sights, sounds, smells, textures, and tastes she encountered when she first arrived at her new home. Think of an occasion when you entered a place

for the first time. What sights, sounds, textures, smells, and tastes made the strongest impressions on you?

Expanding Your Vocabulary

The following words are important to your understanding of this essay. Highlight them throughout the essay before you begin to read. Then refer to this list as you get to these words in the essay.

British Concession: areas the Chinese allowed the British to occupy (paragraph 1)

concubines: women who were part of a man's household and were expected to fulfill his needs (paragraph 14)

mourning: representing grief over a person's death (paragraph 17)

READING CRITICALLY
Making Personal Associations with Your Reading

As you discovered in the Introduction, you can make connections with your reading by writing personal associations in the margins of this essay. Jot down anything that comes to mind. These notes will put your individual stamp on the essay with a set of memories only you can recall. They will also help you understand the essay on an analytical level. Share your notes with one of your classmates.

MAGPIES
by Amy Tan

1   I knew from the beginning our new home would not be an ordinary house. My mother had told me we would live in the household of Wu Tsing, who was a very rich merchant. She said this man owned many carpet factories and lived in a mansion located in the British Concession of Tientsin, the best section of the city where Chinese people could live. We lived not too far from Paima Di, Racehorse Street, where only Westerners could live. And we were also close to little shops that sold only one kind of thing: only tea, or only fabric, or only soap.

2   The house, she said, was foreign-built; Wu Tsing liked foreign things because foreigners had made him rich. And I concluded that was why my mother had to wear foreign-style clothes, in the manner of newly rich Chinese people who liked to display their wealth on the outside. And even though I knew all this before I arrived, I was still amazed at what I saw.

The front of the house had a Chinese stone gate, rounded at the top, with big black lacquer doors and a threshold you had to step over. Within the gates I saw the courtyard, and I was surprised. There were no willows or sweet-smelling cassia trees, no garden pavilions, no benches sitting by a pond, no tubs of fish. Instead, there were long rows of bushes on both sides of a wide brick walkway, and to each side of those bushes was a big lawn area with fountains. And as we walked down the walkway and got closer to the house, I saw this house had been built in the Western style. It was three stories high, of mortar and stone, with long metal balconies on each floor and chimneys at every corner.

When we arrived, a young servant woman ran out and greeted my mother with cries of joy. She had a high scratchy voice: "Oh Taitai, you've already arrived! How can this be?" This was Yan Chang, my mother's personal maid, and she knew how to fuss over my mother just the right amount. She had called my mother Taitai, the simple honorable title of Wife, as if my mother were the first wife, the only wife.

Yan Chang called loudly to other servants to take our luggage, called another servant to bring tea and draw a hot bath. And then she hastily explained that Second Wife had told everyone not to expect us for another week at least. "What a shame! No one to greet you! Second Wife, the others, gone to Peking to visit her relatives. Your daughter, so pretty, your same look. She's so shy, eh? First Wife, her daughters . . . gone on a pilgrimage to another Buddhist temple. Last week, a cousin's uncle, just a little crazy, came to visit, turned out not to be a cousin, not an uncle, who knows who he was."

As soon as we walked into that big house, I became lost with too many things to see: a curved staircase that wound up and up, a ceiling with faces in every corner, then hallways twisting and turning into one room then another. To my right was a large room, larger than I had ever seen, and it was filled with stiff teakwood furniture: sofas and tables and chairs. And at the other end of this long, long room, I could see doors leading into more rooms, more furniture, then more doors. To my left was a darker room, another sitting room, this one filled with foreign furniture: dark green leather sofas, paintings with hunting dogs, armchairs, and mahogany desks. And as I glanced in these rooms, I would see different people, and Yan Chang would explain: "This young lady, she is Second Wife's servant. That one, she is nobody, just the daughter of cook's helper. This man takes care of the garden."

And then we were walking up the staircase. We came to the top of the stairs, and I found myself in another large sitting room. We walked to the left, down a hall, past one room, and then stepped into another. "This is your mother's room," Yan Chang told me proudly. "This is where you will sleep."

And the first thing I saw, the only thing I could see at first, was a magnificent bed. It was heavy and light at the same time: soft rose silk and heavy, dark, shiny wood carved all around with dragons. Four posts held up a silk canopy, and at each post dangled large silk ties holding back curtains. The bed sat on four squat lion's paws, as if the weight of it had crushed the lion underneath. Yan Chang showed me how to use a small step stool to climb onto the bed. And when I tumbled onto the silk coverings, I laughed to discover a soft mattress that was ten times the thickness of my bed in Ningpo.

Sitting in this bed, I admired everything as if I were a princess. This room had a glass door that led to a balcony. In front of the window door was a round table of the same wood as the bed. It too sat on carved lion's legs and was surrounded by four chairs.

A servant had already put tea and sweet cakes on the table and was now lighting the houlu, a small stove for burning coal.

10   It was not that my uncle's house in Ningpo had been poor. He was actually quite well-to-do. But this house in Tientsin was amazing. And I thought to myself, My uncle was wrong. There was no shame in my mother's marrying Wu Tsing.

11   While thinking this, I was startled by a sudden clang! clang! clang! followed by music. On the wall opposite the bed was a big wooden clock with a forest and bears carved into it. The door on the clock had burst open, and a tiny room full of people was coming out. There was a bearded man in a pointed cap seated at a table. He was bending his head over and over again to drink soup, but his beard would dip in the bowl first and stop him. A girl in a white scarf and blue dress was standing next to the table, and she was bending over and over again to give the man more of this soup. And next to the man and girl was another girl with a skirt and short jacket. She was swinging her arm back and forth, playing violin music. She always played the same dark song. I can still hear it in my head after these many years—ni-ah! nah! nah! nah! nah-ni-nah!

12   This was a wonderful clock to see, but after I heard it that first hour, then the next, and then always, this clock became an extravagant nuisance. I could not sleep for many nights. And later, I found I had an ability: To not listen to something meaningless calling to me.

13   I was so happy those first few nights, in this amusing house, sleeping in the big soft bed with my mother. I would lie in this comfortable bed, thinking about my uncle's house in Ningpo, realizing how unhappy I had been, feeling sorry for my little brother. But most of my thoughts flew to all the new things to see and do in this house.

14   I watched hot water pouring out of pipes not just in the kitchen but also into wash-basins and bathtubs on all three floors of the house. I saw chamber pots that flushed clean without servants having to empty them. I saw rooms as fancy as my mother's. Yan Chang explained which ones belonged to First Wife and the other concubines, who were called Second Wife and Third Wife. And some rooms belonged to no one. "They are for guests," said Yan Chang.

15   On the third floor were rooms for only the men servants, said Yan Chang, and one of the rooms even had a door to a cabinet that was really a secret hiding place from sea pirates.

16   Thinking back, I find it hard to remember everything that was in that house; too many good things all seem the same after a while. I tired of anything that was not a novelty. "Oh, this," I said when Yan Chang brought me the same sweet meats as the day before. "I've tasted this already."

17   My mother seemed to regain her pleasant nature. She put her old clothes back on, long Chinese gowns and skirts now with white mourning bands sewn at the bottoms. During the day, she pointed to strange and funny things, naming them for me: bidet, Brownie camera, salad fork, napkin. In the evening, when there was nothing to do, we talked about the servants: who was clever, who was diligent, who was loyal. We gossiped as we cooked small eggs and sweet potatoes on top of the houlu just to enjoy their smell. And at night, my mother would again tell me stories as I lay in her arms falling asleep.

18   If I look upon my whole life, I cannot think of another time when I felt more comfortable: when I had no worries, fears, or desires, when my life seemed as soft and lovely as lying inside a cocoon of rose silk.

Thinking Critically About Content

1. List two details from this essay for each of the five senses: seeing, hearing, touching, smelling, and tasting. How do these details *show* rather than tell the readers the narrator's impressions of her new house?

2. In one or more complete sentences, state the main character's point of view.

3. What does the narrator mean when she says, "If I look upon my whole life, I cannot think of another time when I felt more comfortable: when I had no worries, fears, or desires, when my life seemed as soft and lovely as lying inside a cocoon of rose silk" (paragraph 18)? Why do you think she is so comfortable in these surroundings?

Thinking Critically About Purpose and Audience

4. What dominant impression does the writer create in this description? How does this impression change throughout the essay?

5. Do you think readers who have never been to China can appreciate and enjoy this essay? Explain your answer.

6. What specific observations are most interesting to you? Why? In what ways do these observations help you imagine the entire scene?

Thinking Critically About Paragraphs

7. If a paragraph is unified, all of its sentences are related to one central idea. Based on this explanation, is paragraph 12 unified? Explain your answer.

8. Look closely at paragraph 17. Does it move from general to specific or from specific to general?

9. Choose one body paragraph, and decide if it has enough details. What is the most interesting detail in the paragraph?

10. Write a paragraph describing the inner feelings of the main character when she finally settles into her new home.

To keep track of your critical thinking progress, go to Appendix 1.

LONGING TO DIE OF OLD AGE
by Alice Walker

Focusing Your Attention

1. Do you consider yourself healthy? What keeps you healthy? Do you care about your health?

2. Have you thought about how you might want to die? The essay you are about to read claims that we should all be able to die naturally of old age. Do you agree with this notion? How do you feel when disease gets in the way of this process?

Expanding Your Vocabulary

The following words are important to your understanding of this essay. Highlight them throughout the essay before you begin to read. Then refer to this list as you get to these words in the essay.

enslaved person: slave (paragraph 1)

longevity: long life (paragraph 1)

organic: natural (paragraph 3)

congested: crowded (paragraph 5)

collard greens: a leafy vegetable (paragraph 7)

indelible: permanent (paragraph 12)

self-induced: brought on by one's own actions (paragraph 13)

aberration: abnormality (paragraph 13)

READING CRITICALLY
Making Personal Associations as You Read

As you did with the previous essay, write any personal associations you make with this essay in the margins as you read. This process will give you some good insights into the author's approach to her topic and into her methods of developing her ideas. Write down anything at all that occurs to you. Then share your notes with one of your classmates.

LONGING TO DIE OF OLD AGE
by Alice Walker

1   Mrs. Mary Poole, my "4-greats" grandmother, lived the entire nineteenth century, from around 1800 to 1921, and enjoyed exceptional health. The key to good health, she taught (this woman who as an enslaved person was forced to carry two young children, on foot, from Virginia to Georgia), was never to cover up the pulse at the throat. But, with the benefit of hindsight, one must believe that for her, as for generations of people after her, in our small farming community, diet played as large a role in her longevity and her health as loose clothing and fresh air.

2   For what did the old ones eat?

Alice Walker, "Longing to Die of Old Age" from *Living by the Word: Selected Writings 1973–1987*, copyright © 1985 by Alice Walker, reprinted by permission of Houghton Mifflin Harcourt Publishing Company and The Wendy Weil Agency Inc.

Well, first of all, almost nothing that came from a store. As late as my own child-hood, in the fifties, at Christmas we had only raisins and perhaps bananas, oranges, and a peppermint stick, broken into many pieces, a sliver for each child; and during the year, perhaps, a half-dozen apples, nuts, and a bunch of grapes. All extravagantly expensive and considered rare. You ate *all* of the apple, sometimes, even the seeds. Everyone had a vegetable garden; a garden as large as there was energy to work it. In these gardens peo-ple raised an abundance of food: corn, tomatoes, okra, peas and beans, squash, peppers, which they ate in summer and canned for winter. There was no chemical fertilizer. No one could have afforded it, had it existed, and there was no need for it. From the cows and pigs and goats, horses, mules, and fowl that people also raised, there was always ample organic manure.

Until I was grown, I never heard of anyone having cancer.

In fact, at first cancer seemed to be coming from far off. For a long time if the sub-ject of cancer came up, you could be sure cancer itself wasn't coming any nearer than to some congested place in the North, then to Atlanta, seventy-odd miles away, then to Macon, forty miles away, then to Monticello, twenty miles away. The first inhabitants of our community to die of acknowledged cancer were almost celebrities, because of this "foreign" disease. But now, twenty-odd years later, cancer has ceased to be viewed as a visitor and is feared instead as a resident. Even the children die of cancer now, which, at least in the beginning, seemed a disease of the old.

Most of the people I knew as farmers left the farms (they did not own the land and were unable to make a living working for the white people who did) to rent small apart-ments in the towns and cities. They ceased to have gardens, and when they did manage to grow a few things they used fertilizer from boxes and bottles, sometimes in improba-ble colors and consistencies, which they rightly suspected, but had no choice but to use. Gone were their chickens, cows, and pigs. Gone their organic manure.

To their credit, they questioned all that happened to them. Why must we leave the land? Why must we live in boxes with hardly enough space to breathe? (Of course, indoor plumbing seduced many a one.) Why must we buy all our food from the store? Why is the price of food so high—and so tasteless? The collard greens bought in the supermarket, they said, "tasted like water."

The United States should have closed down and examined its every intention, insti-tution, and law on the very first day a black woman observed that the collard greens tasted like water. Or when the first person of any color observed that store-bought toma-toes tasted more like unripened avocados than tomatoes.

The flavor of food is one of the clearest messages the Universe ever sends to human beings; and we have by now eaten poisoned warnings by the ton.

When I was a child growing up in middle Georgia in the forties and fifties, people still died of old age. Old age was actually a common cause of death. My parents inevitably visited dying persons over the long or short period of their decline; sometimes I went with them. Some years ago, as an adult, I accompanied my mother to visit a very old neighbor who was dying a few doors down the street, and though she was no longer living in the country, the country style lingered. People like my mother were visiting her con-stantly, bringing food, picking up and returning laundry, or simply stopping by to inquire how she was feeling and to chat. Her house, her linen, her skin all glowed with cleanliness. She lay propped against pillows so that by merely turning her head she could watch the postman approaching, friends and relatives arriving, and, most of all, the small children playing beside the street, often in her yard, the sound of their play a lively music.

11   Sitting in the dimly lit, spotless room, listening to the lengthy but warm-with-shared-memories silences between my mother and Mrs. Davis was extraordinarily pleasant. Her white hair gleamed against her kissable black skin, and her bed was covered with one of the most intricately patterned quilts I'd ever seen—a companion to the dozen or more she'd stored in a closet, which, when I expressed interest, she invited me to see.

12   I thought her dying one of the most reassuring events I'd ever witnessed. She was calm; she seemed ready; her affairs were in order. She was respected and loved. In short, Mrs. Davis was having an excellent death. A week later, when she had actually died, I felt this all the more because she had left, in me, the indelible knowledge that such a death is possible. And that cancer and nuclear annihilation are truly obscene alternatives. And surely, teaching this very vividly is one of the things an excellent death is supposed to do.

13   To die miserably of self-induced sickness is an aberration we take as normal; but it is crucial that we remember and teach our children that there are other ways.

14   For myself, for all of us, I want a death like Mrs. Davis's. One in which we will ripen and ripen further, as richly as fruit and then fall slowly into the caring arms of our friends and other people we know. People who will remember the good days and the bad, the names of lovers and grandchildren, the time sorrow almost broke, the time loving friendship healed.

15   It must become a right of every person to die of old age. And if we secure this right for ourselves, we can, coincidentally, assure it for the planet. And that, as they say, will be excellence, which is, perhaps, only another name for health.

Thinking Critically About Content

1. What did the narrator's great-great-great-great grandmother think was the key to good health?

2. Find at least one detail for each of the five senses. Does Walker draw on any one sense more than the others?

3. Why does Walker "want a death like Mrs. Davis's" (paragraph 14)?

Thinking Critically About Purpose and Audience

4. What dominant impression does Walker create in this essay?

5. Who do you think is Walker's primary audience?

6. Explain your understanding of this essay's title.

Thinking Critically About Paragraphs

7. What is the topic sentence of paragraph 12? Do all the sentences in that paragraph relate to its topic sentence? Explain your answer.

8. If a paragraph is coherent, it is considered logical and easy to read. Often, well-chosen transitions help a writer achieve coherence. Underline three transitions Walker uses in paragraph 10. How do these words help this paragraph read smoothly?

9. How are the details organized in paragraph 5—spatially or chronologically?

10. Write a paragraph describing the secret to longevity.

To keep track of your critical thinking progress, go to Appendix 1.

EL HOYO
by Mario Suarez

Focusing Your Attention

1. Think of a place from your childhood that had special meaning for you as you were growing up. Where was this place? Why was it special?

2. In the essay you are about to read, the writer recounts the many sights, sounds, smells, textures, and tastes that he connects with the place where he grew up. What sights, sounds, smells, textures, and tastes do you remember about the city, town, or farm where you grew up? Can you describe the place where you grew up for someone who has never been there?

Expanding Your Vocabulary

The following words are important to your understanding of this essay. Highlight them throughout the essay before you begin to read. Then refer to this list as you come to these words in the essay.

Tucson: city in southeastern Arizona (paragraph 1)

chicanos: Mexican Americans (paragraph 1)

padre: father, priest (paragraph 1)

paisanos: countrymen (paragraph 1)

bicker: quarrel (paragraph 1)

adobe: sun-dried brick (paragraph 1)

chavalos: small boys (paragraph 1)

inundated: flooded (paragraph 1)

Octavio Perea's Mexican Hour: Spanish radio program (paragraph 2)

"Smoke in the Eyes": song (paragraph 2)

solace: comfort (paragraph 2)

benevolent: kind (paragraph 2)

solicited: asked, begged (paragraph 2)

señora: married woman (paragraph 2)

chicanas: Mexican American females (paragraph 2)

Baja California: peninsula along the western coast of Mexico (paragraph 2)

boleros: music for Spanish dances (paragraph 3)

comadres: gossiping women (paragraph 3)

bloodwell: family ancestry (paragraph 3)

conquistador: a Spanish conqueror (paragraph 3)

capirotada: Mexican bread pudding (paragraph 4)

panocha: corn (paragraph 4)

Sermeños: family name (paragraph 4)

READING CRITICALLY
Making Personal Associations with Your Reading

As before, practice making connections with your reading by writing personal associations in the margins of this essay. Jot down anything that comes to mind. These notes will put your individual stamp on the essay with a set of memories only you can recall. They will also help you understand the essay on an analytical level. Share your notes with one of your classmates.

EL HOYO
by Mario Suarez

1   From the center of downtown Tucson, the ground slopes gently away to Main Street, drops a few feet, and then rolls to the banks of the Santa Cruz River. Here lies the section of the city known as El Hoyo. Why it is called El Hoyo is not very clear. In no sense is it a hole as its name would imply; it is simply the river's immediate valley. Its inhabitants are chicanos who raise hell on Saturday night and listen to Padre Estanislao on Sunday morning. While the term *chicano* is the short way of saying Mexicano, it is not restricted to the paisanos who came from old Mexico with the territory or the last famine to work for the railroad, labor, sing, and go on relief. Chicano is the easy way of referring to everybody. Pablo Gut'errez married the Chinese grocer's daughter and now runs a meat department; his sons are chicanos. So are the sons of Killer Jones who threw a fight in Harlem and fled to El Hoyo to marry Cristina Mendez. And so are all of them. However, it is doubtful that

Mario Suárez, "El Hoyo," *Arizona Quarterly*, Summer 1947. Reprinted by permission of The Arizona Board of Regents.

all these spiritual sons of Mexico live in El Hoyo because they love each other—many fight and bicker constantly. It is doubtful they live in El Hoyo because of its scenic beauty—it is everything but beautiful. Its houses are simple affairs of unplastered adobe, wood, and abandoned car parts. Its narrow streets are mostly clearings which have, in time, acquired names. Except for some tall trees which nobody has ever cared to identify, nurse, or destroy, the main things known to grow in the general area are weeds, garbage piles, dark-eyed chavalos, and dogs. And it is doubtful that the chicanos live in El Hoyo because it is safe—many times the Santa Cruz has risen and inundated the area.

2

In other respects, living in El Hoyo has its advantages. If one is born with a weakness for acquiring bills, El Hoyo is where the collectors are less likely to find you. If one has acquired the habit of listening to Octavio Perea's Mexican Hour in the wee hours of the morning with the radio on at full blast, El Hoyo is where you are less likely to be reported to the authorities. Besides, Perea is very popular and sooner or later to everyone "Smoke in the Eyes" is dedicated between the pinto beans and white flour commercials. If one, for any reason whatever, comes on an extended period of hard times, where, if not in El Hoyo, are the neighbors more willing to offer solace? When Teofila Malacara's house burned to the ground with all her belongings and two children, a benevolent gentleman carried through the gesture that made tolerable her burden. He made a list of five hundred names and solicited from each a dollar. At the end of a month, he turned over to the tearful but grateful señora one hundred dollars in cold cash and then accompanied her on a short vacation. When the new manager of a local store decided that no more chicanas were to work behind the counters, it was the chicanos of El Hoyo who, on taking their individually small but collectively great buying power elsewhere, drove the manager out and the girls returned to their jobs. When the Mexican Army was en route to Baja, California, and the chicanos found out that the enlisted men ate only at infrequent intervals, it was El Hoyo's chicanos who crusaded across town with pots of beans and trays of tortillas to meet the train. When someone gets married, celebrating is not restricted to the immediate friends of the couple. Everybody is invited. Anything calls for a celebration, and a celebration calls for anything. On Memorial Day there are no less than half a dozen good fights at the Riverside Dance Hall. On Mexican Independence Day, more than one flag is sworn allegiance to amid cheers for the queen.

3

And El Hoyo is something more. It is this something more which brought Felipe Sanchez back from the wars after having killed a score of Vietnamese with his body resembling a patchwork quilt to marry Julia Armijo. It brought Joe Zepeda, a gunner, back to compose boleros. He has a metal plate for a skull. Perhaps El Hoyo is proof that those people exist, and perhaps exist best, who have as yet failed to observe the more popular modes of human conduct. Perhaps the humble appearance of El Hoyo justifies the indifferent shrug of those made aware of its existence. Perhaps El Hoyo's simplicity motivates an occasional chicano to move away from its narrow streets, babbling comadres, and shrieking children to deny the bloodwell from which he springs and to claim the blood of a conquistador while his hair is straight and his face beardless. Yet El Hoyo is not an outpost of a few families against the world. It fights for no causes except those which soothe its immediate angers. It laughs and cries with the same amount of passion in times of plenty and of want.

4

Perhaps El Hoyo, its inhabitants, and its essence can best be explained by telling a bit about a dish called capirotada. Its origin is uncertain. But, according to the time and the circumstance, it is made of old, new, or hard bread. It is softened with water and then cooked with peanuts, raisins, onions, cheese, and panocha. It is fired with sherry wine. Then it is served hot, cold, or just "on the weather" as they say in El Hoyo. The Sermeños like it one way, the Garcias another, and the Ortegas still another. While it might differ greatly from one home to another; nevertheless, it is still capirotada. And so it is with El Hoyo's chicanos. While being divided from within and from without, like the capirotada, they remain chicanos.

Thinking Critically About Content

1. What does *el hoyo* mean, according to the author?

2. List two details from this essay for each of the five senses: seeing, hearing, touching, smelling, and tasting. How do these details *show* rather than tell the readers the writer's impressions of El Hoyo?

3. What is the main reason people choose to live in El Hoyo?

Thinking Critically About Purpose and Audience

4. What dominant impression does the writer create in this description? Explain your answer in detail.

5. Do you think readers who have never been to this place can appreciate and enjoy this essay? Why or why not?

6. What details about El Hoyo are most interesting to you? Why do you find them interesting?

Thinking Critically About Essays

7. If an essay is unified, all of its paragraphs are related to one central idea. Based on this explanation, is this essay unified? Explain your answer.

8. How does Suarez organize his ideas and observations in this essay? Make a rough outline of the essay.

9. Suarez ends his essay with an analogy that compares El Hoyo to a dish called *capirotada*. Is this an effective end for his essay? Why or why not?

10. Describe as fully as possible the inner feelings of the narrator from inside El Hoyo on a typical day.

To keep track of your critical thinking progress, go to Appendix 1.

DWELLINGS
by Linda Hogan

Focusing Your Attention

1. Think about the place you currently live. Does it serve your purposes? In what ways?

2. The essay you are about to read describes different habitats that suit different animals and humans. If you could move to a new "dwelling," where would you go? Why?

Expanding Your Vocabulary

The following words are important to your understanding of this essay. Highlight them throughout the essay before you begin to read. Then refer to this list as you come to these words in the essay.

eroded: worn down (paragraph 1)

Anasazi: Indian tribe (paragraph 1)

excavations: caves, holes in the earth (paragraph 1)

beetle: jut, project (paragraph 1)

catacombs: tunnels, hollowed-out passageways, burial places (paragraph 2)

droning: monotonous (paragraph 3)

sanctuary: safe place (paragraph 6)

troglodite: caveman (paragraph 7)

utopia: ideal place (paragraph 7)

felled: cut down (paragraph 8)

spired: rising like a church steeple (paragraph 9)

fledglings: baby birds just learning to fly (paragraph 9)

arid: dry (paragraph 10)

pellets: animal droppings (paragraph 13)

fetal: newborn (paragraph 13)

downy: soft (paragraph 14)

rafter: roof beam (paragraph 14)

Zia Pueblo: an Indian village (paragraph 15)

shards: broken pieces (paragraph 15)

sage: an herb (paragraph 16)

READING CRITICALLY
Making Personal Associations with Your Reading

As with the previous essays, write any personal associations you make with this essay in the margins as you read. This process will give you some good insights into the author's approach to her topic and into her methods of developing her ideas. Write down anything at all that occurs to you. Then share your notes with one of your classmates.

DWELLINGS
by Linda Hogan

1   Not far from where I live is a hill that was cut into by the moving water of a creek. Eroded this way, all that's left of it is a broken wall of earth that contains old roots and pebbles woven together and exposed. Seen from a distance, it is only a rise of raw earth. But up close it is something wonderful, a small cliff dwelling that looks almost as intricate and well made as those the Anasazi left behind when they vanished mysteriously centuries ago. This hill is a place that could be the starry skies at night turned inward into the thousand round holes where solitary bees have lived and died. It is a hill of tunneling rooms. At the mouths of some of the excavations, half-circles of clay beetle out like awnings shading a doorway. It is earth that was turned to clay in the mouths of the bees and spit out as they mined deeper into their dwelling places.

2   This place is where the bees reside at an angle safe from rain. It faces the southern sun. It is a warm and intelligent architecture of memory, learned by whatever memory lives in the blood. Many of the holes still contain gold husks of dead bees, their faces dry and gone, their flat eyes gazing out from death's land toward the other uninhabited half of the hill that is across the creek from the catacombs.

3   The first time I found the residence of the bees, it was dusty summer. The sun was hot, and land was the dry color of rust. Now and then a car rumbled along the dirt road, and dust rose up behind it before settling back down on older dust. In the silence, the bees made a soft droning hum. They were alive then and working the hill, going out and returning with pollen, in and out through the holes, back and forth between daylight and the cooler, darker regions of the inner earth. They were flying an invisible map through air, a map charted by landmarks, the slant of light, and a circling story they told one another about the direction of food held inside the center of yellow flowers.

4   Sitting in the hot sun, watching the small bees fly in and out around the hill, hearing the summer birds, the light breeze, I felt right in the world. I belonged there. I thought of my own dwelling places, those real and those imagined. Once I lived in a town called Manitou, which means "Great Spirit," where hot mineral spring water gurgled beneath the streets and rose into open wells. I felt safe there. With the underground movement of water and heat a constant reminder of other life, of what lives beneath us, it seemed to be the center of the world.

5   A few years after that, I wanted silence. My daydreams were full of places I longed to be, shelters and solitudes. I wanted a room apart from others, a hidden cabin to rest in. I wanted to be in a redwood forest with trees so tall the owls called out in the daytime. I daydreamed of living in a vapor cave a few hours away from here. Underground, warm, and moist, I thought it would be the perfect world for staying out of cold winter, for escaping the noise of living.

6   And how often I've wanted to escape to a wilderness where a human hand has not been in everything. But those were only dreams of peace, of comfort, of a nest inside stone or woods, a sanctuary where a dream or life wouldn't be invaded.

Years ago, in the next canyon west of here, there was a man who followed one of those dreams and moved into a cave that could only be reached by climbing down a rope. For years he lived there in comfort, like a troglodite. The inner weather was stable, never too hot, too cold, too wet, or too dry. But then he felt lonely. His utopia needed a woman. He went to town until he found a wife. For a while after the marriage, his wife climbed down the rope along with him, but before long she didn't want the mice scurrying about in the cave or the untidy bats that wanted to hang from the stones of the ceiling. So they built a door. Because of the closed entryway, the temperature changed. They had to put in heat. Then the inner moisture of earth warped the door, so they had to have air-conditioning, and after that the earth wanted to go about life in its own way, and it didn't give in to the people. 7

In other days and places, people paid more attention to the strong-headed will of earth. Once homes were built of wood that had been felled from a single region in a forest. That way, it was thought, the house would hold together more harmoniously, and the family of walls would not fall or lend themselves to the unhappiness or arguments of the inhabitants. 8

An Italian immigrant to Chicago, Aldo Piacenzi, built birdhouses that were dwellings of harmony and peace. They were the incredible spired shapes of cathedrals in Italy. They housed not only the birds, but also his memories, his own past. He painted them the watery blue of his Mediterranean, the wild rose of flowers in a summer field. Inside them was straw and the droppings of lives that laid eggs, fledglings who grew there. What places to inhabit, the bright and sunny birdhouses in dreary alleyways of the city. 9

One beautiful afternoon, cool and moist, with the kind of yellow light that falls on earth in these arid regions, I waited for barn swallows to return from their daily work of food gathering. Inside the tunnel where they live, hundreds of swallows had mixed their saliva with mud and clay, much like the solitary bees, and formed nests that were perfect as a potter's bowl. At five in the evening, they returned all at once, a dark, flying shadow. Despite their enormous numbers and the crowding together of nests, they didn't pause for even a moment before entering the nests, nor did they crowd one another. Instantly they vanished into the nests. The tunnel went silent. It held no outward signs of life. 10

But I knew they were there, filled with the fire of living. And what a marriage of elements was in those nests. Not only mud's earth and water, the fire of sun and dry air, but even the elements contained one another. The bodies of prophets and crazy men were broken down in that soil. 11

I've noticed often how, when a house is abandoned, it begins to sag. Without a tenant, it has no need to go on. If it were a person, we'd say it is depressed or lonely. The roof settles in, the paint cracks, the walls and floorboards warp and slope downward in their own natural ways, telling us that life must stay in everything as the world whirls and tilts and moves through boundless space. 12

One summer day, cleaning up after long-eared owls where I work at a rehabilitation facility for birds of prey, I was raking the gravel floor of a flight cage. Down on the ground, something looked like it was moving. I bent over to look into the pile of bones and pellets I'd just raked together. There, close to the ground, were two fetal mice. They were new to the planet, pink and hairless. They were so tenderly young. Their faces had swollen blue-veined eyes. They were nestled in a mound of feathers, soft as velvet, each one curled up smaller than an infant's ear, listening to the first sounds of earth. But the 13 ants were biting them. They turned in agony, unable to pull away, not yet having the arms or legs to move, but feeling, twisting away from the pain of the bites. I was horrified to see them bitten out of life that way. I dipped them in water, as if to take away the sting, and let the ants fall in the bucket. Then I held the tiny mice in the palm of my hand. Some of the ants were drowning in the water. I was trading one life for another, exchanging the lives of the ants for those of mice, but I hated their suffering, and hated even more that they had not yet grown to a life, and already they inhabited the miserable world of pain. Death and life feed each other. I know that.

14   Inside these rooms where birds are healed, there are other lives besides those of mice. There are fine gray globes the wasps have woven together, the white cocoons of spiders in a corner, the downward tunneling anthills. All these dwellings are inside one small walled space, but I think most about the mice. Sometimes the downy nests fall out of the walls where their mothers have placed them out of the way of their enemies. They are so well made and soft, woven mostly from the chest feathers of birds. Sometimes the leg of a small quail holds the nest together like a slender cornerstone with dry, bent claws. The mice have adapted to life in the presence of their enemies, adapted to living in the thin wall between beak and beak, claw and claw. They move their nests often, as if a new rafter or wall will protect them from the inevitable fate of all our returns home to the deeper, wider nests of earth that houses us all.

15   One August at Zia Pueblo during the corn dance, I noticed tourists picking up shards of all the old pottery that had been made and broken there. The residents of Zia know not to take the bowls and pots left behind by the older ones. They know that the fragments of those earlier lives need to be smoothed back to earth, but younger nations, travelers from continents across the world who have come to inhabit this land, have little of their own to grow on. The pieces of earth that were formed into bowls, even on their way home to dust, provide the new people a lifeline to an unknown land, help them remember that they live in the old nest of earth.

16   It was in early February, during the mating season of the great horned owl. It was dusk, and I hiked up the back of a mountain to where I'd heard the owls a year before. I wanted to hear them again, the voices so tender, so deep, like a memory of comfort. I was halfway up the trail when I found a soft, round nest. It had fallen from one of the bare-branched trees. It was a delicate nest, woven together of feathers, sage, and strands of wild grass. Holding it in my hand in the rosy twilight, I noticed that a blue thread was entwined with the other gatherings there. I pulled at the thread a little, and then I recognized it. It was a thread from one of my skirts. It was blue cotton. It was the unmistakable color and shape of a pattern I knew. I liked it, that a thread of my life was in an abandoned nest, one that had held eggs and new life. I took the nest home. At home, I held it to the light and looked more closely. There, to my surprise, nestled into the gray-green sage, was a gnarl of black hair. It was also unmistakable. It was my daughter's hair, cleaned from a brush and picked up out in the sun beneath the maple tree or the pit cherry where the birds eat from the overladen, fertile branches until only the seeds remain on the trees.

17   I didn't know what kind of nest it was or who had lived there. It didn't matter. I thought of the remnants of our lives carried up the hill that way and turned into shelter. That night, resting inside the walls of our home, the world outside weighed so heavily against the thin wood of the house. The sloped roof was the only thing between us and

the universe. Everything outside of our wooden boundaries seemed so large. Filled with the night's citizens, it all came alive. The world opened in the thickets of the dark. The wild grapes would soon ripen on the vines. The burrowing ones were emerging. Horned owls sat in treetops. Mice scurried here and there. Skunks, fox, the slow and holy porcupine, all were passing by this way. The young of the solitary bees were feeding on the pollen in the dark. The whole world was a nest on its humble tilt, in the maze of the universe, holding us.

Thinking Critically About Content

1. How does each of the dwellings Hogan describes suit its inhabitants? Refer to two specific dwellings to answer this question.

2. Find at least one detail for each of the five senses: seeing, hearing, touching, smelling, and tasting. Does Hogan draw on any one sense more than the others?

3. In paragraph 4, what is Hogan referring to as "the center of the world"? Explain your answer.

Thinking Critically About Purpose and Audience

4. What dominant impression does Hogan create in this essay?

5. Who do you think is Hogan's primary audience?

6. Explain your understanding of this essay's title.

Thinking Critically About Essays

7. Each section of Hogan's essay is about a different dwelling. Is each section unified? Look at the topic sentence of paragraph 7. Do all the sentences in this paragraph relate to its topic sentence? Explain your answer.

8. If a paragraph is coherent, it is logical and easy to read. Often, well-chosen transitions help a writer achieve coherence. Underline the words, phrases, and clauses Hogan uses as transitions in paragraph 13. How do these transitions help this paragraph read smoothly? Explain your answer.

9. Look at Hogan's conclusion. Is it effective for this essay? How does the last sentence ("The whole world was a nest on its humble tilt, in the maze of the universe, holding us") tie the whole essay together?

10. Describe in detail the secret to a perfect dwelling.

To keep track of your critical thinking progress, go to Appendix 1.

Writing Description

This final section gives you opportunities to apply what you have learned in this chapter to your own writing. Following the guidelines for writing a description essay, you will demonstrate that you can go through the entire writing process on your own with occasional feedback from your peers. Review your reading as necessary to study good examples of this type of writing. Then pause at the end of the chapter to reflect briefly on what you have learned.

Guidelines for Writing a Description Essay

1. Decide on a dominant impression—the feeling or mood you want to communicate.
2. Decide how much of your description should be objective (factual) and how much should be subjective (personal reactions).
3. Draw on your five senses to write a good description.
4. When you describe, try to *show* rather than *tell* your readers what you want them to know.
5. Organize your description so that your readers can easily follow it.

Writing About Your Reading

1. In the first selection, Amy Tan draws on impressions from all the senses to show how her main character observes her new home. Think of a place that is very important to you, a place that is a part of your life now or that was a part of your life in the past. Write a description of that place, drawing on as many of the senses as possible—seeing, hearing, touching, smelling, and tasting—so that your readers can experience this place the way you did.

2. How healthy are you? Write a description of the foods you eat and the exercise you get in a normal week. In what ways are you taking good care of yourself so that you have a chance for a long, healthy life?

3. In the third essay, Mario Suarez draws on all five senses to describe this *barrio*. Which of his senses is most active in this essay? Which of your senses is usually most dominant? Write an essay describing a typical day in your life from the point of view of your dominant sense. Give the sense a voice and a mind of its own.

4. How well suited to you is the place where you live now? Write a description of the features of your house or apartment that make it most suitable (or unsuitable) for you.

5. What do you think are the most important features of a good description? Why are they important? What effect do they have on you?

Writing About Your World

1. Place yourself in your favorite natural habitat, and describe it in as much detail as possible. Imagine you can see, hear, smell, taste, and touch everything

near you. What are your sensations? How do you feel? Before you begin to write, decide what dominant impression you want to convey. Then choose your details carefully.

2. Starting college is an important decision for students and everyone associated with them—parents, children, friends, relatives, even the household pets. Describe a person who was helpful with your decision to go to college. Be sure to decide on a dominant impression before you begin to write.

3. You have been asked to write a short statement for your psychology class on the study environment that is best for you. Describe this environment. Where do you study? What sounds do you hear? What do you eat or drink as you study? What do you wear? Help your readers picture your study environment so that they feel they are actually there. Be sure you decide on a dominant impression before you begin to write.

4. A national travel magazine is asking for honest descriptions (positive or negative) of places people have visited. The magazine is offering $100 to the writers of the essays chosen for publication. You may decide to write about a place with a marvelous beach or about an absolutely awful hotel. In either case, remember to begin with the dominant impression you want to communicate.

5. Create your own description assignment (with the help of your instructor), and write a response to it.

Revising

Small Group Activity (5–10 minutes per writer) Working in groups of three or four, read your description essays to each other. Those listening should record their reactions on a copy of the Peer Evaluation Form in Appendix 2A. After your group goes through this process, give your evaluation forms to the appropriate writers so that each writer has two or three peer comment sheets for revising.

Paired Activity (5 minutes per writer) Using the completed Peer Evaluation Forms, work in pairs to decide what you should revise in your essay. If time allows, rewrite some of your sentences, and have your partner look at them.

Individual Activity Rewrite your paper, using the revising feedback you received from other students.

Editing

Paired Activity (5–10 minutes per writer) Swap papers with a classmate, and use the editing portion of your Peer Evaluation Form to identify as many grammar, punctuation, mechanics, and spelling errors as you can. If time allows, correct some of your errors, and have your partner look at them. Record your grammar, punctuation, and mechanics errors in the Error Log (Appendix 3) and your spelling errors in the Spelling Log (Appendix 4).

Individual Activity Rewrite your paper again, using the editing feedback you received from other students.

Reflecting on Your Writing   When you have completed your own essay, answer these six questions.

1. What was most difficult about this assignment?

2. What was easiest?

3. What did you learn about description by completing this assignment?

4. What do you think are the strengths of your description? Place a wavy line by the parts of your essay that you feel are very good.

5. What are the weaknesses, if any, of your paper? Place an X by the parts of your essay you would like help with. Write any questions you have in the margins.

6. What did you learn from this assignment about your own writing process— about preparing to write, about writing the first draft, about revising, and about editing?

Narration: From Reading to Writing

This chapter includes four reading selections and several writing assignments. It also guides you through effective peer evaluation and reflection exercises that teach you how to mark your essay in preparation for your instructor to read it.

Reading Narration

As before, this chapter includes four essays that illustrate good narrative writing. In "Eleven," Sandra Cisneros recalls the humiliation she suffered in front of her classmates as a result of an insensitive teacher. In the second selection, "Choosing the Path with Honor," Michael Arredondo tells a moving story about his education. In "The Sanctuary of School," Lynda Barry tells a story about using her school as an escape from her home life, and in "Writer's Retreat," Stan Higgins talks about his life as a writer in prison. As you read, notice how the writers cover the journalistic questions (who? what? when? where? why? and how?) and use vivid descriptive details to pull you into their narratives, making the main point of the essays all the more meaningful.

ELEVEN
by Sandra Cisneros

Focusing Your Attention

1. Can you recall a time when you felt embarrassed in front of your class-mates? What details do you recall?

2. In the story you are about to read, "Eleven" refers to the age of the main character in the story. Try to remember what your life was like when you

were 11; you would have been in fifth or sixth grade. Were you particularly sensitive about your looks? Did you worry about what your friends thought of you or whether or not you were popular? Have you become more or less self-conscious about these issues as you have gotten older?

Expanding Your Vocabulary

The following word is important to your understanding of this story. Start a vocabulary log of your own by recording any words you don't understand as you read. When you finish reading the essay, write down what you think the words mean. Then check your definitions in the dictionary.

rattling: moving around and making noise (paragraph 5)

READING CRITICALLY
Thinking Aloud as You Read

As demonstrated in the Introduction, "think aloud" as you read. Interject personal references and focused ideas into your oral reading of the essay. The clearer you make your connections, the more deeply you will understand the essay. Read the essay at least two times. Discuss with a classmate the types of ideas you had as you read (focused or random). Which one of you did more focused reading?

ELEVEN
by Sandra Cisneros

1   What they don't understand about birthdays and what they never tell you is that when you're eleven, you're also ten, and nine, and eight, and seven, and six, and five, and four, and three, and two, and one. And when you wake up on your eleventh birthday, you expect to feel eleven, but you don't. You open your eyes and everything's just like yesterday, only it's today. And you don't feel eleven at all. You feel like you're still ten. And you are—underneath the year that makes you eleven.

2   Like some days you might say something stupid, and that's the part of you that's still ten. Or maybe some days you might need to sit on your mama's lap because you're scared, and that's the part of you that's five. And maybe one day when you're all grown up, maybe you will need to cry like if you're three, and that's okay. That's what I tell Mama when she's sad and needs to cry. Maybe she's feeling three.

3   Because the way you grow old is kind of like an onion or like the rings inside a tree trunk or like my little wooden dolls that fit one inside the other, each year inside the next one. That's how being eleven years old is.

You don't feel eleven. Not right away. It takes a few days, weeks even, sometimes even months before you say eleven when they ask you. And you don't feel smart eleven, not until you're almost twelve. That's the way it is.   4

Only today I wish I didn't have only eleven years rattling inside me like pennies in a tin Band-Aid box. Today I wish I was one hundred and two instead of eleven because if I was one hundred and two I'd have known what to say when Mrs. Price put the red sweater on my desk. I would've known how to tell her it wasn't mine instead of just sitting there with that look on my face and nothing coming out of my mouth.   5

"Whose is this?" Mrs. Price says, and she holds the red sweater up in the air for all the class to see. "Whose? It's been sitting in the coatroom for a month."   6

"Not mine," says everybody. "Not me."   7

"It has to belong to somebody," Mrs. Price keeps saying, but nobody can remember. It's an ugly sweater with red plastic buttons and a collar and sleeves all stretched out like you could use it for a jump rope. It's maybe a thousand years old, and even if it belonged to me I wouldn't say so.   8

Maybe because I'm skinny, maybe because she doesn't like me, that stupid Sylvia Saldívar says, "I think it belongs to Rachel." An ugly sweater like that, all raggedy and old, but Mrs. Price believes her. Mrs. Price takes the sweater and puts it right on my desk, but when I open my mouth nothing comes out.   9

"That's not, I don't, you're not ... Not mine," I finally say in a little voice that was maybe me when I was four.   10

"Of course it's yours," Mrs. Price says. "I remember you wearing it once." Because she's older and the teacher, she's right and I'm not.   11

Not mine, not mine, not mine, but Mrs. Price is already turning to page thirty-two, and math problem number four. I don't know why, but all of a sudden I'm feeling sick inside, like the part of me that's three wants to come out of my eyes, only I squeeze them shut tight and bite down on my teeth real hard and try to remember today I am eleven, eleven. Mama is making a cake for me for tonight, and when Papa comes home everybody will sing Happy birthday, happy birthday to you.   12

But when the sick feeling goes away and I open my eyes, the red sweater's still sitting there like a big red mountain. I move the red sweater to the corner of my desk with my ruler. I move my pencil and books and eraser as far from it as possible. I even move my chair a little to the right. Not mine, not mine, not mine.   13

In my head I'm thinking how long till lunchtime, how long till I can take the red sweater and throw it over the schoolyard fence, or leave it hanging on a parking meter, or bunch it up into a little ball and toss it in the alley. Except when math period ends Mrs. Price says loud and in front of everybody, "Now, Rachel, that's enough," because she sees I've shoved the red sweater to the tippy-tip corner of my desk and it's hanging all over the edge like a waterfall, but I don't care.   14

"Rachel," Mrs. Price says. She says it like she's getting mad. "You put that sweater on right now and no more nonsense."   15

"But it's not—"   16

"Now!" Mrs. Price says.   17

This is when I wish I wasn't eleven, because all the years inside of me—ten, nine, eight, seven, six, five, four, three, two, and one—are pushing at the back of my eyes when I put one arm through one sleeve of the sweater that smells like cottage cheese, and then   18

19   the other arm through the other and stand there with my arms apart like if the sweater hurts me and it does, all itchy and full of germs that aren't even mine.

That's when everything I've been holding in since this morning, since when Mrs. Price put the sweater on my desk, finally lets go, and all of a sudden I'm crying in front of everybody. I wish I was invisible but I'm not. I'm eleven and it's my birthday today and I'm crying like I'm three in front of everybody. I put my head down on the desk and bury my face in my stupid clown-sweater arms. My face all hot and spit coming out of my mouth because I can't stop the little animal noises from coming out of me, until there aren't any more tears left in my eyes, and it's just my body shaking like when you have the hiccups, and my whole head hurts like when you drink milk too fast.

20   But the worst part is right before the bell rings for lunch. That stupid Phyllis Lopez, who is even dumber than Sylvia Saldívar, says she remembers the red sweater is hers! I take it off right away and give it to her, only Mrs. Price pretends like everything's okay.

21   Today I'm eleven. There's a cake Mama's making for tonight, and when Papa comes home from work we'll eat it. There'll be candles and presents and everybody will sing Happy birthday, happy birthday to you, Rachel, only it's too late.

22   I'm eleven today. I'm eleven, ten, nine, eight, seven, six, five, four, three, two, and one, but I wish I was one hundred and two. I wish I was anything but eleven, because I want today to be far away already, far away like a runaway balloon, like a tiny *o* in the sky, so tiny-tiny you have to close your eyes to see it.

Thinking Critically About Content

1. Why do you think Cisneros pays such close attention to Rachel's age and to the fact that it is her birthday?

2. What does Rachel mean when she says that although there will be a cake and candles and presents and singing that evening at her home, "it's too late" (paragraph 21)?

3. What details does Cisneros use to show that Rachel is far more sensitive and intelligent than her teacher, Mrs. Price, thinks she is?

Thinking Critically About Purpose and Audience

4. What do you think Cisneros's purpose is in this essay? Explain your answer.

5. What type of audience would most understand and appreciate this recollection?

6. Does the writer succeed in making the audience feel the pain and hurt of an 11-year-old? How does she accomplish this?

Thinking Critically About Paragraphs

7. In this story, Cisneros adopts the point of view of an 11-year-old girl, using the language, thought processes, and behavior of a child that age. Paragraph 19 is an especially good example of the author's point of view in this essay. How would this paragraph be different if it were told by Rachel as an adult remembering the incident?

8. In this essay, Cisneros uses several comparisons called *similes*. A simile uses "like" or "as" in a comparison between two unlike items. These comparisons help us understand an item the author is trying to explain. Here are some examples:

> Because the way you grow old is kind of like an onion or like the rings inside a tree trunk or like my little wooden dolls that fit one inside the other, each year inside the next one. That's how being eleven years old is. (paragraph 3)

Find two more similes, and explain why they are effective.

9. Record three specific details from paragraph 9. What do they add to the paragraph?

10. Rachel feels terribly frustrated because her teacher simply does not understand the significance of making Rachel claim ownership for the ugly red sweater. Pretend you are Mrs. Price, and rewrite this event from her point of view, portraying her frustration over Rachel's behavior.

To keep track of your critical thinking progress, go to Appendix 1.

CHOOSING THE PATH WITH HONOR
by Michael Arredondo

Focusing Your Attention

1. Have you ever wanted something you couldn't have? What was it? Why couldn't you have it?

2. This narrative is about a person who, since he was six years old, had a dream he didn't know if he could achieve. Have you ever had a dream that seemed impossible? What have you done to keep that dream alive?

Expanding Your Vocabulary

The following words are important to your understanding of this essay. Start a vocabulary log of your own by recording any words you don't understand as you read. When you finish reading the essay, write down what you think the words mean. Then check your definitions in the dictionary.

ruptured: burst (paragraph 1)

fragmented: broken into pieces (paragraph 2)

deployed: sent off (paragraph 15)

fibrillators: medical tools that help control an abnormal heartbeat (paragraph 17)

ablation: process of melting away (paragraph 17)

empowering: enabling (paragraph 23)

predominantly: mainly (paragraph 27)

READING CRITICALLY
Thinking Aloud As You Read

As you did with the previous essay, "think aloud" as you read this essay by Michael Arredondo. This process will give you some good insights into the author's approach to his topic. Write down any new ideas you discover. As you continue to read critically, you will deepen your understanding of this essay. Read the essay at least two times. Discuss with a classmate the types of ideas you had as you read (focused or random). Which one of you did more focused reading?

CHOOSING THE PATH WITH HONOR
by Michael Arredondo

1   I get my Shawnee blood from my mother's side of the family. Her father was Shawnee, and her mother was Turtle Mountain Chippewa. My father's family is from Mexico. My great, great grandfather, David Dushane, was chief of the Eastern Shawnee in the 1940s, who died in 1976 of a ruptured appendix. The Shawnee were involuntarily placed in Oklahoma. But of course we were promised the land would always be ours and it would never be owned by whites.

2   As we all know, in 1907 Oklahoma, land of the Red people, home of the Red people, became the 46th state. The Shawnee were fragmented into three tribes—the Loyal, the Absentee, and the Eastern extreme.

3   We have about 1,000 tribal members, and if my math is correct, it's only two to three percent that are fluent in our language. There is no way to learn our language unless you go home. There is no other way to learn the language. You have to go home and attend language class on Wednesday nights. Being a student here at Cornell, it is just impossible for me to be in Oklahoma on Wednesday nights. I understand the elders reasoning for doing that. However, it is a difficult thing to accept.

4   The Shawnee never received a reservation. Instead, we received offers to buy tracts of land for individual ownership.

5   I have two older sisters, and my father took a look at the poverty, high unemployment, poor health, and the welfare system and said, "I cannot raise my family here. I need to go where I can do the best for them." So he moved us to Albuquerque, New Mexico. You know, they say if you don't like Mexicans and you don't like Indians, don't go to Albuquerque.

6   So we fit right in there, and that is where we grew up. My mom's parents were also there. My grandfather sat me down as he would from time to time and told me about all the bad things I would hear about being Native.

7   As my life unfolded, I saw that it was indeed true. I did hear those things. In paralleling Sitting Bull's words, in his time, he told me that I had been born into a white man's world and that I would be walking on a white man's road.

He said, "You should acquire the white man's medicine and his skills and his planning, and you bring them back to us. We will be waiting for you."   8

I have been trying my whole life to get to college. It has been quite a long road. I learned about college while watching TV. I caught about the last five minutes of a TV program, and I went and found my mom after it was over, and I asked her what an Ivory Leaf school was.   9

She was chuckling for about as long as you are, and she told me that it was a school that you could go to if you had a lot of money. I asked her if we had enough.   10

She looked at me, and she said, "It might be a little while." So this college thing sounded pretty good, and if I was going to go, I was definitely going to go to the best, because that was what the TV program said.   11

So I went out, and I got all the jobs a little kid can get at that age. I raked leaves and picked up old cans and that sort of thing. They were all too happy to pay me to do odd jobs to contribute to my Ivory Leaf school fund. After some time, I put all this money together and took it to my mom, and I asked her if I had enough yet to go to the best school.   12

She didn't bother to count it. She only looked at me, and she said, "You know, it might be a while." So this continued for some time, but I noticed that a very indirect and subtle message began to appear. Over time as I got older, it came to be a very direct message. I was told by various people in the school system that certain programs, institutions, and educational opportunities weren't for me. Weren't for Indians. Weren't for people of color. And that perhaps I should make other plans.   13

So I quit talking about it so much, and by the time I got to high school, I quit talking about it altogether. In four years of high school, I did not have one teacher, one administrator, one coach, one advisor, one counselor ask me if I wanted to go to college. Not one.   14

So after high school, I joined the U.S. Navy to get the G.I. bill so I could go to college, because I knew my parents couldn't help me. Shortly thereafter I was deployed to the Gulf War. Being medical personnel in the Gulf on the USS *Iwo Jima* put me in a pretty bad position. We had what was termed the worst accident in the history of the Gulf War. I had never seen and I hope I never see again bodies that were burned that bad, beyond recognition. Using their dental records to identify their remains, preparing them to be shipped back home, I could only stop and think, this is not what I had in mind. I just wanted to get money to go to school.   15

But you know what they say, join the service, see the world, get money for your education. When I got back from the Gulf, I applied and was accepted to the cardiovascular school of medicine in Bethesda, Maryland. To give you a very brief idea of what a cardiovascular technologist does, we function in place of a physician's assistant to the cardiologist. We scrub in with the physician at the table in the OR. We are a cross between a physician's assistant and first assistant in the operating room.   16

Along with the doctor, we know all the procedures that clear out the blockages in the heart. We know how to program and implant internal fibrillators that will restore an abnormal heartbeat. We know how to map the electricity inside the heart, find the abnormal pathways, and fry them out with radio frequency ablation to restore normal rhythms.   17

I really love what I do, what I have been doing for ten years already. When I got out of the Navy five years ago, I was 26. I had to stop and think, do I still want to be assisting physicians in ten years? In ten years, I could be a physician.   18

19   So I had three goals ahead of me. I needed to get out of debt. I am a skydiver. I have been skydiving for six years now, and I stopped counting jumps at 200, which is a whole other story. But I had to master a significant amount of debt. I needed to get in school, because as we all know, being outside of the school system and getting to the point where you are sitting down in the classroom and taking classes can be quite a hurdle.

20   I also wanted to find a way to finance my education and cost of living. I looked around for about six months. I found a job in Seattle, and I moved up there. In a year, I pounded down about $17 grand worth of debt, and I got into school.

21   I reduced my hours to part-time at work, which in my field is about 30 hours a week. And while taking chemistry, calculus, physics, organic chemistry, biology, and all those sorts of classes, I found that it was becoming just too much, the stress of my work and my classes.

22   So I wrote a letter to the richest man in the world, explaining my plight to accomplish my third goal. The richest man in the world wrote me back and said, I understand your situation. I understand what you have been up against. I understand that not very many people have given you a chance. I'll take a chance on you.

23   It's really been quite a thing to think that somebody that I don't even know has decided to back me like that. For every semester that I successfully complete, along my pathway, I get funding from the Bill and Linda Gates Foundation, and it covers my tuition, my books and my fees, cost of living, groceries and electricity bill, food plan. It's really quite a deal. It is one of the most empowering things that has ever happened to me.

24   So, this last spring, a letter came in the mail from an Ivory Leaf school.

25   I opened that letter up, and it told me that the dream that I had inside for 25 years, the dream of a six-year-old child, had finally come true.

26   This past summer, I sold most of what I owned and loaded the rest in a U-Haul and took six days to drive out here to Cornell, to finish my pre-med requirements. I am here at Cornell.

27   The Native students here, we face our own issues. We wonder if we got accepted for our blood. I've talked with other Native people, not here at Cornell, that feel perhaps we have sold out, come to a predominantly white institution, that what we need is to attend our own schools and tribal colleges.

28   When you look at all the physicians in the United States, divide them up by race, and point to all of them that are Indian, it's one tenth of one one-hundredth. When you look at all of the applicants in the Cornell pre-med pool every year, out of everybody that applies to medical school from Cornell University every year, on the average 81 percent get in. Those are huge numbers when you compare that to other institutions.

29   I came here to increase my chances, to take the road that gives me the best chance to accomplish my dream. Unfortunately the reality is that if I blow my grades, I blow my ride. It's that simple.

30   I imagine with my heritage I could just as well work for indigenous people from Mexico. But I wasn't nurtured that way. I know that in the end, when I stand before the Creator and look him in the eye, I know that I have chosen the more narrow, more difficult path, but one with great honor.

31   That will be my message to those that are yet to come, not to be self-serving. To pick that most difficult path, to come back and serve your own, to be proud of who you are, be proud of being Indian and where you come from. To be humble before the Creator, to listen to the children, for they will be sitting where you sit and I will sit. They'll be the only ones.

Thinking Critically About Content

1. What race is the author? When do we learn this fact?

2. What is the author's dream for his future?

3. According to Arredondo, what was "one of the most empowering things that has ever happened to me" (paragraph 23)?

Thinking Critically About Purpose and Audience

4. Explain your understanding of this essay's title.

5. Who do you think is Arredondo's primary audience?

6. Arredondo uses a very informal tone in this essay, which makes the readers feel he is actually talking to them. Do you feel this is an effective way to get his message across? Explain your answer.

Thinking Critically About Paragraphs

7. Find four details in Arredondo's essay that help us understand the difficult time the author had getting to college.

8. How does Arredondo organize his details in paragraph 22? Is this an effective order for this paragraph?

9. Why does Arredondo focus on children in his final paragraph? Is this an effective ending to his essay?

10. Write a paragraph describing what you believe Arredondo's mother was thinking the first time he asked her about college.

To keep track of your critical thinking progress, go to Appendix 1.

THE SANCTUARY OF SCHOOL
by Lynda Barry

Focusing Your Attention

1. Can you recall a time in your life when you felt particularly lonely or afraid? Write down as many facts, impressions, and memories as you can recall about that period of your life.

2. In the essay you are about to read, the writer describes a person who had a lasting impact on her. Have you ever had such an impact on someone that he or she wrote an essay about you? Have you had such an impact on more than one person? Who are these people? What would they say about you in their recollections?

Expanding Your Vocabulary

The following words are important to your understanding of this essay. Start a vocabulary log of your own by recording any words you don't understand as you read. When you finish reading the essay, write down what you think the words mean. Then check your definitions in the dictionary.

sanctuary: safe place (title)

nondescript: not distinctive (paragraph 7)

monkey bars: playground equipment (paragraph 8)

breezeway: covered passage between two buildings (paragraph 13)

READING CRITICALLY
Thinking Aloud as You Read

As before, "think aloud" as you read. Interject personal references and focused ideas into your oral reading of the essay. The clearer you make your connections, the more deeply you will understand the essay. Read the essay at least two times. Discuss with a classmate the types of ideas you had as you read (focused or random). Which one of you did more focused reading?

THE SANCTUARY OF SCHOOL
by Lynda Barry

1   I was 7 years old the first time I snuck out of the house in the dark. It was winter, and my parents had been fighting all night. They were short on money and long on relatives who kept "temporarily" moving into our house because they had nowhere else to go.

2   My brother and I were used to giving up our bedroom. We slept on the couch, something we actually liked because it put us that much closer to the light of our lives, our television.

3   At night when everyone was asleep, we lay on our pillows watching it with the sound off. We watched Steve Allen's mouth moving. We watched Johnny Carson's mouth moving. We watched movies filled with gangsters shooting machine guns into packed rooms, dying soldiers hurling a last grenade, and beautiful women crying at windows. Then the sign-off finally came, and we tried to sleep.

4   The morning I snuck out, I woke up filled with a panic about needing to get to school. The sun wasn't quite up yet, but my anxiety was so fierce that I just got dressed, walked quietly across the kitchen, and let myself out the back door.

It was quiet outside. Stars were still out. Nothing moved, and no one was in the street. It was as if someone had turned the sound off on the world.

I walked the alley, breaking thin ice over the puddles with my shoes. I didn't know why I was walking to school in the dark. I didn't think about it. All I knew was the feeling of panic, like the panic that strikes kids when they realize they are lost.

That feeling eased the moment I turned the corner and saw the dark outline of my school at the top of the hill. My school was made up of about 15 nondescript portable classrooms set down on a fenced concrete lot in a rundown Seattle neighborhood, but it had the most beautiful view of the Cascade Mountains. You could see them from anywhere on the playfield, and you could see them from the windows of my classroom—Room 2.

I walked over to the monkey bars and hooked my arms around the cold metal. I stood for a long time just looking across Rainier Valley. The sky was beginning to whiten, and I could hear a few birds.

In a perfect world, my absence at home would not have gone unnoticed. I would have had two parents in a panic to locate me, instead of two parents in a panic to locate an answer to the hard question of survival during a deep financial and emotional crisis.

But in an overcrowded and unhappy home, it's incredibly easy for any child to slip away. The high levels of frustration, depression, and anger in my house made my brother and me invisible. We were children with the sound turned off. And for us, as for the steadily increasing number of neglected children in this country, the only place where we could count on being noticed was at school.

"Hey there, young lady. Did you forget to go home last night?" It was Mr. Gunderson, our janitor, whom we all loved. He was nice and he was funny and he was old with white hair, thick glasses, and an unbelievable number of keys. I could hear them jingling as he walked across the playfield. I felt incredibly happy to see him.

He let me push his wheeled garbage can between the different portables as he unlocked each room. He let me turn on the lights and raise the window shades, and I saw my school slowly come to life. I saw Mrs. Holman, our school secretary, walk into the office without her orange lipstick on yet. She waved.

I saw the fifth-grade teacher, Mr. Cunningham, walking under the breezeway eating a hard roll. He waved.

And I saw my teacher, Mrs. Claire LeSane, walking toward us in a red coat and calling my name in a very happy and surprised way, and suddenly my throat got tight and my eyes stung and I ran toward her crying. It was something that surprised both of us.

It's only thinking about it now, 28 years later, that I realize I was crying from relief. I was with my teacher, and in a while I was going to sit at my desk, with my crayons and pencils and books and classmates all around me, and for the next six hours I was going to enjoy a thoroughly secure, warm, and stable world. It was a world I absolutely relied on. Without it, I don't know where I would have gone that morning.

Mrs. LeSane asked me what was wrong, and when I said, "Nothing," she seemingly left it at that. But she asked me if I would carry her purse for her, an honor above all honors, and she asked if I wanted to come into Room 2 early and paint.

5

6

7

8

9

10

11

12

13

14

15

16

17   She believed in the natural healing power of painting and drawing for troubled children. In the back of her room there was always a drawing table and an easel with plenty of supplies, and sometimes during the day she would come up to you for what seemed like no good reason and quietly ask if you wanted to go to the back table and "make some pictures for Mrs. LeSane." We all had a chance at it—to sit apart from the class for a while to paint, draw, and silently work out impossible problems on 11 × 17 sheets of newsprint.

18   Drawing came to mean everything to me. At the back table in Room 2, I learned to build myself a life preserver that I could carry into my home. . . .

19   By the time the bell rang that morning, I had finished my drawing, and Mrs. LeSane pinned it up on the special bulletin board she reserved for drawings from the back table. It was the same picture I always drew—a sun in the corner of a blue sky over a nice house with flowers all around it.

Thinking Critically About Content

1. Notice how the writer describes herself and her brother as "children with the sound turned off" (paragraph 10) and their environment "as if someone had turned the sound off on the world" (paragraph 5). Is this an effective image? Why? What effect does it have on you? What does it tell you about Lynda Barry's childhood?

2. Why do you think the writer uses warm and vivid details to describe the arrival of school employees (paragraphs 11 through 16)? What effect does this description have on you, compared with the description of her home life?

3. Does this essay make you compare your own childhood to Lynda Barry's?

Thinking Critically About Purpose and Audience

4. What do you think Barry's purpose is in writing this narrative essay? Explain your answer.

5. What readers do you think would most understand and appreciate this recollection?

6. In your opinion, why doesn't the writer tell us more about her parents' problems?

Thinking Critically About Essays

7. Describe in a complete sentence the writer's point of view in this essay.

8. How does Barry organize the details in this essay? Is this an effective order?

9. Explain Barry's title for this essay.

10. Explain in detail how this essay would be different if it were written by Lynda Barry's parents.

To keep track of your critical thinking progress, go to Appendix 1.

WRITER'S RETREAT
by Stan Higgins

Focusing Your Attention

1. Can you remember a time in your life when you were frustrated trying to meet a goal you set for yourself? Write down as many facts, impressions, and memories as you can about this feeling.

2. In the essay you are about to read, the writer describes a person who is trying to write in prison. What do you think is his motivation? Have you ever wanted to do something so much you would even do it in prison? Explain your answer.

Expanding Your Vocabulary

The following words are important to your understanding of this essay. Start a vocabulary log of your own by recording any words you don't understand as you read. When you finish reading the essay, write down what you think the words mean. Then check your definitions in the dictionary.

within a pole vault: a few yards away (paragraph 1)

the Muse: inspiration (paragraph 2)

staccato: consisting of short, sharp sounds (paragraph 2)

ransacked: torn apart (paragraph 3)

confiscated: taken away (paragraph 3)

contraband: prohibited items (paragraph 3)

lock down: lock all prisoners in their cells (paragraph 4)

Bugler: brand of tobacco (paragraph 7)

mud: coffee (paragraph 16)

tier: row of prison cells (paragraph 23)

persevere: continue (paragraph 30)

tantamount: equal (paragraph 32)

misdemeanors: minor crimes (paragraph 32)

subsides: decreases (paragraph 34)

nebulous: vague, uncertain (paragraph 34)

girth: size (paragraph 41)

obscenities: offensive comments (paragraph 42)

READING CRITICALLY
Thinking Aloud as You Read

As with the previous essays, "think aloud" as you read this essay by Stan Higgins. This process will give you some good insights into the author's approach to his topic. Write down any new ideas you discover. As you continue to read critically, you will deepen your understanding of this essay. Read the essay at least two times. Discuss with a classmate the types of ideas you had as you read (focused or random). Which one of you did more focused reading?

WRITER'S RETREAT
by Stan Higgins

1   Sandwiched between mountain snow and desert sand, hidden by sandstone walls 150 years old within a pole vault of the Arkansas River, it just doesn't get any better than this writer's retreat I call home. I write from a Colorado prison cell.

2   During the day I wash dishes, clean tables, and mop floors. They call it Vocational Training. And today, as every day at three p.m., I return to my cozy, bathroom-size suite and drag out my tiny portable. We've all night, just the two of us, my blue typewriter that has been my steady cell-mate for six years, through seven facilities across two states, and I. Today's goal is three pages. I blow dust from the cover and clean the keys. The Muse calls. *Tack-tack. Tack. Tack-tack-tack.* My typewriter sings its staccato song as I search for a fertile word or idea, some harmonious junction of thought and paper. Locked in solitary combat with my machine, nothing exists outside my cell, or so I pretend. I type a line. My door opens. Two blue-uniformed guards stand there grinning. "Guess what?" one says. "Your number came up."

3   Somehow I know he doesn't mean the Lottery. One begins searching my cell. The other pats me down as I leave. I return twenty minutes later to find my house ransacked, my bed torn up, papers scattered, pencils and pens strewn about, socks, shorts, and type-writer piled in a heap on the floor. Taped to the shelf above my desk is a slip of yellow paper with a fancily scrawled list of books, magazines, and other confiscated contraband. I can't help but question their appreciation for the written word.

4   I put my house back in order. We lock down, and the guards count us. After ten minutes the Count is cleared. My hands tremble. I can't write, not now. It's time for the ultimate challenge to a prisoner's courage . . . Chow!

5   Buoyed at having survived another meal, I return to my cell and begin anew. *Tack-tack-tack.*

6   "Hey, Bro," a green-uniformed inmate named O'Neil hollers from my doorway. "Think I can get a pinch of tobacco?"

7   This, too, is part of the territory. I pause to hand him a can of Bugler. My attention returns to writing as I study the list of disjointed, unrelated words I have accumulated, but I see out of the corner of my eye that I still have company.

Stan Higgins, "Writer's Retreat," *The Writer* (1991).

"Think I can get a rolling paper?" O'Neil asks as he pops the lid off the can.   8

With a deep breath, I fish him a pack of papers from my pocket and hand them over.   9
He fumbles with the paper as I reread my typed words.

"Think you could roll it for me, Bro?"   10

"What else, O'Neil?" I say whisking the paper and tobacco from his hands and   11
rolling him a quick, crooked cigarette. He asks for a light as I usher him to the door.

Tack-tack-tack-tack, I resume. Just more words. I pinch my lips and study the nearly   12
blank sheet of paper. *Write what you know,* memories of books past suggest. What do I
know? Steel and concrete, jingling keys, and slamming doors. *Tack-tack-tack. Tack-tack.*

"M-m-Mr. Higgins?" another prisoner interrupts. It's a skinny kid in oversize greens,   13
and his voice squeaks. "W-would you maybe have a dictionary I could, you know, sorta read,
please?" He hesitates at the door in his stiff, fresh-out-of-the-package uniform that reminds
me of pajamas, eyeing my bookshelf from a safe distance until I stand. I pull a *Webster's New
Collegiate Dictionary* from my shelf above the desk and sit down again as he thumbs through
it. He clears his throat. "Uh, excuse me, how do you spell *the?*"

"With two *r*'s instead of one," I tell him, shooing him away with the back of my hand.   14

Tack-tack. Tack-tack, tack-tack-tack, tack. Bones of steel, concrete skin, I type, and a   15
soul as slippery as time.

Digger B. struts into my house. "Ya got a cup a mud I can get or what?" He pushes his   16
empty cup in front of me, and as I fill it, he peers over my shoulder. "So what ya doin'?"

"Trying to write about trying to write."   17

"Man," he says and slurps coffee from his cup. "Whyn't ya write about somethin'   18
interestin', know what I mean? Murder, war, sex, ya know—interestin'!"

I love encouragement. He wanders out.   19

I stare at my typewriter. I wait a few minutes. Nothing. My fingers creep back into   20
place. *Tack-tack-tack.*

"Got a weed?" asks a gruff voice. It's Thunder. Six-foot-six and almost as wide, 300   21
pounds of beard and tattoo, he slides sideways into my cell. I quickly roll him a cigarette
and light it.

"Anything else, Mr. Thunder?"   22

"Heared you typing clean down the tier," he grumbles. "What you doing?"   23

"Typing. Trying to type. Trying to write, I guess."   24

"You ain't writing 'bout me, are you?" He stares at me with eyes like rocks.   25

"No, sir, Mr. Thunder," I assure him, pointing to my almost blank paper. "Check it out."   26

He squints at it. "Don't like people writing 'bout me 'hind my back."   27

"I wouldn't do that, Mr. Thunder."   28

"Just so you ain't. 'At's all I care." He turns and sidles out the doorway. Thunder is   29
unpredictable. Thunder hears voices. Thunder caught a guy in the shower once and
stabbed him 53 times with a sharpened Number 2 pencil; he thought the man was talking about him. All in all, I figure it's not a bad idea to get along with Mr. Thunder.

The sun is setting. I've completed three sentences. My goal of three pages for the   30
day is becoming as gray as my cell. At this rate I'm confident I can finish an 800-word
article by my 2006 discharge date. *Persevere!* I get up and flip on the light.

Back to my typewriter; back on track. *Tack-tack-tack. Tack-tack, tack-tackity-tack.*   31
I'm into it finally, my head is there, I'm on the verge of something . . . when Thunder stops
at my door and pokes his woolly head in. "You sure you ain't writing things 'bout me?"

32   In prison, opening a can of tobacco, a bag of potato chips, or brewing a pot of coffee—like trying to type—is tantamount to throwing a side of beef into shark-infested waters. But these are minor distractions … misdemeanors. Prison overcrowding being what it is, Colorado officials have on several occasions sent inmates to faraway places for temporary storage. Two years ago guards came to my door with a green duffel bag and ordered me to pack up. I surveyed my four-year accumulation of books, magazines, and notes that converted my six-by-ten-foot cell into a private classroom. Each book and magazine, then highlighted for frequent reference, had been a hard-collected treasure. There were works-in-progress scattered on my desk. "Now!" a guard encouraged. "You're going to Washington state. If your stuff don't all fit …," he reassured me with a glint in his eye and a broad sweep of his arm, "… you don't need it!" A year later, I was returned to sender. Back in Colorado, I set up housekeeping, mailed out another batch of address changes.

33   An aluminum trash can falls to the floor from an upper tier, perhaps with a little help. I try to type. The cell block explodes in cheering and clapping. Pop cans rain from above. I hesitate at the keyboard. It might be boredom; it might be a fight or a stabbing. It might be a riot. Then again, it might be they just discovered what was for breakfast tomorrow.

34   It is dark outside. The noise subsides. I sit for a few minutes blissfully alone, rescuing my thoughts, pondering my last sentence, imagining some nebulous, faraway, fairy tale future where everything is happily-ever-after. I imagine a steak dinner, the meat still sizzling, its pink and brown juice puddling the plate beneath a twice-baked potato and fresh asparagus, steam rising. . . .

35   "You ain't writing 'bout me!?" Thunder startles me. This time I didn't hear or see him fill my doorway.

36   "No, sir," I tell him, cigarette smoke replacing the scent of steak. "Not one word, Mr. Thunder."

37   He scratches his beard and stares. He steps in and looks over my shoulder. When he speaks again, after some moments, his voice is uncharacteristically soft and plaintive. "Not one word?"

38   I shake my head.

39   "Ain't I good enough to be in your stories?"

40   For a minute I think he is about to cry. I tell him I'll write something about him if he likes. He reaches across the desk for the can of Bugler, rolls a cigarette, pats me on the back, and leaves.

41   I sigh into the typewriter keys and look up in time to see a couple of guards making the rounds, parading their girth like badges of authority, jingling keys. "Attention on the Block! Attention on the Block!" blares the loudspeaker. "Five minutes to Count! Lock up now!"

42   Inmates shout obscenities, but they are just pretending. They filter off to their cells. Visions of solitude dance in my head. Alone! Just me and my typewriter! Now I'll get something done. But maybe I am pretending also. Maybe we are all just pretending.

43   I get up and stretch, close my door, return to my desk, and wait.

44   "Count!" the loudspeaker squawks. "Count!"

45   Doors slam shut. Suddenly it is quiet. I pause to savor the silence. A plastic Salvation Army cup rests next to my typewriter, its contents cold, thick, and dark, but it is the best cup I've had all day. For a moment I think I hear crickets, distant, anonymous traffic, dogs barking, the hum of street lights.

Tickticktick . . . complains my clock, its face turned away, hiding time.   46

This is it. I'm either going to write, or I'm not. I remove a three-by-five-inch wire-bound notebook: musings for the day, observations carried with me through the day. Flipped open and set on the desk beside my typewriter, it reminds me that place can also be irrelevant. I turn a page and begin typing. *Tack-tack, tack-tack, tack-tackity-tack. Tack-tack.* What is it like to write from a prison cell? I write. *Tack-tack.*   47

The glare of a flashlight hits me in the eyes. There is a pounding at my door. A guard is aiming his light in my face. "What're ya doing this time of night?" he asks.   48

I take a deep breath and count to ten before answering. Writing from prison, I tell myself, just ain't what it used to be. Maybe it never was. I count to twenty.   49

"Baking a cake," I finally answer.   50

He grins. "Yeah? Is it fun?"   51

"I don't know," I say. "I'll tell you when it's done."   52

Thinking Critically About Content

1. What characterizes this "writer's retreat"?
2. What is Higgins writing about on his typewriter?
3. How does Higgins deal with all the interruptions? In what ways are these incidents part of his writing process?

Thinking Critically About Purpose and Audience

4. Explain your understanding of the writer's main point in this essay.
5. Who do you think Higgins's primary audience is?
6. Why was Higgins frustrated trying to meet his goal of three pages of writing for the day?

Thinking Critically About Essays

7. Describe Higgins's point of view in this essay. Does it change throughout the essay? If so, in what ways?
8. Higgins uses many details to illustrate his frustration as he tries to write. Which details communicate his frustration most clearly to you?
9. Higgins talks about baking a cake in his conclusion. Is this an effective ending? Why or why not?
10. Tell this same story from Mr. Thunder's perspective.

To keep track of your critical thinking progress, go to Appendix 1.

Writing Narration

This section asks you to apply what you have learned in this chapter to your own writing. It provides guidelines for writing a narration essay and for peer evaluation. Be sure to review the model narration essays in this chapter as needed. Pause at the end of the chapter to reflect briefly on what you have learned.

Guidelines for Writing a Narration Essay

1. Make sure your essay has a point.
2. Use the five *W*s and one *H* to construct your story.
3. Develop your narrative with vivid details.
4. Build excitement in your narrative with careful pacing.
5. Organize your narration so that your readers can easily follow it.

Writing About Your Reading

1. If being eleven, according to Cisneros, is also being ten, nine, eight, seven, six, and so on, what is being twenty? thirty? Choose an age older than eleven, and write a narrative to explain it to other students in your class.

Answer →

2. How clear are your goals? Arredondo set his career objectives at six years old and then worked twenty-five years just to get into pre-med school. What are your main goals in life? How do you plan to reach them? Explain your goals for the future.

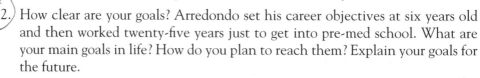

3. In "The Sanctuary of School," Lynda Barry recalls the way her school and her teachers provided a sanctuary, a place where she could escape from the problems of home. Write an essay in which you recall a place, a person, or an event that made you feel safe, secure, and welcome.

4. We all deal with frustration in different ways. Explain the coping strategies you have observed in friends and relatives. Do they work? Are they effective? Write a narrative essay focusing on various coping strategies you have observed.

5. What do you think are the most important features of a good story? Why are they important? What effect do they have on you?

Writing About Your World

1. Your old high school has asked you, as a graduate, to submit an essay to the newsletter recalling a job or volunteer experience you enjoyed. The editors want to inform current high school students about options for volunteer and paid work. Your purpose is to tell your story in enough interesting detail so that you convince the current high school students that the job you had is worth looking into.

2. Your college class is putting together a collection of essays that explain how classmates decided to go to their college. What happened first? When did you decide? What helped you decide? What activities or people influenced your decision the most? Tell your story in vivid detail.

3. We have all had experiences that began as carefree adventures and ended up as misadventures. Imagine that a national magazine is asking for honest stories about experiences that turned bad unexpectedly. The winning story will be published, and the author will win $200. You decide to enter the competition. The directions are to explain an experience in such a way that you reveal your feelings about this activity. Be sure to decide on a main point before you begin to write.

4. Your high school's alumni newsletter has asked you to explain an episode that influenced the values you hold today. Recall an event that influenced the kind of person you are today. First, identify one of your core values such as honesty, hard work, a strong sense of responsibility, independence, or patience. Then think back to what happened to give you this particular value, and write a paragraph telling the story about that value. The purpose of this narrative is to give current high school students some sense of how values might form in their own lives. Where can they look? How do values develop? Be sure to decide on a main point before you begin to write.

5. Create your own narration assignment (with the help of your instructor), and write a response to it.

Revising

Small Group Activity (5–10 minutes per writer) Working in groups of three or four, read your narration essays to each other. Those listening should record their reactions on a copy of the Peer Evaluation Form in Appendix 2A. After your group goes through this process, give your evaluation forms to the appropriate writers so that each writer has two peer comment sheets for revising.

Paired Activity (5 minutes per writer) Using the completed Peer Evaluation Forms, work in pairs to decide what you should revise in your essay. If time allows, rewrite some of your sentences, and have your partner look at them.

Individual Activity Rewrite your paper, using the revising feedback you received from other students.

Editing

Paired Activity (5–10 minutes per writer) Swap papers with a classmate, and use the editing portion of your Peer Evaluation Form to identify as many grammar, punctuation, mechanics, and spelling errors as you can. If time allows, correct some of your errors, and have your partner look at them. Record your grammar, punctuation, and mechanics errors in the Error Log (Appendix 3) and your spelling errors in the Spelling Log (Appendix 4).

Individual Activity Rewrite your paper again, using the editing feedback you received from other students.

Reflecting on Your Writing   When you have completed your own essay, answer these six questions.

1. What was most difficult about this assignment?

2. What was easiest?

3. What did you learn about narration by completing this assignment?

4. What do you think are the strengths of your narration? Place a wavy line by the parts of your essay that you feel are very good.

5. What are the weaknesses, if any, of your paper? Place an X by the parts of your essay you would like help with. Write any questions you have in the margins.

6. What did you learn from this assignment about your own writing process—about preparing to write, about writing the first draft, about revising, and about editing?

Illustration: From Reading to Writing

This chapter, as the others, includes four reading selections and several writing assignments. It leads you through peer evaluation and some reflection exercises that will help you annotate your final draft to create a productive dialogue on your paper with your instructor.

Reading Illustration

Here are four essays that use examples to make their point: "Mute in an English-Only World," written by Chang-Rae Lee, uses examples to show her mother's painful adjustment to the English language; in "Walk On By," Brent Staples uses some examples from his own experience to send a warning to kids in gangs; "Dawn's Early Light" by Richard Rodriguez gives examples from his experience to show how immigrants in the United States have changed us; and "The Decorated Body" by France Borel uses examples to talk about the importance of altering our physical appearance.

MUTE IN AN ENGLISH-ONLY WORLD
by Chang-Rae Lee

Focusing Your Attention

1. Can you think of a time in your life when you had trouble adjusting to a new situation? How did you handle it?

2. The essay you are about to read explains through well-chosen examples how it feels to live in a country where you don't understand the language. Have you ever had this experience? If so, how did you feel? if not, how do you think you would feel?

Expanding Your Vocabulary

The following words are important to your understanding of this essay. Organize this list into two columns—words you know and words you don't know. Write the definitions of the words you don't know over the words in the essay.

proliferation: rapid increase (paragraph 1)

vital: important (paragraph 1)

exclusionary: something that excludes others (paragraph 2)

aping: mimicking like an ape (paragraph 5)

sundry: of various kinds (paragraph 7)

harrowing: causing distress (paragraph 8)

deft: quick and skilled (paragraph 8)

READING CRITICALLY
Chunking Your Reading

As you learned in the Introduction, circle the main idea of the following essay, and then separate each example with horizontal lines. Label the examples in the margin. Then, share your marks with a classmate, justifying each of your decisions.

MUTE IN AN ENGLISH-ONLY WORLD
by Chang-Rae Lee

1   When I read of the troubles in Palisades Park, New Jersey, over the proliferation of Korean-language signs along its main commercial strip, I unexpectedly sympathized with the frustrations, resentments, and fears of the longtime residents. They clearly felt alienated and even unwelcome in a vital part of their community. The town, like seven others in New Jersey, has passed laws requiring that half of any commercial sign in a foreign language be in English.

2   Now I certainly would never tolerate any exclusionary ideas about who could rightfully settle and belong in the town. But having been raised in a Korean immigrant family, I saw every day the exacting price and power of language, especially with my mother, who was an outsider in an English-only world. In the first years we lived in America, my mother could speak only the most basic English, and she often encountered great difficulty whenever she went out.

We lived in New Rochelle, New York, in the early seventies, and most of the local businesses were run by the descendants of immigrants who, generations ago, had come to the suburbs from New York City. Proudly dotting Main Street and North Avenue were Italian pastry and cheese shops, Jewish tailors and cleaners, and Polish and German butchers and bakers. If my mother's marketing couldn't wait until the weekend, when my father had free time, she would often hold off until I came home from school to buy the groceries.

Though I was only six or seven years old, she insisted that I go out shopping with her and my younger sister. I mostly loathed the task, partly because it meant I couldn't spend the afternoon off playing catch with my friends but also because I knew our errands would inevitably lead to an awkward scene and that I would have to speak up to help my mother.

I was just learning the language myself, but I was a quick study, as children are with new tongues. I had spent kindergarten in almost complete silence, hearing only the high nasality of my teacher and comprehending little but the cranky wails and cries of my classmates. But soon, seemingly mere months later, I had already become a terrible ham and mimic, and I would crack up my father with impressions of teachers, his friends, and even himself. My mother scolded me for aping his speech, and the one time I attempted to make light of hers I rated a roundhouse smack on my bottom.

For her, the English language was not very funny. It usually meant trouble and a good dose of shame and sometimes real hurt. Although she had a good reading knowledge of the language from university classes in South Korea, she had never practiced actual conversation. So in America she used English flash cards and phrase books and watched television with us kids. And she faithfully carried a pocket workbook illustrated with stick-figure people and compound sentences to be filled in.

But none of it seemed to do her much good. Staying mostly at home to care for us, she didn't have many chances to try out sundry words and phrases. When she did, say, at the window of the post office, her readied speech would stall, freeze, sometimes altogether collapse.

One day was unusually harrowing. We ventured downtown in the new Ford Country Squire my father had bought her, an enormous station wagon that seemed as long—and deft—as an ocean liner. We were shopping for a special meal for guests visiting that weekend, and my mother had heard that a particular butcher carried fresh oxtails, which she needed for a traditional soup.

We'd never been inside the shop, but my mother would pause before its window, which was always lined with whole hams, crown roasts, and ropes of plump handmade sausages. She greatly esteemed the bounty with her eyes, and my sister and I did also, but despite our desirous cries she'd turn us away and instead buy the packaged links at the Finast supermarket, where she felt comfortable looking them over and could easily spot the price—and, of course, not have to talk.

But that day she was resolved. The butcher store was crowded, and as we stepped inside, the door jingled a welcome. No one seemed to notice. We waited for some time, and people who entered after us were now being served. Finally an old woman nudged my mother and waved a little ticket, which we hadn't taken. We patiently waited again, until one of the beefy men behind the glass display hollered our number.

My mother pulled us forward and began searching the cases, but the oxtails were nowhere to be found. The man, his big arms crossed, sharply said, "Come on, lady, whaddya want?" This unnerved her, and she somehow blurted the Korean word for oxtail, *soggori*.

12   The butcher looked as if my mother had put something sour in his mouth, and he glanced back at the lighted board and called the next number.

13   Before I knew it, she had rushed us outside and back in the wagon, which she had double-parked because of the crowd. She was furious, almost vibrating with fear and grief, and I could see she was about to cry.

14   She wanted to go back inside, but now the driver of the car we were blocking wanted to pull out. She was shooing us away. My mother, who had just earned her driver's license, started furiously working the pedals. But in her haste she must have flooded the engine, for it wouldn't turn over. The driver started honking, and then another car began honking as well, and soon it seemed the entire street was shrieking at us.

15   In the following years, my mother grew steadily more comfortable with English. In Korean she could be fiery, stern, deeply funny, and ironic; in English just slightly less so. If she was never quite fluent, she gained enough confidence to make herself clearly known to anyone, and particularly to me.

16   Five years ago she died of cancer, and some months after we buried her I found myself in the driveway of my father's house, washing her sedan. I liked taking care of her things; it made me feel close to her. While I was cleaning out the glove compartment, I found her pocket English workbook, the one with the silly illustrations. I hadn't seen it in nearly twenty years. The yellowed pages were brittle and dog-eared. She had fashioned a plain paper wrapping for it, and I wondered whether she meant to protect the book or hide it.

17   I don't doubt that she would have appreciated doing the family shopping on the new Broad Avenue of Palisades Park. But I like to think, too, that she would have understood those who now complain about the Korean-only signs.

18   I wonder what these same people would have done if they had seen my mother studying her English workbook—or lost in a store. Would they have nodded gently at her? Would they have lent a kind word?

Thinking Critically About Content

1. What examples from the essay illustrate the mother's discomfort with the English language during her first few years in America?

2. How does the author's mother learn to speak English?

3. Why is the English workbook an important part of this story?

Thinking Critically About Purpose and Audience

4. Why do you think the author wrote this essay?

5. What type of audience do you think would most understand and appreciate this essay?

6. Are you one of the people who would criticize foreign signs in your community?

Thinking Critically About Paragraphs

7. The author writes this essay predominantly in the past tense until paragraph 17 when she shifts to the present. What does this shift represent in the essay?

8. Look closely at paragraph 9. Is it unified? Do the examples the author uses in this paragraph support its topic sentence? Explain your answer.

9. How does the writer organize her details in paragraph 16? Is this an effective order?

10. Write a paragraph introducing a difficult adjustment you have made in your life.

To keep track of your critical thinking progress, go to Appendix 1.

WALK ON BY
by Brent Staples

Focusing Your Attention

1. Do you intimidate people with any of your behavior? Are you intimidated by anyone in particular?

2. The essay you are about to read discusses the image of African American males as criminals or suspects. It is written by someone who doesn't deserve this reputation. Have you ever been blamed for something you didn't do? What were you blamed for? Why were you blamed?

Expanding Your Vocabulary

The following words are important to your understanding of this essay. Organize this list into two columns—words you know and words you don't know. Write the definitions of the words you don't know over the words in the essay.

affluent: wealthy (paragraph 1)

impoverished: poor (paragraph 1)

uninflammatory: giving no cause for concern (paragraph 1)

billowing: waving (paragraph 1)

menacingly: dangerously (paragraph 1)

unwieldy: large, unmanageable (paragraph 2)

insomnia: sleeplessness (paragraph 2)

wayfarers: wanderers, travelers (paragraph 2)

dismayed: horrified (paragraph 2)

accomplice: associate, helper (paragraph 2)

tyranny: cruelty (paragraph 2)

errant: out of place (paragraph 2)

crowd cover: presence of large numbers of people (paragraph 4)

SoHo: a neighborhood of Manhattan, south of Houston Street (paragraph 4)

taut: strained, intense (paragraph 4)

ruthless: cruel (paragraph 5)

extols: praises (paragraph 5)

panhandlers: beggars (paragraph 5)

warrenlike: crowded (paragraph 6)

bandolier style: over one shoulder (paragraph 6)

lethality: deadliness (paragraph 7)

flailings: flinging one's arms in the air (paragraph 8)

mark: victim (paragraph 8)

cowered: cringed (paragraph 8)

valiant: brave, courageous (paragraph 8)

bravado: false bravery (paragraph 9)

perilous: dangerous (paragraph 10)

proprietor: owner (paragraph 11)

Doberman pinscher: a large breed of dog (paragraph 11)

skittish: easily frightened (paragraph 13)

congenial: friendly (paragraph 13)

constitutionals: walks (paragraph 14)

Beethoven: 1770–1827, a German composer (paragraph 14)

Vivaldi: 1678–1741, an Italian composer (paragraph 14)

READING CRITICALLY
Chunking Your Reading

Once again, circle the thesis of the following essay, and draw horizontal lines in the essay to show the different examples the author has chosen to support his thesis. Label the examples in the margins. Then, compare your marks with those of a classmate, and justify your divisions to each other.

WALK ON BY
by Brent Staples

My first victim was a woman—white, well dressed, probably in her early twenties. I came upon her late one evening on a deserted street in Hyde Park, a relatively affluent neighborhood in an otherwise mean, impoverished section of Chicago. As I swung onto the avenue behind her, there seemed to be a discreet, uninflammatory distance between us. Not so. She cast back a worried glance. To her, the youngish black man—a broad six feet two inches with a beard and billowing hair, both hands shoved into the pockets of a bulky military jacket—seemed menacingly close. After a few more quick glimpses, she picked up her pace and was soon running in earnest. Within seconds she disappeared into a cross street.

That was more than a decade ago. I was 22 years old, a graduate student newly arrived at the University of Chicago. It was in the echo of that terrified woman's footfalls that I first began to know the unwieldy inheritance I'd come into—the ability to alter public space in ugly ways. It was clear that she thought herself the quarry of a mugger, a rapist, or worse. Suffering a bout of insomnia, however, I was stalking sleep, not defenseless wayfarers. As a softy who is scarcely able to take a knife to a raw chicken—let alone hold it to a person's throat—I was surprised, embarrassed, and dismayed all at once. Her flight made me feel like an accomplice in tyranny. It also made it clear that I was indistinguishable from the muggers who occasionally seeped into the area from the surrounding ghetto. That first encounter, and those that followed, signified that a vast, unnerving gulf lay between nighttime pedestrians—particularly women—and me. And I soon gathered that being perceived as dangerous is a hazard in itself. I only needed to turn a corner into a dicey situation, or crowd some frightened, armed person in a foyer somewhere, or make an errant move after being pulled over by a policeman. Where fear and weapons meet—and they often do in urban America—is always the possibility of death.

In the first year, my first away from my hometown, I was to become thoroughly familiar with the language of fear. At dark, shadowy intersections in Chicago, I could cross in front of a car stopped at a traffic light and elicit the *thunk, thunk, thunk, thunk* of the driver—black, white, male, or female—hammering down the door locks. On less traveled streets after dark, I grew accustomed to but never comfortable with people who crossed to the other side of the street rather than pass me. Then there were the standard unpleasantries with police, doormen, bouncers, cab drivers, and others whose business it is to screen out troublesome individuals *before* there is any nastiness.

I moved to New York nearly two years ago, and I have remained an avid night walker. In central Manhattan, the near-constant crowd cover minimized tense one-on-one street encounters. Elsewhere—visiting friends in SoHo, where sidewalks are narrow and tightly spaced, buildings shut out the sky—things can get very taut indeed.

Black men have a firm place in New York mugging literature. Norman Podhoretz in his famed (or infamous) 1963 essay, "My Negro Problem—and Ours," recalls growing up in terror of black males; they "were tougher than we were, more ruthless," he writes—and as an adult on the Upper West Side of Manhattan, he continues, he cannot constrain his nervousness when he meets black men on certain streets. Similarly, a decade later, the essayist and novelist Edward Hoagland extols a New York where once "Negro bitterness

1

2

3

4

5

Brent Staples, "Walk On By," *Ms.* magazine (1986). Reprinted by permission of the author.

bore down mainly on other Negroes." Where some see mere panhandlers, Hoagland sees "a mugger who is clearly screwing up his nerve to do more than just *ask* for money." But Hoagland has "the New Yorker's quick-hunch posture for broken-field maneuvering," and the bad guy swerves away.

6 I often witness that "hunch posture" from women after dark on the warrenlike streets of Brooklyn where I live. They seem to set their faces on neutral and, with their purse straps strung across their chests bandolier style, they forge ahead as though bracing themselves against being tackled. I understand, of course, that the danger they perceive is not a hallucination. Women are particularly vulnerable to street violence, and young black males are drastically overrepresented among the perpetrators of that violence. Yet these truths are no solace against the kind of alienation that comes of being ever the suspect, against being set apart, a fearsome entity with whom pedestrians avoid making eye contact.

7 It is not altogether clear to me how I reached the ripe old age of 22 without being conscious of the lethality nighttime pedestrians attributed to me. Perhaps it was because in Chester, Pennsylvania, the small, angry industrial town where I came of age in the 1960s, I was scarcely noticeable against a backdrop of gang warfare, street knifings, and murders. I grew up one of the good boys, had perhaps a half-dozen fist fights. In retrospect, my shyness of combat has clear sources.

8 Many things go into the making of a young thug. One of those things is the consummation of the male romance with the power to intimidate. An infant discovers that random flailings send the baby bottle flying out of the crib and crashing to the floor. Delighted, the joyful babe repeats those motions again and again, seeking to duplicate the feat. Just so, I recall the points at which some of my boyhood friends were finally seduced by the perception of themselves as tough guys. When a mark cowered and surrendered his money without resistance, myth and reality merged—and paid off. It is, after all, only manly to embrace the power to frighten and intimidate. We, as men, are not supposed to give an inch of our lane on the highway; we are to seize the fighter's edge in work and in play and even in love; we are to be valiant in the face of hostile forces.

9 Unfortunately, poor and powerless young men seem to take all this nonsense literally. As a boy, I saw countless tough guys locked away; I have since buried several. They were babies, really—a teenage cousin, a brother of 22, a childhood friend in his mid-twenties— all gone down in episodes of bravado played out in the streets. I came to doubt the virtues of intimidation early on. I chose, perhaps even unconsciously, to remain a shadow—timid, but a survivor.

10 The fearsomeness mistakenly attributed to me in public places often has a perilous flavor. The most frightening of these confusions occurred in the late 1970s and early 1980s when I worked as a journalist in Chicago. One day, rushing into the office of a magazine I was writing for with a deadline story in hand, I was mistaken for a burglar. The office manager called security and, with an ad hoc posse, pursued me through the labyrinthine halls, nearly to my editor's door. I had no way of proving who I was. I could only move briskly toward the company of someone who knew me.

11 Another time I was on assignment for a local paper and killing time before an interview. I entered a jewelry store on the city's affluent Near North Side. The proprietor excused herself and returned with an enormous red Doberman pinscher straining at the end of a leash. She stood, the dog extended toward me, silent to my questions, her eyes bulging nearly out of her head. I took a cursory look around, nodded, and bade her good

night. Relatively speaking, however, I never fared as badly as another black male journalist. He went to nearby Waukegan, Illinois, a couple of summers ago to work on a story about a murderer who was born there. Mistaking the reporter for the killer, police hauled him from his car at gunpoint and but for his press credentials would probably have tried to book him. Such episodes are not uncommon. Black men trade tales like this all the time.

In "My Negro Problem—and Ours," Podhoretz writes that the hatred he feels for   12
blacks makes itself known to him through a variety of avenues—one being his discomfort with that "special brand of paranoid touchiness" to which he says blacks are prone. No doubt he is speaking here of black men. In time, I learned to smother the rage I felt at so often being taken for a criminal. Not to do so would surely have led to madness—via that special "paranoid touchiness" that so annoyed Podhoretz at the time he wrote the essay.

I began to take precautions to make myself less threatening. I move about with care,   13
particularly late in the evening. I give a wide berth to nervous people on subway platforms during the wee hours, particularly when I have exchanged business clothes for jeans. If I happen to be entering a building behind some people who appear skittish, I may walk by, letting them clear the lobby before I return, so as not to seem to be following them. I have been calm and extremely congenial on those rare occasions when I've been pulled over by the police.

And on late-evening constitutionals along streets less traveled by, I employ what has   14
proved to be an excellent tension-reducing measure: I whistle melodies from Beethoven and Vivaldi and the more popular classical composers. Even steely New Yorkers hunching toward nighttime destinations seem to relax, and occasionally they even join in the tune. Virtually everybody seems to sense that a mugger wouldn't be warbling bright, sunny selections from Vivaldi's *Four Seasons*. It is my equivalent of the cowbell that hikers wear when they know they are in bear country.

Thinking Critically About Content

1. According to Staples, what reputation do African American men have?
2. When did the author become aware of this reputation?
3. What is Staples's opinion of "young thugs" (paragraph 8)? How did you come to this conclusion?

Thinking Critically About Purpose and Audience

4. What do you think Staples's purpose is in this essay?
5. Who do you think is Staples's primary audience?
6. Which of Staples's examples convince you that people are sometimes intimidated by African American men?

Thinking Critically About Paragraphs

7. What is the topic sentence of paragraph 3? Do all the sentences in that paragraph support that topic sentence? Explain your answer.
8. Staples begins his essay with the words "My first victim." What is he implying by these words? Is this an effective beginning? Explain your answer.

9. What is the organization of paragraph 9? Is this an effective order for these details? Explain your answer.

10. Write a paragraph using examples to explain one of your opinions about society today.

To keep track of your critical thinking progress, go to Appendix 1.

DAWN'S EARLY LIGHT
by Richard Rodriguez

Focusing Your Attention

1. What are your current opinions on border control in the United States? Who should be allowed to be an American? What guidelines do you suggest we use in deciding who can become Americans?

2. The essay you are about to read considers our current problems in the United States with immigration. What role do immigrants play in our country's economy? In our social structure? In our workplace?

Expanding Your Vocabulary

The following words are important to your understanding of this essay. Organize this list into two columns—words you know and words you don't know. Which of the words you don't know can you guess from their sentences?

amnesty: an official pardon (paragraph 1)

feckless: unthinking and irresponsible (paragraph 5)

stamina: the ability to sustain prolonged effort (paragraph 9)

undermine: weaken (paragraph 11)

exalted: praised highly (paragraph 11)

Trabajo: work (paragraph 11)

Señor: Sir (paragraph 11)

Barato: cheap (paragraph 11)

READING CRITICALLY
Chunking as You Read

As you learned earlier, circle the main idea of the following essay, and then separate each example with horizontal lines. Label the examples in the margins. Then, share your marks with a classmate, justifying each of your decisions.

DAWN'S EARLY LIGHT
by Richard Rodriguez

We see them lined up on American streets at dawn's early light. Depending on our point of view, we call them "illegal" or "undocumented." The question preoccupying us now as a nation, from the White House on down, is "them"—what to do with them? Grant them amnesty? Send them all back? Make them guest workers?

But I wonder about us. How they have changed us, even while we have paid them cheaply to wash our restaurant dishes and to pick our apples and to sit with a dying grandparent.

For much of the 20th century, we employed Mexicans when it suited us. For example, during the war, we needed Mexicans to harvest our crops. Slowly, mutual dependence was established. A rumor of dollars spread through Mexican villages, and Americans grew accustomed to cheap laboring hands.

Now they come, children following the footsteps of parents and grandparents, often at the risk of death or injury. We say about them that they are disrespectful of American laws. But for every illegal worker employed today in America, there is an employer—equally disrespectful of American law. Mexicans reveal our hypocrisy to ourselves.

They, in their relentless movement back and forth, are forcing us to see America within the Americas. Long before diplomats and politicians spoke of NAFTA or feckless college students headed to Cancun for spring break, Mexican peasants saw the Americas whole. They—in Peruvian villages, they know when apples are being picked in the Yakima Valley. Brazilian teenagers know when fishing companies are hiring in Alaska. They—they know all about us.

But now they are forcing us to acquire a working knowledge of them. Because of them, Spanish is, unofficially, the second language of the United States, apparent on signs all over the city. Though we are the employers dispensing dollars at the end of the day or short-changing them or threatening to call the police if they complain, they leave us with an odd sense of powerlessness, for we are not in control of the movement of people across the border.

We are not in control because the movement of people across the earth is an aspect of tragedy, of circumstances—drought, plague, civil war, poverty. Peasants all over the world are in movement, violating borders.

Even President Bush, in announcing his sympathetic proposals for how to deal with them, assumed the given: They are here. We pay them as little as we can, of course, which is how the undocumented undercut America's working class, white and black. We say about them, sometimes, that "the illegals work very hard, work harder for less than we can get Americans to work."

On a carefree weekend, we might suddenly see them on the horizon working amidst rows of dusty green. They force us to wonder if we have the courage of such labor or the stamina. Sometimes, Americans will compare these people to their own great-grandparents. The difference, people say, is that these Mexicans and central Americans are illegally here, whereas our ancestors came here legally.

10   Consider the familiar images of those ships headed for Ellis Island, which have become commonplace in American legend. We picture those immigrants enthralled to the Goddess of Liberty and the freedom she represents.

11   Today's undocumented workers do not speak of the *Federalist Papers* or of Thomas Jefferson. They want only a job. They undermine the romanticism we harbor about earlier generations and about ourselves. They, today's illegal immigrants, may lead us to wonder whether for our ancestors America was not simply an exalted vision, but also partook of tragedy: A loaf of stale bread. A backbreaking job. A terrible loneliness. "¿*Trabajo*? Cheap, *Señor*, cheap. Roof? Digging? *Barato, sí, barato.*"

Thinking Critically About Content

1. Based on Richard Rodriguez's essay, describe "them" in your own words.

2. In what ways are Mexicans "disrespectful of American laws" (paragraph 4)? Give an example from Rodriguez's essay to support your answer.

3. In what ways do immigrants force us "to see America within the Americas" (paragraph 4)?

Thinking Critically About Purpose and Audience

4. What do you think Rodriguez's purpose is in this essay? Explain your answer.

5. What type of audience do you think would most understand and appreciate this essay?

6. What do you think Rodriguez's title means?

Thinking Critically About Essays

7. Does Rodriguez give you enough examples to understand his learning environment in high school? Explain your answer.

8. Is this essay unified? Does each of the author's topic sentences support the essay's thesis statement? Explain your answer.

9. What is Rodriguez's thesis in this essay? Where is it located?

10. Explain your opinion on immigration today. What are the problems? How can we solve these problems? Respond to these questions in detail.

To keep track of your critical thinking progress, go to Appendix 1.

THE DECORATED BODY
by France Borel

Focusing Your Attention

1. In what ways have you changed your natural appearance—hair color, makeup, tattoos, piercings, and the like? Why do you make these alterations? What messages do they send to others?

2. The essay you are about to read deals with the ways we decorate our bodies. These methods vary according to someone's culture. Why do you think people change their appearance in the United States? What physical decorations are appealing to you? Which are unappealing? Why do you think you have these various reactions?

Expanding Your Vocabulary

The following words are important to your understanding of this essay. Organize this list into two columns—words you know and words you don't know. Which of the words you don't know can you guess from their sentences?

unfathomably: impossible to measure (paragraph 1)

artifice: device used to trick people (paragraph 2)

millennia: thousands of years (paragraph 3)

prevalent: widespread (paragraph 3)

aesthetically: concerned with appearances (paragraph 4)

amorous: pertaining to love (paragraph 4)

scarification: scarring of the skin (paragraph 6)

pretexts: false justifications (paragraph 8)

malleable: easily influenced (paragraph 9)

eludes: evades or escapes from (paragraph 12)

homogenous: of the same kind (paragraph 12)

tacit: implied (paragraph 12)

adhere: stick to (paragraph 13)

READING CRITICALLY
Chunking as You Read

Once again, circle the thesis of the following essay, and draw horizontal lines in the essay to show the different examples the author has chosen to support his thesis. Label the examples in the margins. Then, compare your marks with those of a classmate, and justify your decisions to each other.

THE DECORATED BODY
by France Borel

"Nothing goes as deep as dress nor as far as the skin; ornaments have the dimensions of the world."

—Michel Serres, *The Five Senses*

1   Human nakedness, according to social custom, is unacceptable, unbearable, and dangerous. From the moment of birth, society takes charge, managing, dressing, forming, and deforming the child—sometimes even with a certain degree of violence. Aside from the most elementary caretaking concerns—the very diversity of which shows how subjective the motivation is—an unfathomably deep and universal tendency pushes families, clans, and tribes to rapidly modify a person's physical appearance.

2   One's genuine physical makeup, one's given anatomy, is always felt to be unacceptable. Flesh, in its raw state, seems both intolerable and threatening. In its naked state, body and skin have no possible existence. The organism is acceptable only when it is transformed, covered with signs. The body only speaks if it is dressed in artifice.

3   For millennia, in the four quarters of the globe, mothers have molded the shape of their newborn babies' skulls to give them silhouettes conforming to prevalent criteria of beauty. In the nineteenth century, western children were tightly swaddled to keep their limbs straight. In the so-called primitive world, children were scarred or tattooed at a very early age in rituals which were repeated at all the most important steps of their lives. At a very young age, children were fitted with belts, necklaces, or bracelets; their lips, ears, or noses were pierced or stretched.

4   Some cultures have designed sophisticated appliances to alter physical structure and appearance. American Indian cradleboards crushed the skull to flatten it; the Mangbetus of Africa wrapped knotted rope made of bark around the child's head to elongate it into a sugar-loaf shape, which was considered to be aesthetically pleasing. The feet of very young Chinese girls were bound and spliced, intentionally and irreversibly deforming them, because this was seen to guarantee the girls' eventual amorous and matrimonial success.[1]

5   Claude Lévi-Strauss said about the Caduveo of Brazil: "In order to be a man, one had to be painted; whoever remained in a natural state was no different from the beasts."[2] In Polynesia, unless a girl was tattooed, she would not find a husband. An unornamented hand could not cook, nor dip into the communal food bowl. Pink lips were despicable and ugly. Anyone who refused the test of the tattoo was seen to be marginal and suspect.

6   Among the Tivs of Nigeria, women called attention to their legs by means of elaborate scarification and the use of pearl leg bands; the best decorated calves were known for miles around. Tribal incisions behind the ears of Chad men rendered the skin "as smooth and stretched as that of a drum." The women would laugh at any man lacking these incisions, and they would never accept him as a husband. Men would subject themselves willingly to this custom, hoping for scars deep enough to leave marks on their skulls after death.

7   At the beginning of the eighteenth century, Father Laurent de Lucques noted that any young girl of the Congo who was not able to bear the pain of scarification and who

Le Vêtement incarné, les métamorphoses du corps by France Borel © Editions Calmann-Lévy, 1992.

cried so loudly that the operation had to be stopped was considered "good for nothing."[3] That is why, before marriage, men would check to see if the pattern traced on the belly of their intended bride was beautiful and well-detailed.

The fact that such motivations and pretexts depend on aesthetic, erotic, hygienic, or even medical considerations has no influence on the result, which is always in the direction of transforming the appearance of the body. Such a transformation is wished for, whether or not it is effective.

8

The body is a supple, malleable, and transformable prime material, a kind of modeling clay, easily molded by social will and wish. Human skin is an ideal subject for inscription, a surface for all sorts of marks which make it possible to differentiate the human from the animal. The physical body offers itself willingly for tattooing or scarring so that, visibly and recognizably, it becomes a social entity.

9

The absolutely naked body is considered as brutish, reduced to the level of nature where no distinction is made between man and beast. The decorated body, on the other hand, dressed (if even only in a belt), tattooed, or mutilated, publicly exhibits humanity and membership in an established group. As Theophile Gautier said, "The ideal disturbs even the roughest nature, and the taste for ornamentation distinguishes the intelligent being from the beast more exactly than anything else. Indeed, dogs have never dreamed of putting on earrings."

10

So, it is by their categorical refusal of nakedness that human beings are distinguished from nature. The "mark makes unremarkable"—it creates an interval between what is biologically and brutally given in the animal realm and what is won in the cultural realm. The body is tamed continuously; social custom demands, at any price—including pain, constraint, or discomfort—that wildness be abandoned.

11

Each civilization chooses—through a network of elective relationships which are difficult to determine—which areas of the body deserve transformation. These areas are as difficult to define and as shifting as those of eroticism or modesty. An individual alone eludes bodily modifications; they are the expression of a homogeneous collectivity which, at a chosen moment, comes to a tacit agreement to attack one or another part of the anatomy.

12

Whatever the choices, options, or differences may be, that which remains constant is the transformation of appearance. In spite of our contemporary western belief that the body is perfect as it is, we are constantly changing it: clothing it in musculature, suntan, or makeup; dying its head hair or pulling out its bodily hair. The seemingly most innocent gestures for taking care of the body very often hide a persistent and disguised tendency to make it adhere to the strictest of norms, reclothing it in a veil of civilization. The total nudity offered at birth does not exist in any region of the world. Man puts his stamp on man. The body is not a product of nature, but of culture.

13

Notes

1. Of course, there are also many different sexual mutilations, including excisions and circumcisions, which we will not go into at this time as they constitute a whole study in themselves.
2. C. Lévi-Strauss, *Tristes Tropiques* (Paris: Plon, 1955), p. 214.
3. J. Cuvelier, *Relations sur le Congo du Père Laurent de Lucques* (Brussels: Institut royal colonial belge, 1953), p. 144.

Thinking Critically About Content

1. What does Borel mean when he says, "The body only speaks if it is dressed in artifice" (paragraph 2)?

2. According to Borel, what are the primary reasons people make changes in their appearance? Do you notice any common thread in these reasons?

3. In what ways is tattooing "a social entity" (paragraph 9)?

Thinking Critically About Purpose and Audience

4. What do you think France Borel's purpose is in this essay?

5. Do you think all students would be interested in this essay? What other groups would find this essay interesting? Why?

6. Do you think this essay might change someone's opinion about body decorations? Explain your answer.

Thinking Critically About Essays

7. What is the thesis of this essay?

8. Why do you think Borel divides this essay into two parts? What is the main idea of each part? Is this an effective way to break up this essay? Explain your answer.

9. In what way does the last sentence serve as a summary for the essay?

10. Were your views on any forms of body decoration changed as a result of reading this essay? If so, in what way? Explain your answer in detail.

To keep track of your critical thinking progress, go to Appendix 1.

Writing Illustration

This section gives you opportunities to apply what you have learned in this chapter to your own writing. It provides guidelines for writing an illustration essay and for peer evaluation. Review the readings in this chapter when you need samples of good illustration essays. Pause at the end of the chapter to reflect briefly on what you have learned.

Guidelines for Writing an Illustration Essay

1. State your main point in the last sentence of your introduction.
2. Choose examples that are relevant to your point.
3. Choose examples your readers can identify with.
4. Use a sufficient number of examples to make your point.
5. Organize your examples to make your point in the clearest, strongest way.

Writing About Your Reading

1. Contemporary American society rewards compulsive, fast-moving people. But some people just can't keep up for any number of reasons. Have you ever felt the way Lee says her mother feels in her essay? Discuss any similarities you see between yourself and Lee's mother.

2. What are some of the main dangers on the streets in your hometown? What characterizes these dangers? How do you deal with them?

3. Current American society can't make up its mind about illegal immigrants. In some cases, Americans want to allow illegal immigrants to stay in the country; in other instances, Americans say that illegal immigrants should return to their home countries. How do you think this feud will be resolved? Give examples to explain your reasoning.

4. What are some of the differences between the generations regarding body decorations? What do you think accounts for these differences? Give examples to support your claims.

5. What do you think writers should consider first when choosing examples in an essay? How should the examples be related to the thesis statement? Why are these criteria important when working with examples?

Writing About Your World

1. Share with your classmates one of your opinions about the United States government, and use examples to explain it.

2. Use examples or illustrations to explain your observations about the increased interest in fitness among Americans.

3. Share with your classmates your opinion on a specific national issue such as capital punishment, abortion, or gun laws. Use examples in your body paragraphs to support your main point.

4. Why do you think Americans are interested in exercise and weight loss? What actions illustrate this attitude? Use examples or illustrations to explain your observations on the current interest in health and weight among Americans.

5. Create your own illustration assignment (with the help of your instructor), and write a response to it.

Revising

Small Group Activity (5–10 minutes per writer) Working in groups of three or four, read your illustration essays to each other. Those listening should record their reactions on a copy of the Peer Evaluation Form in Appendix 2A. After your group goes through this process, give your evaluation forms to the appropriate writers so that each writer has two or three peer comment sheets for revising.

Paired Activity (5 minutes per writer) Using the completed Peer Evaluation Forms, work in pairs to decide what you should revise in your essay. If time allows, rewrite some of your sentences, and have your partner look at them.

Individual Activity Rewrite your paper, using the revising feedback you received from other students.

Editing

Paired Activity (5–10 minutes per writer) Swap papers with a classmate, and use the editing portion of your Peer Evaluation Form to identify as many grammar, punctuation, mechanics, and spelling errors as you can. If time allows, correct some of your errors, and have your partner look at them. Record your grammar, punctuation, and mechanics errors in the Error Log (Appendix 3) and your spelling errors in the Spelling Log (Appendix 4).

Individual Activity Rewrite your paper again, using the editing feedback you received from other students.

Reflecting on Your Writing When you have completed your own essay, answer these six questions.

1. What was most difficult about this assignment?

2. What was easiest?

3. What did you learn about illustration by completing this assignment?

4. What do you think are the strengths of your illustration? Place a wavy line by the parts of your essay that you feel are very good.

5. What are the weaknesses, if any, of your paper? Place an X by the parts of your essay you would like help with. Write any questions you have in the margins.

6. What did you learn from this assignment about your own writing process—about preparing to write, about writing the first draft, about revising, and about editing?

Process Analysis:
From Reading to Writing

This chapter includes four reading selections and several writing assignments. It also takes you through the routine of peer evaluation and reflection on your writing that focuses on productive ways to annotate your own essay for your instructor to read.

Reading Process Analysis

The following essays explain different events or processes; in other words, they tell you how to do something or how something happened the way it did. The first, "Getting Out of Debt (and Staying Out)" by Julia Bourland, offers practical suggestions for dealing with debt. It demonstrates how to do something. "Coming Over," by Russell Freedman, explains what people had to go through at Ellis Island to immigrate to the United States around the turn of the twentieth century. It demonstrates the how-something-happened process analysis. "How to Protect Your Identity" by Brian O'Connell explains how to prevent identity theft (how to do something), and "Why We Have a Moon" by David Levy explains the role of the moon in relation to the Earth (how something happens). As you read, notice how the writers explain every step of the process carefully and completely.

GETTING OUT OF DEBT (AND STAYING OUT)
by Julia Bourland

Focusing Your Attention

1. Think of a time when you had to explain to someone how to do something. Was it an easy or a difficult task? Did the person understand you? Was the person able to follow your directions?

2. In the process analysis essay you are about to read, the writer tells us how to manage money and control debt. Do you manage your money efficiently? Have you ever been in debt? Do you know how to avoid debt?

Expanding Your Vocabulary

The following words are important to your understanding of this essay. As you read, circle any words you don't know beyond this list. Then break into groups, and help each other figure out the meanings of these unknown words.

assumption: claim (paragraph 1)

incurred: gained (paragraph 1)

deferring: putting off (paragraph 2)

vulnerable: capable of being hurt (paragraph 5)

meager: small (paragraph 8)

insatiable: unsatisfied (paragraph 8)

conscientious: careful (paragraph 8)

inundated: swamped (paragraph 8)

gingerly: with caution (paragraph 8)

diligent: hardworking (paragraph 9)

accrue: gain (paragraph 10)

amassed: gathered (paragraph 10)

uber-exorbitant: very extreme (paragraph 15)

READING CRITICALLY
Graphing Your Reading

As you learned in the Introduction, practice drawing graphic organizers for the ideas in this essay. Exchange "pictures" with someone in your class, and write a brief statement of what your classmate's drawing communicates to you.

GETTING OUT OF DEBT (AND STAYING OUT)
by Julia Bourland

1   I'm going to make the bold assumption that you have incurred a little debt during your great entrance into adulthood, from either student loans, devilish credit cards, or that car loan you recently signed with its 36 easy installment payments. If you haven't tasted

debt, you are abnormally perfect and un-American and can just skip on down to the next section on retirement planning and chill out until the rest of us catch up with you.

Some debt, such as student loans, is money well borrowed and an investment in your future. Because of their relatively low interest rates, manageable (though seemingly eternal) repayment plans, and reasonable deferment options, student loans should not be the source of midnight panic attacks during your second semester of senior year, even if you've incurred thousands and thousands of dollars to fund your education and still don't have a job that suggests that all the debt was worth it. If you haven't graduated yet, toward the end of your final semester, your college student loan officer will give you all the dirty details of your repayment schedule (hopefully armed with ample tissue for the tears that are certain to flood your contacts), as well as tell you how to defer paying back your loans if you aren't employed by the time your repayment grace period is up, as was my case. The cheery thing I discovered about deferring repayment is that the groovy government actually paid the interest I owed during my six-month deferment. That's not the case with all student loans, but you'll find that out when you start reading the fine print.

If you're like me, you may have several loans to repay. Again, you probably got (or will get) the skinny from your financial aid administrator at college, but in case he or she is on drugs, I'll summarize. There are a few consolidation plans that can make the whole process of paying back your loans less horrifying. Consolidating means that you will be able to merge all of your loans into one giant superloan that offers a low interest rate, as well as various options for shortening or lengthening your repayment schedule (which will increase or decrease the amount you owe each month, thereby increasing or decreasing the amount of interest you ultimately end up paying). But the best reason to consolidate your loans is that you will receive only one bill every month, which means you have to think and stress about all the student loan money you owe only once every 30 days! I highly recommend consolidation, if only for that.

If you have several loans from one financial institution, contact your lender directly about its consolidation options, or try these two programs: Federal Direct Consolidation Loan Program (800–557–7392; www.ed.gov/directloan) and Student Loan Marketing Association (a.k.a. Sallie Mae) Smart Loan Account (800–524–9100; www.salliemae.com).

Student loans are much less threatening and guilt-provoking than credit card debt, to which we 20-somethings are painfully vulnerable. There are so many things we want and need. Credit card companies seize upon our vulnerability, especially during college, sending us application after application with such enticing incentives as a *free water bottle, a two-pound bag of M&Ms, a 10% discount on first purchases, free checks* to spend anywhere we please, our very own *head shot* on the card, a *4.9% introductory interest rate,* and *bonus airline miles.* My first advice on the whole matter of credit card debt is to avoid it like the devil! I know many honest, smart girls who've become submerged in debt through the seductive power of plastic.

Our society once thrived without credit, so it *is* possible to stay out of debt as we begin our adult lives. But since you will probably experiment with credit despite the danger, memorize these eight guidelines compliments of those who've battled the plastic demons:

1. No Department Store Credit Cards

In-store credit usually carries a much higher interest rate than credit cards issued by banks. If you don't pay your debt back right away, what you buy is going to cost you much more than you bargained for. The only exception is if you have money to pay off your debt as soon as the bill arrives, and signing up for a card gives you a substantial discount on your first purchase. In these cases, get the card (and discount), pay your bill in full, and immediately cancel the card and shred it into a million pieces, lest you be tempted to use it again without the discount and money to pay for it. Note: If the discount isn't more than $10 or $20, don't even bother, because when you sign on, you'll probably get put on some annoying direct-mail list that will be sold to a bunch of trashy companies who will send you junk mail every single day.

2. One Card Only

8   The fewer little plastic rectangles you have, the less you'll be tempted to live beyond your meager means (and the fewer hysteria-provoking bills you'll receive). Ideally, you should use your card only for items that you know you can pay off with your next paycheck or for unavoidable emergencies, like getting new brakes for your clunker or fillings for your insatiable sweet tooth. The ideal cards have fixed annual percentage rates ranging from 9 to 12 percent, or less if you can find them, no annual fee, and a grace period that doesn't start charging interest on what you buy until the bill's due date. If you are a conscientious customer, you will be inundated with appealing offers for new cards boasting Platinum status and $25,000 credit lines. When you receive these, gingerly toss them into the recycling bin. Opening them will only lead you into trouble. There is one exception to this rule, but I'll get to that when we talk about transferring balances. First, a few more basic tips.

3. Use Your ATM Credit/Debit Card Instead

9   If you're diligent about balancing your checkbook, there's no reason to fear the credit card capabilities of your ATM card, which most banks are offering these days. Keep the receipt for whatever you purchase with your card as you would had you withdrawn money from the bank, and record the amount in your checkbook ledger as you would a check. Your debit card is just as convenient as a credit card, but your purchase won't accrue interest, which will save you money. Definitely use your debit card instead of a real credit card when grocery shopping or buying little things at the pharmacy, unless you like the idea of paying 18 percent interest on cereal and tampons. Trust your elders: the interest on all the little things makes them as costly as a raging girl's night out.

4. Pay Back as Much as You Can, as Soon as You Can

10   If we take the *minimum* payment request on our monthly statements to heart, we may not pay off our account in full until we qualify for social security. That's because interest continues to accrue on our balance each month. If we don't pay off everything we owe, the remainder plus the interest we've amassed will be charged interest the following month, and the month after that, which means our balance continues to grow at the speed of our card's annual percentage rate (APR) despite the fact that we pay our minimum due every month and have hidden our credit card in the closet under five shoe boxes. That's how credit card companies make so much money and why we should avoid getting into debt in every humanly possible (but legal) way.

11   If you have debt from several sources, pay back whatever has higher interest rates first—usually your credit cards—then tackle the typically lower-rated student loan and

car loan debts. If your credit card debt is spiraling out of control, you could refinance your student or car loans so that you will owe less on them each month, using the extra money to pay off your credit cards. Then, when your costlier debts have been paid off (and cards dumped in the nearest incinerator), you can designate all your funds to paying back your temporarily neglected student and car loans as quickly as you can.

5. Trash Those Credit Card Checks That Come with Your Statement, and Shun Cash Advances from the ATM

Both checks and cash advances will cost you dearly, since many card companies tack on an additional finance charge to your bill when you use them, plus impose an interest rate for the amount you borrow that's much higher than the rate you have for normal purchases. That means that if you withdraw $100 from your card at a bank or ATM or use one of those checks for your rent, you'll be paying back your credit card company a lot more than the amount you borrowed.

6. Switch to a Card with a Lower Interest Rate

I said earlier that you should throw away offers for additional credit cards, and that is a good rule unless you are carrying a balance on a card (or cards) with an outrageous interest rate, say more than 12 percent. In that case, it's a good financial move to transfer your balance(s) to one card with the lowest rate you can find. Some offer temporary introductory interest rates as low as 2.9 percent on all transferred balances; when you apply, make sure you note the expiration date for those low rates on your calendar, and have another card offer lined up and ready to take on the load when the time comes. I know this sounds tedious, but careful organization and diligence will save you money as you attempt to pay the whole balance off.

If you play credit card musical chairs, keep three things in mind. First, some balance transfer offers have associated fees or finance charges that aren't exactly highlighted in their promotions. Always inquire about transfer fees, and try to talk them out of it; many issuers are willing to waive the fees upon request. Second, even after you transfer your balance in full, the account remains open. To close it, you must officially cancel. The issuing bank won't automatically cancel a zero-balance account, so if you don't, your access to that credit line will remain on your credit report. That could be problematic later on when you're applying for a mortgage and have thousands of dollars worth of potential debt in your financial profile—something that makes lenders skittish. The other reason to cancel is to avoid the temptation to start using that clean slate of credit that your old card suddenly presents. And the third caveat: When you transfer your balance, do not use this new card to purchase new things. Declare it a debt repayment card only, and stick that shiny piece of plastic in the file where you keep your monthly statements. Here's why:

When you charge new items on a card that has adopted old debt, many card issuers apply a different (and uber-exorbitant) interest rate to those new purchases. The higher interest rate will remain on the amount of your new purchases until your entire debt has been repaid. Therefore, when you are trying to pay off a large debt, you should try to have two credit cards—one with a very low balance-transfer interest rate for your main debt and another with a reasonable interest rate on new purchases that you will use for emergencies only, since you are, after all, trying to get

12

13

14

15

out of the hole, not rack up new debt. A good resource for finding low-rate, no-fee cards is a company called CardWeb.com, Inc., which publishes a newsletter called CardTrak that lists these desirable cards. You can access the newsletter and other credit card consumer information on its website (www.cardweb.com) or by calling (800) 344–7714.

7. Apply for a Secured Credit Card If Your Credit Is Screwed

16   If you have damaged your credit rating by defaulting on a loan or debt, your main priority (besides coming up with a repayment plan that suits all your creditors) is to rebuild your credit. Secured credit cards can help. You give the issuer a certain sum of money up front, which is kept in an account for you as a security deposit. Depending on the terms of your agreement, you can then charge a specified amount on that card. Once you've proved that you can repay your debts in this secured way, you may be offered a new card with real credit that doesn't require you to put up money ahead of time. CardWeb.com, Inc. (cited in the previous entry) can provide a list of secured credit cards as well as low-rate, no-fee cards.

17   If you are in a bad situation and creditors are calling you about monster debt that you can't currently pay off, don't pack up and move to North Dakota, thinking creditors won't be able to find you—they will. A couple of nonprofit credit counseling organizations can help with debt-repayment planning assistance: Consumer Credit Counseling Services, associated with the National Foundation for Consumer Credit (800–388–2227; www.nfcc.org), and Debt Counselors of America (800–698–5182; www.dca.org).

8. Check Your Credit Report

18   I've already expounded on why a clean credit report is so important, so I won't beat that dead horse, but I will add that it's wise to check up on your report every now and then to make sure there are no surprises (or mistakes) that need mending. There are three agencies that compile credit reports, and they all get their information separately, so what one company says is part of your credit history may differ from what another company includes. You can get copies of your credit report from each company for $8 or less, depending on your state of residence. If you have had bad credit in the past but believe you've been exonerated (usually after seven years), you should make sure all three companies are showing you in the proper light.

19   The three agencies keeping tabs are Experian (formerly TRW) (888–397–3742; www.experian.com/ecommerce/consumercredit.html); Equifax (800–685–1111; www.econsumer.equifax.com); and Trans Union (800–888–4213; www.transunion.com/CreditReport/).

Thinking Critically About Content

1. According to Bourland, what types of debt are worthwhile?

2. What are Bourland's eight guidelines for avoiding credit card debt? Summarize each guideline.

3. How can you check your credit rating?

Thinking Critically About Purpose and Audience

4. What do you think Bourland's purpose is in writing this essay?

5. Who do you think is Bourland's primary audience? Does debt play any part in their lives?

6. Which of Bourland's guidelines are most likely to help you now and in the future? Explain your answer.

Thinking Critically About Paragraphs

7. Summarize Bourland's essay. Make sure you cover all her main points.

8. Choose a paragraph from this essay, and explain why it is well developed.

9. How is the information in paragraph 3 organized? Why is this an effective order for this topic?

10. Write a paragraph trying to convince a bill collector that you will pay a specific overdue bill next month.

To keep track of your critical thinking progress, go to Appendix 1.

COMING OVER
by Russell Freedman

Focusing Your Attention

1. If you could immigrate to another country, which one would you go to and why?

2. The following essay chronicles the experiences of Europeans trying to immigrate into the United States around 1900. Do you know any recent immigrants to the United States? What did they do to get into the United States? Was it a traumatic experience for them?

Expanding Your Vocabulary

The following words are important to your understanding of this essay. As you read, circle any words you don't know beyond this list. Then break into groups, and help each other figure out the meanings of these unknown words.

impoverished: poor (paragraph 1)

fervent: intense (paragraph 1)

narrows: a strait connecting two bodies of water (paragraph 6)

jabbered conversation: rapid talk that can't be understood (paragraph 6)

din: continuous noise (paragraph 6)

flustered: confused (paragraph 13)

indomitable: unable to be conquered (paragraph 15)

READING CRITICALLY
Graphing Your Reading

As you did with the previous essay, draw a graphic organizer for the ideas in the following essay. Make the drawing so accurate that someone could look at it and understand the basic concepts in the essay. Compare your drawing with someone else's in your class, and write a brief statement about the reading from your partner's graphic organizer.

COMING OVER
by Russell Freedman

1   In the years around the turn of the [twentieth] century, immigration to America reached an all-time high. Between 1880 and 1920, 23 million immigrants arrived in the United States. They came mainly from countries of Europe, especially from impoverished towns and villages in southern and eastern Europe. The one thing they had in common was a fervent belief that in America life would be better.

2   Most of these immigrants were poor. Somehow they managed to scrape together enough money to pay for their passage to America. Many immigrant families arrived penniless. Others had to make the journey in stages. Often the father came first, found work, and sent for his family later. Immigrants usually crossed the Atlantic as steerage passengers. Reached by steep, slippery stairways, the steerage lay deep down in the hold of the ship. It was occupied by passengers paying the lowest fare.

3   Men, women, and children were packed into dark, foul-smelling compartments. They slept in narrow bunks stacked three high. They had no showers, no lounges, and no dining rooms. Food served from huge kettles was dished into dinner pails provided by the steamship company. Because steerage conditions were crowded and uncomfortable, passengers spent as much time as possible up on deck.

4   The voyage was an ordeal, but it was worth it. They were on their way to America.

5   The great majority of immigrants landed in New York City at America's busiest port. They never forgot their first glimpse of the Statue of Liberty.

6   Edward Corsi, who later became United States Commissioner of Immigration, was a 10-year-old Italian immigrant when he sailed into New York harbor in 1907:

My first impression of the New World will always remain etched in my memory, particularly that hazy October morning when I first saw Ellis Island. The steamer *Florida*, fourteen days out of Naples, filled to capacity with 1600 natives of Italy, had weathered one of the worst storms in our captain's memory; and glad we were, both children and grown-ups, to leave the open sea and come at last through the Narrows into the Bay.

My mother, my stepfather, my brother, Giuseppe, and my two sisters, Liberta and Helvetia, all of us together, happy that we had come through the storm safely, clustered on the foredeck for fear of separation and looked with wonder on this miraculous land of our dreams.

Giuseppe and I held tightly to Stepfather's hands, while Liberta and Helvetia clung to Mother. Passengers all about us were crowding against the rail. Jabbered conversation, sharp cries, laughs and cheers—a steadily rising din filled the air. Mothers and fathers lifted up babies so that they too could see, off to the left, the Statue of Liberty. . . .

Finally the *Florida* veered to the left, turning northward into the Hudson River, and now the incredible buildings of lower Manhattan came very close to us.

The officers of the ship . . . went striding up and down the decks shouting orders and directions and driving the immigrants before them. Scowling and gesturing, they pushed and pulled the passengers, herding us into separate groups as though we were animals. A few moments later we came to our dock, and the long journey was over.

But the journey was not yet over. Before they could be admitted to the United States, immigrants had to pass through Ellis Island, which became the nation's chief immigrant processing center in 1892. There they would be questioned and examined. Those who could not pass all the exams would be detained; some would be sent back to Europe. And so their arrival in America was filled with great anxiety. Among the immigrants, Ellis Island was known as "Heartbreak Island."   7

When their ship docked at a Hudson River pier, the immigrants had numbered identity tags pinned to their clothing. Then they were herded onto special ferryboats that carried them to Ellis Island. Officials hurried them along, shouting "Quick! Run! Hurry!" in half a dozen languages.   8

Filing into an enormous inspection hall, the immigrants formed long lines separated by iron railings that made the hall look like a great maze.   9

Now the examinations began. First, the immigrants were examined by two doctors of the United States Health Service. One doctor looked for physical and mental abnormalities. When a case aroused suspicion, the immigrant received a chalk mark on the right shoulder for further inspection: L for lameness, H for heart, X for mental defects, and so on.   10

The second doctor watched for contagious and infectious diseases. He looked especially for infections of the scalp and at the eyelids for symptoms of trachoma, a blinding disease. Since trachoma caused more than half of all medical detentions, this doctor was greatly feared. He stood directly in the immigrant's path. With a swift movement, he would grab the immigrant's eyelid, pull it up, and peer beneath it. If all was well, the immigrant was passed on.   11

Those who failed to get past both doctors had to undergo a more thorough medical exam. The others moved on to the registration clerk, who questioned them with the aid of an interpreter: What is your name? Your nationality? Your occupation? Can you read and write? Have you ever been in prison? How much money do you have with you? Where are you going?   12

Some immigrants were so flustered that they could not answer. They were allowed to sit and rest and try again.   13

14 About one immigrant out of every five or six was detained for additional examinations or questioning.

15 The writer Angelo Pellegrini has recalled his own family's detention at Ellis Island:

16 Most immigrants passed through Ellis Island in about one day. Carrying all their worldly possessions, they left the examination hall and waited on the dock for the ferry that would take them to Manhattan, a mile away. Some of them still faced journeys overland before they reached their final destination. Others would head directly for the teeming immigrant neighborhoods of New York City.

Thinking Critically About Content

1. What common belief did the American immigrants share?

2. Make a chart of the stages of the immigration process in 1900, starting with receiving identity tags.

3. Why were families who wanted to move to the United States so anxious when they reached Ellis Island?

Thinking Critically About Purpose and Audience

4. What do you think is the purpose of this essay?

5. Who would be most interested in this essay?

6. Does the excerpt by Edward Corsi (paragraph 6) capture the excitement the new immigrants probably felt when they saw Ellis Island for the first time?

Thinking Critically About Paragraphs

7. Why do you think Freedman includes the paragraph written by Angelo Pellegrini (paragraph 15)? Do the details in this paragraph support its topic sentence? Explain your answer.

8. This essay has a number of well-chosen transitions in every paragraph to help move the readers through the author's ideas. Look closely at paragraph 10, and underline three transition words or phrases.

9. What is the topic sentence of paragraph 7? Do all the sentences in that paragraph support this topic sentence? Explain your answer.

10. Pretend (if necessary) you and your family came to the United States from another country. Write a paragraph explaining the process you went through to get admitted to the country. If any members of your family actually went through the immigration process to be allowed into the United States, you might want to talk to them before you write.

To keep track of your critical thinking progress, go to Appendix 1.

HOW TO PROTECT YOUR IDENTITY
by Brian O'Connell

Focusing Your Attention

1. Think of a time when you had to explain to someone how to do something. Was it an easy or a difficult task? Did the person understand you? Was the person able to follow your directions?

2. In the process analysis essay you are about to read, the writer explains how to prevent identity theft. Have you ever told someone how to prevent something from happening? Was it useful information to those you were talking to?

Expanding Your Vocabulary

The following words are important to your understanding of this essay. As you read, circle any words you don't know beyond this list. Then break into groups, and help each other figure out the meanings of these unknown words.

cyber-means: using the Internet (paragraph 2)

breaches: security flaws (paragraph 2)

transactions: business dealings (paragraph 2)

vulnerable: open to attack (paragraph 2)

fraudulently: deceitfully (paragraph 5)

phishing: dealing with Internet theft (paragraph 7)

opt out: choose not to participate (paragraph 8)

rummage: search, dig (paragraph 8)

affidavit: a written statement (paragraph 9)

common denominator: something in common (paragraph 10)

READING CRITICALLY
Graphing Your Reading

Once again, practice drawing graphic organizers for the ideas in this essay. Exchange "pictures" with someone in your class, and write a brief statement of what your classmate's drawing communicates to you.

HW:

Read →

HOW TO PROTECT YOUR IDENTITY
by Brian O'Connell

1   There's an old Chinese proverb that says whoever steals an egg will steal an ox. Fast forward to the 21st century, replace "egg" with a credit card number and "ox" with your Social Security number, and you've tapped into one of the biggest threats to the information age—identity theft.

2   Identity theft—the act of having your personal and financial information stolen from you, often by cyber-means—is a burgeoning problem. According to an April 15, 2008, study of identity theft victims by the Poneman Institute, a Michigan-based research group, 55 percent suffered two or more information breaches in the past two years. According to a February 2009 report by Javelin Strategy and Research, in 2008 the number of identity fraud victims grew 25 percent—affecting 9.9 million people. This is the first time since the report began in 2004 that the numbers have increased. In 2007, about 8.4 million people were victims of identity theft, one person every four seconds, which was down from more than 9 million the year before. On Jan. 20, 2008, Heartland Payment Systems, a financial transactions company, announced a security breach that occurred in late 2008 that left tens of millions of credit cards vulnerable to cyber-fraud. Heartland doesn't know yet how many accounts were breached, but it handles payment processing for 250,000 customers, 40 percent of which are restaurants. Heartland processes over 100 million transactions each month, according to company chief financial officer Robert Baldwin.

3   The good news is that taking action to stem ID theft is both easy and doable. CreditCards.com asked some leading information security experts what steps to take to secure your personal identity and here is what they had to say:

4   1. **Be aware:** First, how do you know your identity has been breached? Bruce Cornelius, chief marketing officer at Canoga Park, California-based CreditReport.com, says you'll know when you start getting letters and phone calls saying your application for credit has been approved or rejected, or you notice that your credit card statement has charges you never approved. Another red flag is getting phone calls from collection agencies saying you owe money.

5   2. **Act fast:** The key is to get out in front of the problem as soon as possible—before heavier damage can be done. "Oftentimes thieves will use your credit card data to commit non-financial identity theft crimes which become much larger problems," says Justin Yurek, president of Denver-based IDWatchdog.com. "As thieves begin to truly clone your identity, they can move from buying items in your name to committing crimes in your name, or obtaining employment benefits in your name, or obtaining medical services in your name. Unlike a thief fraudulently purchasing products in your name, there is no easy reversal for these crimes, and the consequences to the victim are much more severe."

6   3. **Prevention defense:** ID theft specialists say that the real key in stopping identity breaches is in prevention. "To prevent identity theft, cardholders need to guard

their cards and keep secret any identifying information about their accounts," says Scott Crawford, CEO of DebtGoal.com. "This includes shredding account statements and keeping account and personal information secret. Look through your statement carefully to identify transactions that you didn't initiate, and take advantage of alerts that your credit institution offers. Many allow you to get alerts for abnormal transactions that can warn you of potential fraud on your account."

4. **Check URLs:** Always check a Web site's URL and security certificate before entering in your personal information. "With phishing schemes becoming increasingly sophisticated, it is important to ensure that you are doing business with the person you think you are and not an imposter," says Yurek. "Also, never send your personal information, such as a Social Security number or credit card number, in a non-secure format, such as an e-mail."

7

5. **Play it close to the vest:** Always keep your personal information as private as possible, and take concrete steps to eliminate your "financial footprint." "Don't give out your Social Security number unless it is absolutely necessary," says Scott Stevenson, founder and CEO of Eliminate ID Theft. "If you do not want credit offers to come to you, contact the three credit reporting agencies and 'opt out' of these offers. They should remove your name for two years from mailing and telemarketing lists. Don't carry your Social Security card, passport, or birth certificate in your wallet or purse, and only carry the credit cards that you need." Stevenson also advocates checking the "inquiry" section of your credit report to see if there are unsolicited creditors reviewing your credit that you haven't done business with. Be careful about your mail habits too. "Don't mail bills or any documents like tax forms from your personal mailbox. Take them directly to the post office or pay them online. Thieves will rummage through your mailbox and take your valuable information."

8

6. **Contact the authorities:** If you've been the victim of an identity theft crime, contact the police as soon as possible. CreditReport.com's Cornelius also advises to close all accounts you didn't open and ones that were taken over. "Also use the Federal Trade Commission's identity theft affidavit from the FTC Web site, to file a complaint that can be used to investigate identity theft," adds Cornelius. "Then file a report with your local police department and in the community where the identity theft occurred. Get copies of this police report to help you prove to credit card companies and banks that your identity was stolen."

9

One common denominator among all ID theft experts? Get ahead of the problem before it gets ahead of you. That way, both your egg and your ox are well protected.

10

Thinking Critically About Content

1. How does O'Connell explain the "egg" and the "ox" (paragraph 1) in the twenty-first century?
2. What is one example the author cites to explain the current magnitude of identity theft?
3. What are the six steps to O'Connell's plan for preventing identity theft?

Thinking Critically About Purpose and Audience

4. What is O'Connell's purpose in this essay?

5. Who do you think would benefit from the information in this essay? Explain your answer.

6. Which piece of O'Connell's advice do you find most useful for your lifestyle?

Thinking Critically About Essays

7. Describe in a complete sentence the author's point of view in his last paragraph.

8. How does O'Connell organize his essay? Write a rough outline to show his method of organization.

9. Choose a paragraph from his essay, and explain how it is developed.

10. Explain in detail why identity theft is such an enormous problem in the information age.

To keep track of your critical thinking progress, go to Appendix 1.

WHY WE HAVE A MOON
by David Levy

Focusing Your Attention

1. Astronomy is the study of planets and stars. What interests you about the world of astronomy?

2. In the essay you are about to read, the writer explains his research on how the moon was formed and what its role is in relation to the earth. Have you ever been interested enough in something that you took the time to look into its origins or related facts?

Expanding Your Vocabulary

The following words are important to your understanding of this essay. As you read, circle any words you don't know beyond this list. Then break into groups, and help each other figure out the meanings of these unknown words.

orbit: the path of a planet, moon, or satellite (paragraph 3)

gravitational pull: the pull of a planet on an object near its surface (paragraph 3)

supercolossal: extremely large (paragraph 3)

plummeted: fell (paragraph 4)

devastation: severe damage (paragraph 4)

promontory: a piece of land that juts out into the sea (paragraph 7)

mottled: spotted (paragraphs 11 and 12)

exhalations: letting air out (paragraph 12)

meteors, comets, asteroids: bodies of rock and air in space (paragraph 13)

imminent: about to happen (paragraph 16)

carbon: a chemical element (paragraph 17)

hydrogen, nitrogen, oxygen: gases in the earth's atmosphere (paragraph 17)

READING CRITICALLY
Graphing Your Reading

As you did for the previous essays, draw a graphic organizer for the ideas in the following essay. Make the drawing so accurate that someone could look at it and understand the basic concepts in the essay. Compare your drawing with someone else's in your class, and write a brief statement about the reading from the graphic organizer.

WHY WE HAVE A MOON
by David Levy

I remember the beautiful clear sky the day my granddaughter, then 14 months old, first fell under its spell. She called it the "oon." Soon, I knew, she'd be asking, "How did the Moon get there? Did people really walk on it? Will *I* someday?"—the same questions asked by Moonwatchers of all ages. So, how *did* the Moon get there?   1

About 4.5 billion years ago, the Earth had a bad day. The Sun was shining on our young world, which had no oceans yet and no life, but a surface filled with erupting volcanoes. The sky was awash with stars, though not the ones we see now. But the familiar planets were there—Venus, Jupiter, Saturn, Mars—and another planet the size of Mars but much closer.   2

Had we been alive back then, we would have noticed this other planet looping again and again around the Sun in an odd orbit that brought it very close to Earth, then farther away. On this day, that odd planet, approaching us again, became brighter than ever before, filling the sky and getting bigger by the minute, its gravitational pull now so great that rocks began to stretch and rumble. Then, with unimaginable energy and deafening noise, it sideswiped the Earth, bounced off and, seconds later, tore right back into our planet with a supercolossal force.   3

That Mars-size world broke apart, and huge chunks of Earth's crust flew off into space. Two rings of debris, their particles much larger than those in the fine-grained rings of Saturn, grew and circled the Earth. For many days, pieces of the inner ring plummeted down again, adding to the Earth's devastation. Pieces of the outer ring slowly gathered together around its largest chunks. In just a year, those pieces formed a large new world, a world that we can still see. That world we call the Moon.   4

5   So goes the prevailing theory, developed in the 1970s. In its earliest days, our Moon was probably no more than 10,000 miles away. The Earth spun around faster then, in a 10-hour day. But over time, the Moon slowly veered away from Earth, its gravity forever slowing Earth's rotation. By the time of the dinosaurs, more than 4 billion years after the Moon's formation, a day was about 22 hours long. With our day now at 24 hours, the Moon, still inching away at approximately 3 feet every century, is about 240,000 miles away. But even at this distance, it has a powerful influence on the Earth's waters.

The Moon and the Tides

6   We have tides on Earth because of the gravitational pull of the Moon (and the Sun, especially when the two are in alignment) across the diameter of the Earth. If you've ever been to an ocean beach, you have felt the Moon's whisper as its gravity brings the water in, then out, twice each day. One day in Nova Scotia, I felt the Moon roar.

7   At the eastern end of Canada's Bay of Fundy, a flow of water equal to the combined currents of all the rivers on Earth thunders through the Minas Channel into the Minas Basin twice a day for six hours. To see this marvelous sight, I traveled to a remote Nova Scotia promontory called Cape Split. I arrived as the incoming tidal flow was at its maximum.

8   A first-quarter Moon hung in the sky as a *million* gallons of water poured into the Minas Basin. I found it incredible that the Moon, from a distance of 240,000 miles, was responsible for the tremendous noise in the channel below. After a few hours, the flow slowed, then stopped. For a half hour or so, the water was still. Then the huge basin began to empty, flowing *in reverse* like a movie running backward, the noise rising once again. Such is the power of the Moon's gravity.

9   The shape of the land makes the tides stronger. In midocean, the daily tidal bulge is about a yard. But at Minas Basin, it's 45 feet—the largest tidal flow on the planet—owing to the peculiar geography of the Gulf of Maine, the Bay of Fundy, the Minas Channel and basin. It's like a child playing in a bathtub, pushing the water to the front, then letting it flow back. A rhythm builds. If the child lifts up slightly each time, the water sloshes toward one end. Eventually, the water rides up the side of the tub and spills out. The child's movement is "in sync" with the natural motion of the water in the tub. The water's increased momentum, plus the confining shape of the tub, results in more force on the water—just as the Moon's gravity, aided by the shape of the land, strengthens the force of the Fundy tides.

The Moon Is a Mirror

10   When we look at the Moon, we see on its uneven surface a record of billions of years of bashing. The Moon's face is trying to tell us something about Earth's own past. If the Moon has been hit so often, the Earth, being a much bigger target, must have been struck even more often.

11   The first thing you notice about the Moon is its uneven, mottled surface. With binoculars, the unevenness appears more pronounced, with clear evidence of dark and bright spots. What are they?

12   To the ancient Greeks, the Moon's "spots" were exhalations from the Earth that rose all the way to the Moon. By the 1500s, it was common to compare the Moon to green cheese—not because of its mysterious color but because "green cheese" meant round, uncut cheese with a mottled surface. As recently as 1960, most scientists believed craters were the result of volcanic forces beneath the Moon's surface.

That was before Gene Shoemaker appeared on the scene. A young geologist, he was studying craters formed by underground nuclear testing near Las Vegas in the late 1950s. He noted that these craters, formed by far greater heat and pressure than a volcano could produce, resembled some of the great natural craters on Earth. Perhaps the latter—as well as the craters on the Moon—had resulted from impacts by meteors, comets or asteroids, whose energy would have been closer to that of an atomic bomb.   13

By 1960, Shoemaker had proved that a 1.2-mile-wide crater near Flagstaff, Arizona, was the result of the crash of an asteroid some 50,000 years ago. By studying detailed photographs of craters on the Moon, plus images taken by the *Ranger* and *Surveyor* spacecraft, Shoemaker established that the Moon's surface was a story of impacts over billions of years.   14

In 1972, the astronaut Harrison Schmidt went to the Moon on *Apollo 17* and confirmed Shoemaker's theory live on television. "Gene defined what the characteristics of the Moon's surface layer would be," Schmidt told me.   15

But the Moon's surface revealed a far more important story—that of the solar system's violent past, when the planets, including Earth, were bombarded by comets and meteors. On March 25, 1993, Shoemaker, his wife, Carol, and I discovered that a collision in the solar system was imminent. And 16 months later, as the world watched, comet Shoemaker-Levy 9 slammed into Jupiter at 37 miles per second—the equivalent of going from New York to Los Angeles *in 70 seconds*.   16

The spectacle of these comets hitting Jupiter was a replay of an ancient scenario in which comets—comprised of carbon, hydrogen, nitrogen, and oxygen—crashed into Earth, starting a slow process that eventually led to the earliest life here.   17

Is the Moon still being bombarded today? On July 10, 1941, Walter Haas, one of the world's most experienced observers, saw a speck of light move across Gassendi, a large lunar crater. Did Haas see a meteorite striking the Moon at enormous speed? Smaller particles did hit the Moon on Nov. 17, 1999, during the Leonid meteor shower.   18

If small objects still hit the Moon, can large ones? In 1178, some monks near Canterbury, England, reported a terrifying experience on a night of a crescent Moon: "Suddenly," the account reads, "the upper horn split in two. From the division, a flaming torch sprang up, spewing out, over a considerable distance, fire, hot coals, and sparks."   19

Could they have seen a major impact on the Moon? Conceivably, a 20-mile crater on the Moon's far side, called Giordano Bruno, was caused by a large impact. We may never know the answer, but there's a clue.   20

In the 1970s, the McDonald Observatory in Texas, bouncing laser beams off the Moon, found that it "sways" by a few yards about every three years. Like a huge bell vibrating after being clanged, the Moon is acting as if it had been struck by a large object within the last 1,000 years. Perhaps, someday, my granddaughter, caught by the Moon's wondrous pull, will walk there as others once did and find an answer.   21

Thinking Critically About Content

1. Writers often use personal stories to get the reader's attention or understanding. Where does Levy use stories in this essay? What effect do they have?

2. What were the steps in the moon's formation 4.5 billion years ago?

3. According to Levy, what is the relationship between the moon and the oceans?

Thinking Critically About Purpose and Audience

4. What do you think the purpose of this essay is?

5. How do you think a general audience would respond to the author's description of the moon as a mirror of the earth's past?

6. Levy often relates scientific information to everyday occurrences—like comparing the motion of the tides to a child playing in the bathtub (paragraph 9). Find one other example of this technique. As a reader, how do you respond to this strategy?

Thinking Critically About Essays

7. Describe in a complete sentence the writer's point of view.

8. Why do you think Levy introduces current research on the moon in the last section of his essay?

9. What are the three main parts of Levy's essay? Why do you think he arranges these topics in this order?

10. If Levy were writing this essay for a publication to be read only by scientists, how might it be different? How might it be the same? Rewrite the introduction or the conclusion for an audience of scientists.

To keep track of your critical thinking progress, go to Appendix 1.

Writing Process Analysis

This section gives you the opportunity to apply what you have learned in this chapter to your own writing. It provides you with guidelines for a process analysis essay and then lets you go through your own writing process with feedback from your peers. Refer to the readings, as necessary, for examples of good process analysis writing. Finally, pause at the end of the chapter to reflect briefly on what you have learned.

Guidelines for Writing a Process Analysis Essay

1. State in the thesis statement what the reader should be able to do or understand by the end of the essay.
2. Know your audience.
3. Explain the process clearly in the body of your essay.
4. Organize your material logically.
5. End your essay by considering the process as a whole.

Writing About Your Reading

1. In the first essay, Julia Bourland discusses debt as a normal part of life. Have you ever thought of debt in this way? Explain a process from your experience that is another normal part of life.

2. Think of something in life that you want as much as the Europeans described in Freedman's essay wanted to come to the United States. Then explain your plan for achieving this goal or accomplishing this mission you have set for yourself.

3. O'Connell talks about how we need to "get ahead of the problem before it gets ahead of you." Are you aware of a need for this timing in other aspects of your life? How can thoughtful timing get you what you want? Explain a process that involved getting something you wanted by timing your words and/or actions with care.

4. Think of something in life that you want to study as much as Levy wants to study the moon and stars. Then discuss your plans for achieving your goals in this area of study.

5. Which type of process analysis do you find most interesting—the how-to essays or the background explanations? Explain your answer.

Writing About Your World

1. Choose an appliance or a piece of equipment you understand well, and write a process analysis essay explaining how it works. Don't identify the item in your essay. Then see if the class members can guess what device you are talking about.

2. Research the history of your college or university, and write an essay explaining its background to prospective students. Be sure to give a focus to your study and decide on a purpose before you begin write.

3. Tell your classmates about a sport or hobby you enjoy. Include what it takes to get started in this activity and why you enjoy it. For example, how would a person get started playing the guitar, collecting stamps, or snowboarding? And what could it lead to?

4. Your college newspaper is running a special edition on study habits, and the editor has asked you to write an article explaining how you manage all the demands on your time, including studying, socializing, working, and keeping family obligations. Prepare your explanation for the next edition of the paper.

5. Create your own process analysis assignment (with the help of your instructor), and write a response to it.

Revising

Small Group Activity (5–10 minutes per writer) In groups of three or four, read your process analysis essays to each other. Those listening should record their reactions on a copy of the Peer Evaluation Form in Appendix 2A. After your group goes through this process, give your evaluation forms to the appropriate writers so that each writer has two or three peer comment sheets for revising.

Paired Activity (5 minutes per writer) Using the completed Peer Evaluation Forms, work in pairs to decide what you should revise in your essay. If time allows, rewrite some of your sentences, and have your partner look at them.

Individual Activity Rewrite your paper, using the revising feedback you received from other students.

Editing

Paired Activity (5–10 minutes per writer) Swap papers with a classmate, and use the editing portion of your Peer Evaluation Form to identify as many grammar, punctuation, mechanics, and spelling errors as you can. If time allows, correct some of your errors, and have your partner look at them. Record your grammar, punctuation, and mechanics errors in the Error Log (Appendix 3) and your spelling errors in the Spelling Log (Appendix 4).

Individual Activity Rewrite your paper again, using the editing feedback you received from other students.

Reflecting on Your Writing   When you have completed your own essay, answer these six questions.

1. What was most difficult about this assignment?
2. What was easiest?
3. What did you learn about process analysis by completing this assignment?
4. What do you think are the strengths of your process analysis? Place a wavy line by the parts of your essay that you feel are very good.
5. What are the weaknesses, if any, of your paper? Place an X by the parts of your essay you would like help with. Write any questions you have in the margins.
6. What did you learn from this assignment about your own writing process— about preparing to write, about writing the first draft, about revising, and about editing?

Comparison and Contrast: From Reading to Writing

This chapter includes four reading selections and several writing assignments. It offers guidance in peer evaluation and reflection, ending with suggestions about how to lead your instructor through your writing in ways that will benefit both of you.

Reading Comparison/Contrast

The following essays show how comparison and contrast work in a complete essay. The first, "The Barrio" by Ernesto Galarza, is from his book *Barrio Boy*, which traces Galarza's move from Tepic, Mexico, to California. The second essay, "It's a Girls' World, After All: The New Imbalance in the Information Age" by David Brooks, compares and contrasts the performance of males and females in the new age of information. The third, "American Space, Chinese Place" by Yi-Fu Tuan, compares the concept of space in two different cultures, and "Between Worlds" by Tony Cohan compares and contrasts a writer's life in two separate locations. As you read, notice how the writers make their points through thoughtful, detailed comparisons and contrasts.

THE BARRIO
by Ernesto Galarza

Focusing Your Attention

1. Have you ever watched someone merge two cultures or tried to blend two cultures yourself? What are the advantages of merging cultures? What are the disadvantages?

2. In the essay you are about to read, the writer compares and contrasts various characteristics of American and Latin American life from the

perspective of someone who has come to America for the first time. What do you think are some of the differences between these two cultures? Some of the similarities?

Expanding Your Vocabulary

The following words are important to your understanding of this essay. Start a vocabulary log of your own by recording any words you don't understand as you read. When you finish reading the essay, write down what you think the words mean. Then check your definitions in the dictionary.

barrio: Spanish-speaking neighborhood (title)

mercados: marketplaces (paragraph 1)

chiquihuite: basket (paragraph 1)

pilón: sugar candy (paragraph 1)

Mazatlán: a city in Mexico (paragraph 1)

Judases: images of the disciple who betrayed Jesus (paragraph 2)

Holy Week: the week leading up to Easter (paragraph 2)

promenades: parades (paragraph 2)

plaza: public square (paragraph 2)

cathedral: large church (paragraph 2)

Palacio de Gobierno: town hall (paragraph 2)

vecindades: close-knit neighborhoods (paragraph 3)

mirth: fun, laughter (paragraph 4)

boisterous: noisy (paragraph 4)

compadre: godfather (paragraph 5)

comadre: godmother (paragraph 5)

cherubs: angels depicted as babies with wings (paragraph 5)

mica: a mineral (paragraph 5)

atole: a drink (paragraph 5)

corridos: songs (paragraph 5)

paddy wagon: police van (paragraph 6)

IOU's: debts (paragraph 8)

pochos: Mexicans living in the United States who grew up in the United States (paragraph 9)

chicanos: Mexicans living in the United States who grew up in Mexico (paragraph 9)

READING CRITICALLY
Peer Teaching Your Reading

For this reading, practice peer teaching by dividing the following essay into logical pieces and teaching it to each other. You could divide the essay into topics (Mexican and American) or sections (a certain number of paragraphs). Once you decide on the divisions, break the class up into just as many groups. Study your material as deeply as you can in the time allowed. Then teach it to the rest of the class.

THE BARRIO
by Ernesto Galarza

1   We found the Americans as strange in their customs as they probably found us. Immediately we discovered that there were no *mercados* and that when shopping you did not put the groceries in a *chiquihuite.* Instead, everything was in cans or in cardboard boxes, or each item was put in a brown paper bag. There were neighborhood grocery stores at the corners and some big ones uptown, but no *mercado.* The grocers did not give children a *pilón,* and they did not stand at the door and coax you to come in and buy, as they did in Mazatlán. The fruits and vegetables were displayed on counters instead of being piled up on the floor. The stores smelled of fly spray and oiled floors, not of fresh pineapple and limes.

2   Neither was there a plaza, only parks which had no bandstands, no concerts every Thursday, no Judases exploding on Holy Week, and no promenades of boys going one way and girls the other. There were no parks in the *barrio,* and the ones uptown were cold and rainy in winter, and in summer there was no place to sit except on the grass. When there were celebrations, nobody set off rockets in the parks, much less on the street in front of your house to announce to the neighborhood that a wedding or a baptism was taking place. Sacramento did not have a *mercado* and a plaza with the cathedral to one side and the Palacio de Gobierno on another to make it obvious that there and nowhere else was the center of the town.

3   It was just as puzzling that the Americans did not live in *vecindades,* like our block on Leandro Valle. Even in the alleys, where people knew one another better, the houses were fenced apart, without central courts to wash clothes, talk, and play with the other children. Like the city, the Sacramento *barrio* did not have a place which was the middle of things for everyone.

4   In more personal ways, we had to get used to the Americans. They did not listen if you did not speak loudly, as they always did. In the Mexican style, people would know that you were enjoying their jokes tremendously if you merely smiled and shook a little, as if you were trying to swallow your mirth. In the American style, there was little difference between a laugh and a roar, and until you got used to them you could hardly tell whether the boisterous Americans were roaring mad or roaring happy.

5   The older people of the *barrio,* except in those things which they had to do like the Americans because they had no choice, remained Mexican. Their language at home was Spanish. They were continuously taking up collections to pay somebody's funeral expenses or to help someone who had had a serious accident. Cards were sent to you to attend a burial where you would throw a handful of dirt on top of the coffin and listen to tearful speeches at the graveside. At every baptism, a new *compadre* and a new *comadre* joined the family circle. New Year greeting cards were exchanged, showing angels and cherubs in bright colors sprinkled with grains of mica so that they glistened like gold dust. At the family parties the huge pot of steaming tamales was still the center of attention, the *atole* served on the side with chunks of brown sugar for sucking and crunching. If the party lasted long enough, someone produced a guitar; the men took over and the singing of *corridos* began.

6   In the *barrio* there were no individuals who had official titles or who were otherwise recognized by everybody as important people. The reason must have been that there was no place in the public business of the city of Sacramento for the Mexican immigrants. We only rented a corner of the city and as long as we paid the rent on time everything else was decided at City Hall or the County Court House, where Mexicans went only when they were in trouble. Nobody from the *barrio* ever ran for mayor or city councilman. For us, the most important public officials were the policemen who walked their beats, stopped fights, and hauled drunks to jail in a paddy wagon we called *La Julia.*

7   The one institution we had that gave the *colonia* some kind of image was the *Comisión Honorífica,* a committee picked by the Mexican Consul in San Francisco to organize the celebration of the *Cinco de Mayo* and the Sixteenth of September, the anniversaries of the battle of Puebla and the beginning of our War of Independence. These were the two events which stirred everyone in the *barrio,* for what we were celebrating was not only the heroes of Mexico but also the feeling that we were still Mexicans ourselves. On these occasions, there was a dance preceded by speeches and a concert. For both the *cinco* and the sixteenth, queens were elected to preside over the ceremonies.

8   Between celebrations, neither the politicians uptown nor the *Comisión Honorífica* attended to the daily needs of the *barrio.* This was done by volunteers—the ones who knew enough English to interpret in court, on a visit to the doctor, a call at the county hospital, and who could help make out a postal money order. By the time I had finished the third grade at the Lincoln School, I was one of these volunteers. My services were not professional, but they were free, except for the IOU's I accumulated from families who always thanked me with "God will pay you for it."

9   My clients were not *pochos,* Mexicans who had grown up in California, probably had even been born in the United States. They had learned to speak English of sorts

and could still speak Spanish, also of sorts. They knew much more about the Americans than we did and much less about us. The *chicanos* and the *pochos* had certain feelings about one another. Concerning the *pochos,* the *chicanos* suspected that they considered themselves too good for the *barrio* but were not, for some reason, good enough for the Americans. Toward the *chicanos,* the *pochos* acted superior, amused at our confusions but not especially interested in explaining them to us. In our family, when I forgot my manners, my mother would ask me if I was turning *pochito.*

Turning *pocho* was a half-step toward turning American. And America was all   10
around us, in and out of the *barrio.* Abruptly we had to forget the ways of shopping in a *mercado* and learn those of shopping in a corner grocery or in a department store. The Americans paid no attention to the Sixteenth of September, but they made a great commotion about the Fourth of July. In Mazatlán, Don Salvador had told us, saluting and marching as he talked to our class, that the *Cinco de Mayo* was the most glorious date in human history. The Americans had not even heard about it.

Thinking Critically About Content

1. Explain three differences between American and Latin American customs.

2. What difference between these customs is most interesting to you? Why?

3. What does Galarza mean when he says, "Turning *pocho* was a half-step toward turning American" (paragraph 10)?

Thinking Critically About Purpose and Audience

4. What is Galarza's purpose in writing this essay?

5. Who do you think is his primary audience?

6. Why does Galarza call his essay "The Barrio"? What is his point of view toward the *barrio*?

Thinking Critically About Paragraphs

7. Explain how the topic sentence works in paragraph 4. Does it supply the controlling idea for the entire paragraph?

8. Choose a paragraph from this essay, and underline all of its transitional words and phrases. Do these transitions help move the reader through the paragraph? Explain your answer.

9. Galarza sprinkles Spanish words throughout his essay. What effect does the addition of Spanish words have on the essay?

10. Write a paragraph responding to some of Galarza's observations. What are some of his confusions?

To keep track of your critical thinking progress, go to Appendix 1.

IT'S A GIRLS' WORLD, AFTER ALL: THE NEW IMBALANCE OF THE INFORMATION AGE
by David Brooks

Focusing Your Attention

1. What differences between males and females do you find most obvious?

2. In the essay you are about to read, the author explains why females are beginning to succeed in the world today at a higher rate than males. What evidence of this observation do you see in your immediate environment?

Expanding Your Vocabulary

The following words are important to your understanding of this essay. Start a vocabulary log of your own by recording any words you don't understand as you read. When you finish reading the essay, write down what you think the words mean. Then check your definitions in the dictionary.

crucial: critical (paragraph 1)

accumulate: build up (paragraph 3)

persistent: continuing or recurring (paragraph 3)

median: in the middle (paragraph 4)

monumental: of great importance (paragraph 5)

patriarchy: male dominated society (paragraph 7)

quaint: old fashioned (paragraph 7)

anachronism: something appropriate to a period other than the one it belongs in (paragraph 7)

machismo: strong masculine pride (paragraph 8)

READING CRITICALLY
Peer Teaching Your Reading

As with the previous reading, divide the following paragraph into logical pieces and teach it to each other in class. You could divide the essay into topics (males and females) or sections (a certain number of paragraphs). Once you decide on the divisions, break the class up into just as many groups. Study your material as deeply as you can in the time allowed. Then teach it to the rest of the class.

IT'S A GIRLS' WORLD, AFTER ALL:
THE NEW IMBALANCE OF THE INFORMATION AGE
by David Brooks

1   Once upon a time, it was a man's world. Men possessed most of the tools one needed for power and success: muscles, connections, control of the crucial social institutions.

2   But then along came the information age to change all that. In the information age, education is the gateway to success. And that means this is turning into a woman's world, because women are better students than men.

3   From the first days of school, girls outperform boys. The gap is sometimes small, but over time slight advantages accumulate into big ones. In surveys, kindergarten teachers report that girls are more attentive than boys and more persistent at tasks. Through elementary school, girls are less likely to be asked to repeat a grade. They are much less likely to be diagnosed with a learning disability.

4   In high school, girls get higher grades in every subject, usually by about a quarter of a point, and have a higher median class rank. They are more likely to take advanced placement courses and the hardest math courses and are more likely to be straight-A students. They have much higher reading and writing scores on national assessment tests. Boys still enjoy an advantage on math and science tests, but that gap is smaller and closing. Girls are much more likely to be involved in the school paper or yearbook, to be elected to student government, and to be members of academic clubs. They set higher goals for their post-high-school careers. (These data are all from the Department of Education.)

5   The differences become monumental in college. Women are more likely to enroll in college, and they are more likely to have better applications, so now there are hundreds of schools where the female–male ratio is 60 to 40. About 80 percent of those majoring in public administration, psychology, and education are female. And here's the most important piece of data: Until 1985 or so, male college graduates outnumbered female college graduates. But in the mid-'80s, women drew even, and ever since they have been pulling away at a phenomenal rate.

6   This year, 133 women will graduate from college for every 100 men. By decade's end, according to Department of Education projections, there will be 142 female graduates for every 100 male graduates. Among African Americans, there are 200 female grads for every 100 male grads.

7   The social consequences are bound to be profound. The upside is that by sheer force of numbers, women will be holding more and more leadership jobs. On the negative side, they will have a harder and harder time finding marriageable men with comparable education levels. One thing is for sure: In 30 years the notion that we live in an oppressive patriarchy that discriminates against women will be regarded as a quaint anachronism.

8   There are debates about why women have thrived and men have faltered. Some say men are imprisoned by their anti-intellectual machismo. Others say the educational system has been overly feminized. Boys are asked to sit quietly for hours at a stretch under conditions where they find it harder to thrive.

9   But Thomas G. Mortensen of the Pell Institute observes that these same trends—thriving women, faltering men—are observable across the world. In most countries and in nearly all developed countries, women are graduating from high school and college at much higher rates than men. Mr. Mortensen writes, "We conclude that the issue is far less driven by a nation's culture than it is by basic differences between males and females in the modern world."

10   In other words, if we want to help boys keep up with girls, we have to have an honest discussion about innate differences between the sexes. We have to figure out why poor girls who move to middle-class schools do better, but poor boys who make the same move often do worse. We have to absorb the obvious lesson of every airport bookstore, which is that men and women like to read totally different sorts of books, and see if we can apply this fact when designing curriculums. If boys like to read about war and combat, why can't there be books about combat on the curriculum?

11   Would elementary school boys do better if they spent more time outside the classroom and less time chained to a desk? Or would they thrive more in a rigorous, competitive environment?

12   For 30 years, attention has focused on feminine equality. During that time, honest discussion of innate differences has been stifled (ask Harvard President Larry Summers). It's time to look at the other half.

Thinking Critically About Content

1. What is the main idea that David Brooks presents in this essay?

2. Do you see any evidence of Brooks's points about men and women in higher education at your college?

3. What do you think Brooks means when he says, "It's time to look at the other half" (paragraph 12)?

Thinking Critically About Purpose and Audience

4. Why do you think Brooks wrote this essay?

5. Who would be most interested in this essay?

6. How does this essay make you feel about the American education system in general?

Thinking Critically About Paragraphs

7. What examples does Brooks use in paragraph 5 to explain his topic sentence? Do these examples get his point across in this paragraph?

8. If a paragraph is unified, all of its sentences refer to the idea expressed in the topic sentence. In paragraph 7, three sentences follow the topic sentence. How do these three sentences relate to the paragraph's topic sentence?

9. Brooks begins his essay like a fable ("Once upon a time..."). Is this an effective beginning for this essay? Explain your answer.

10. Write a paragraph exploring another comparison or contrast about men and women.

To keep track of your critical thinking progress, go to Appendix 1.

AMERICAN SPACE, CHINESE PLACE
by Yi-Fu Tuan

Focusing Your Attention

1. Are you aware of how most Americans respond to space in our culture? Do you generally like open spaces or closed spaces?

2. The essay you are about to read compares the American concept of space with that of the Chinese. Do you know any culture that thinks differently than we do about space? What are the differences? The similarities? What is the source of these differences and similarities?

Expanding Your Vocabulary

The following words are important to your understanding of this essay. Start a vocabulary log of your own by recording any words you don't understand as you read. When you finish reading the essay, write down what you think the words mean. Then check your definitions in the dictionary.

exurbia: prosperous areas beyond the suburbs (paragraph 1)

vistas: pleasant views (paragraph 1)

ambiance: the atmosphere of a place (paragraph 2)

terrestrial: relating to the Earth (paragraph 2)

wanderlust: a strong desire to travel (paragraph 3)

pecuniary: relating to money (paragraph 3)

nostalgia: sentimental longing for the past (paragraph 4)

beckons: encourages someone to approach (paragraph 5)

READING CRITICALLY
Peer Teaching Your Reading

Once again, practice peer teaching by dividing the following essay into logical pieces and teaching it to each other. This time, get into five small groups (one for each paragraph), and study your paragraph as deeply as you can in the time allowed. Then teach it to the rest of the class.

AMERICAN SPACE, CHINESE PLACE
by Yi-Fu Tuan

1   Americans have a sense of space, not of place. Go to an American home in exurbia, and almost the first thing you do is drift toward the picture window. How curious that the first compliment you pay your host inside his house is to say how lovely it is outside his house! He is pleased that you should admire his vistas. The distant horizon is not merely a line separating earth from sky, it is a symbol of the future. The American is not rooted in his place, however lovely: his eyes are drawn by the expanding space to a point on the horizon, which is his future. By contrast, consider the traditional Chinese home. Blank walls enclose it.

2   Step behind the spirit wall and you are in a courtyard with perhaps a miniature garden around the corner. Once inside the private compound, you are wrapped in an ambiance of calm beauty, an ordered world of....buildings, pavement, rock, and decorative vegetation. But you have no distant view: nowhere does space open out before you. Raw nature in such a home is experienced only as weather, and the only open space is the sky above. The Chinese is rooted in his place. When he has to leave, it is not for the promised land on the terrestrial horizon, but for another world altogether along the vertical, religious axis of his imagination.

3   The Chinese tie to place is deeply felt. Wanderlust is an alien sentiment. The Taoist classic Tao Te Ching captures the ideal of rootedness in place with these words: "Though there may be another country in the neighborhood so close that they are within sight of each other and the crowing of cocks and barking of dogs in one place can be heard in the other, yet there is no traffic between them; and throughout their lives the two peoples have nothing to do with each other." In theory if not in practice, farmers have ranked high in Chinese society. The reason is not only that they are engaged in the "root" industry of producing food but that, unlike pecuniary merchants, they are tied to the land and do not abandon their country when it is in danger.

4   Nostalgia is a recurrent theme in Chinese poetry. An American reader of translated Chinese poems will be taken aback—even put off—by the frequency as well as the sentimentality of the lament for home. To understand the strength of this sentiment, we need to know that the Chinese desire for stability and rootedness in place is prompted by the constant threat of war, exile, and the natural disasters of flood and drought.

5   Forcible removal makes the Chinese keenly aware of their loss. By contrast, Americans move, for the most part, voluntarily. Their nostalgia for home town is really longing for childhood to which they cannot return: in the meantime the future beckons and the future is "out there" in open space. When we criticize American rootlessness we tend to forget that it is a result of ideals we admire, namely, social mobility and optimism about the future. When we admire Chinese rootedness, we forget that the word "place" means both location in space and position in society: to be tied to place is also to be bound to one's station in life, with little hope of betterment. Space symbolizes hope, place, achievement, and stability.

Yi-Fu Tuan, "American Space, Chinese Place." Reprinted by permission of Yi-Fu Tuan, Ph.D.

Thinking Critically About Content

1. What are the main differences between American homes and Chinese homes? Where is the focus in both of these settings?

2. What is "exurbia" (paragraph 1)?

3. In what ways are the Chinese rooted in their places?

Thinking Critically About Purpose and Audience

4. Why do you think Tuan wrote this essay?

5. Who do you think is his main audience?

6. How could space symbolize "hope, place, achievement, and stability" (paragraph 5)? How are all these notions related?

Thinking Critically About Essays

7. What is Tuan's thesis statement? How does he lead up to this thesis?

8. Explain how the topic sentence works in paragraph 5. Does it supply the controlling idea for the entire paragraph?

9. This is one of the shortest essays in this collection. Does Tuan get his point across effectively in this essay or does he need more paragraphs? Explain your answer.

10. Do you agree or disagree with his general conclusions about the Chinese and American concepts of space? Write a detailed response to some of Tuan's observations.

To keep track of your critical thinking progress, go to Appendix 1.

BETWEEN WORLDS
by Tony Cohan

Focusing Your Attention

1. Do you ever feel like you live in two or more different worlds? What are they?

2. In the essay you are about to read, the author compares and contrasts the "worlds" of San Miguel de Allende in Mexico and Los Angeles from a writer's point of view. What similarities and differences do you imagine that Cohan discovered?

Expanding Your Vocabulary

The following words are important to your understanding of this essay. Start a vocabulary log of your own by recording any words you don't understand as you read. When you finish reading the essay, write down what you think the words mean. Then check your definitions in the dictionary.

entwine: weave (paragraph 1)

revelatory: revealing (paragraph 1)

mired: buried (paragraph 1)

recession: decline (paragraph 1)

unkempt: messy, untidy (paragraph 4)

la frontera: border (paragraph 5)

calibrations: adjustments (paragraph 6)

referent: point of reference (paragraph 7)

jargon: specialized language (paragraph 7)

deciphering: figuring out (paragraph 7)

corrido: run (paragraph 8)

Proustian: emotional (paragraph 8)

feigned: pretend (paragraph 9)

reticent: uncommunicative, silent (paragraph 9)

xenophobic: afraid of strangers or foreigners (paragraph 9)

primordial: primitive (paragraph 9)

brujos: wizards (paragraph 9)

audibility: hearing (paragraph 10)

near-monastic: almost monk-like (paragraph 13)

muster: create (paragraph 13)

sabor: flavor (paragraph 13)

ambiente: atmosphere (paragraph 13)

celebratory: festive (paragraph 14)

norte–o bands: bands from northern Mexico (paragraph 14)

patina: shine (paragraph 14)

conditional: tentative (paragraph 14)

corrugated: with parallel ridges (paragraph 17)

lumpen detritus: accumulated debris (paragraph 17)

READING CRITICALLY
Peer Teaching Your Reading

As with the previous readings, teach the following essay to each other in class. This time, divide into two large groups and then break those groups in half (one for California and one for Mexico). So each large group will study both cultures in this essay. After separate discussions in your groups, you will present your findings to the rest of the class. With two groups working on each culture, this is an excellent way to make sure you understand all the details in a complex essay.

BETWEEN WORLDS
by Tony Cohan

Our fourth year in Mexico. We live between worlds these days, frequent flyers. The Mexican cycles of seasons and holidays entwine us deeper in town and country. Friends come and go, fall in love, split up; babies are born. Our life in San Miguel de Allende remains the intimate sum of our days—sensual, revelatory, engaged. Mexico, still mired in post-earthquake recession, muddles through somehow. New friends emerge: Arnaud, a Haitian poet in exile who has awakened me to Caribbean culture; a Chilean painter and his wife; a Mexican professor. 1

Our world widens southward. The sprawling lands below the Rio Grande, a mere blip on CNN or ABC, remain to us norteamericanos, after all these centuries, the New World. Often after a flight from California we remain in Mexico City to explore, see new friends, venture out into other regions—Oaxaca, Guerrero, Yucatán, Chiapas—before returning to San Miguel, the heart's abode. 2

Still we feel unsettled at times, uneasily poised between cultures: losing a foothold in the old country, still on tourist visas in the new one. Masako's art bursts with imagery found here. Slowly Mexico takes root in my work, too: yet the language I hear and speak every day is not the one I write in. Gore Vidal, in an introduction to Paul Bowles's collected short stories, touches on the problem: "Great American writers are supposed not only to live in the greatest country in the world....but to write about that greatest of all human themes: the American Experience." A novelist friend I work with in PEN, the international writers group, says only half jokingly, "Careful you don't become a *desaparecido,* a disappeared person, yourself." 3

Sometimes I do fear liking Mexico too much, getting lost in it. One day I saw a scraggly, unkempt gringo on the Mexico City metro around my age with bad teeth and a bad haircut, tangled in another land, beyond return. He reminded me of Russians I'd seen in China, poor and disheveled, hunched atop bundles in train stations—the ones who'd stayed on too long. 4

On plane trips back to California, I gaze down at the Sea of Cortez: tidal blue stripes graduating from pale agate to turquoise to aquamarine. Salty inlets and rust basins, 5 green algal meadows. Violet badlands etched with tiny straight-line roads, barren as Mars. We cross *la frontera,* that invisible, charged border, and belly down over L.A.'s carpet of light. From the back of a taxi running up the 405, the city spreads away before us, a bobbing, firefly-infested lake.

6   We stay on friends' couches, house-sit, sublet. We see people necessary to the work we do, thumbing our Rolodexes, trying to make the days count. Observing age's effects upon our parents, we make careful calibrations between desire and duty. Sometimes we talk of buying another place in L.A. just to have an anchor in the home country, but we can't summon the interest. We hurry through our tasks so we can leave all the sooner.

7   Old friends are busy climbing up, clinging to, falling off career ladders. The conversation is the same one we checked out on six months earlier, different only in detail, with television and movies the referent, not live experience or books. I'm losing the jargon, the codes, the names of things. In conversations I blank on celebrities' names, hip expressions. Car alarms go off like crazy toys. Helicopters throb overhead, spotlighting evil. The nightly news imbues pedestrian acts with hysterical urgency. Few people walk for pleasure. There's little time to talk, and seldom of important things. It's easier to get some tasks done, as long as you don't need another human: I spend hours deciphering new telephone message menus, wading through oceans of calling options, waiting on hold. Arnaud, my Haitian poet friend in San Miguel, refers to revisiting his beloved Haiti as *the exile of return.*

8   Mexico in memory can be flat, flavorless, a postcard—like trying to remember sex or a good meal. It lives in the senses, not the mind, collapsing all abstractions into the brimming moment. Yet hearing a *corrido* on the radio or Spanish spoken in an L.A. market can unleash a near-overwhelming, Proustian effect, bringing tears. Now I understand better the mariachis' howling laments of memory and loss.

9   In California we don't talk much about Mexico. We've grown tired of the blank stares, the feigned interest, the allusions to Tijuana and the border towns, the beaches of Cabo or Cancún. Now I know why Mina and Paul used to be so reticent. In glossy, xenophobic, dollar-grubbing late-eighties U.S.A., Mexico is buzzless: a torpid blank somewhere south. Mexico, grail to generations of artists, site of primordial revelation—Mayan temples, *brujos,* muralists, hallucinatory mushrooms—has fallen off the map. This whorled, ornate neighbor civilization, secretly and essentially entwined with ours, is invisible, its people among us silent, nameless wraiths who clip lawns and clear tables.

10   In a West Hollywood eatery, we sit with friends, poking at endive salad, designer pizza. A plate glass window offers a view of the foothills behind the Strip. A Sade tape teases the threshold of lyric audibility. Noticing the nine-dollar taco on the menu, we glance at each other.

11   "Yes, but what do you *do* there?" one friend asks.

12   How to describe a trip to the Tuesday market? A four-hour dinner with Carlos, Elenita, Arnaud, and Colette in our patio by the Quebrada bridge? Waking up to the bells' sweet clangor? Hurrying along the cobbles in the rain, ducking under archways? How to describe Friday lunches at El Caribe or checking out Thomas More's *Utopia* at the little bilingual library and actually reading it through? It's as if we have a secret life, in a secret place.

13   I used to like L.A.: the cool speed, the indifference to history, the near-monastic life of house, car, house. It freed the mind to run along some ever widening horizon line. Flatness, the absence of affect: not a bad place for a writer. There's no world out there so

you invent one. I can't muster that appreciation any longer. I want taste, smell, *sabor, ambiente*. I want the human shape to my days.

In another sense, though, Mexico has redeemed L.A. to me. I've discovered a buried 14 city there—a Latino L.A., warm and celebratory, where Spanish traces an invisible heart line deeper than place. In the course of my days, I may encounter a man or woman hailing from Guanajuato or Jalisco or Oaxaca, and matters of truth and fullness of heart may pass between us, and much laughter: riches invisible to most of my other friends. I can trace Los Lobos riffs back to *norte-o* bands that come through our part of Mexico: Los Tigres del Norte, Los Bukis. California street names and foods reveal their origins. Suddenly the century-old Anglo patina looks flimsy, conditional.

Sometimes I get energy off the displacement, the dislocation, the back-and-forth. 15 Each country seems the antidote to the other's ills. "In Rio, dreaming of New England/In New England, dreaming of Rio," the poet Elizabeth Bishop wrote.

Sometimes it feels like the two countries, through me, dream each other. 16

Invariably our L.A. trips end with a visit to the storage bin in Glendale. We intro- 17 duce the seven-digit code, pass through the security gates, inch down aisles of identical metal containers and cinder-block structures. We remove the lock, raise the corrugated door, and consider the lumpen detritus of our former life.

We shut the door, lock it, drive off. 18

Finally, our lists checked off, we head back to Mexico. At journey's end, the Flecha 19 Amarilla bus pulls into the dusty turnaround at the foot of San Miguel. We step out into darkness, as on that first night four years ago. The street dogs, the boys who want a coin to help with the baggage, the waiting taxi driver—those shades that so alarmed us then— appear to us now as town greeters, familiars. Wending up unlit streets once mysterious but intimate now from walking them, we make small talk with the taxi driver. "*Si*," he says. "*Un poco frio*." A little chilly. At Calle Quebrada we drag our bags down the dark stairwell, brush past a pair of young lovers. We open the door. The dusky smell of the last mesquite fire we'd built hits us. Our luggage slumps to the stone floor, our hands unclench. We're back.

Thinking Critically About Content

1. What do you think is Cohan's main point in this essay?
2. Why does Cohan call San Miguel "the heart's abode" (paragraph 2)?
3. In what ways is Cohan "poised between cultures" (paragraph 3)

Thinking Critically About Purpose and Audience

4. Why do you think Cohan wrote this essay?
5. Who would be most interested in this essay?
6. How does this essay make you feel about your hometown?

Thinking Critically About Essays

7. Name four points of comparison and four points of contrast in this essay.
8. How are most of the paragraphs in this essay organized? Use one paragraph to explain your answer.

9. Is Cohan's title effective? Explain your answer.

10. Write a short fable about a similarity or difference between two cities you know.

To keep track of your critical thinking progress, go to Appendix 1.

Writing Comparison/Contrast

This final section provides opportunities for you to apply what you have learned in this chapter to your own writing. It furnishes guidelines for writing a comparison/contrast essay and for peer evaluation. Return to the readings in the chapter as necessary to review good examples of comparison/contrast writing. Then pause at the end of the chapter to reflect briefly on what you have learned.

Guidelines for Writing a Comparison/Contrast Essay

1. Decide what point you want to make with your comparison, and state it in your thesis statement.
2. Choose items to compare and contrast that will make your point most effectively.
3. Use as many specific details and examples as possible to expand your comparison.
4. Develop your comparison in a balanced way.
5. Organize your essay subject by subject or point by point—or combine the two approaches.

Writing About Your Reading

1. In the first essay, Ernesto Galarza talks about the differences he sees on a daily basis between two cultures. Compare and contrast your family's rituals and practices with those of another family.

2. Expand the comparison you wrote in response to question 10 after David Brooks's essay.

3. Yi-Fu Tuan talks about the changes he sees in two countries' concept of space. But even in a single culture, we often think in different ways about space. Some people like to be physically close to others, some touch people while they talk, and others keep their distance at all times. Compare and contrast your personal notion of space with that of another person. What is the same between you two? What is different?

4. Expand the fable you wrote in response to question 10 after Tony Cohan's essay by adding more characters and more points.

5. What process do you have to go through to come up with an interesting comparison or contrast? How is it different from the process you go through for other rhetorical modes?

Writing About Your World

1. Discuss the similarities and differences between your high school life and your college life. Are your classes more difficult? Do you still hang out with your friends from high school? Are you treated differently by your parents, school officials, or old classmates? Have your expectations of yourself changed? Do you now have to juggle school and work?

2. You have been hired by your local newspaper to compare and contrast various aspects of daily life. For example, you might compare two musical groups, good drivers and bad drivers, two malls, or two kinds of pets. Decide on the point you want to make before you begin writing.

3. Choose a job advertised in your local newspaper's classified section, and write a cover letter to the employer comparing yourself to your probable competition. What are your best qualifications compared to others who might be applying for this job? What are your weaknesses in comparison to them? Why would you be the best candidate for the job?

4. Discuss the similarities and differences between two cities you know well. How are they the same? How are they different? What do you think accounts for these similarities and differences? When you write your essay, consider whether a subject-by-subject or a point-by-point organization would be more effective.

5. Create your own comparison/contrast assignment (with the help of your instructor), and write a response to it.

Revising

Small Group Activity (5–10 minutes per writer) Working in groups of three or four, read your comparison/contrast essays to each other. Those listening should record their reactions on a copy of the Peer Evaluation Form in Appendix 2A. After your group goes through this process, give your evaluation forms to the appropriate writers so that each writer has two or three peer comment sheets for revising.

Paired Activity (5 minutes per writer) Using the completed Peer Evaluation Forms, work in pairs to decide what you should revise in your essay. If time allows, rewrite some of your sentences, and have your partner look at them.

Individual Activity Rewrite your paper, using the revising feedback you received from other students.

Editing

Paired Activity (5–10 minutes per writer) Swap papers with a classmate, and use the editing portion of your Peer Evaluation Form to identify as many grammar, punctuation, mechanics, and spelling errors as you can. If time allows, correct some of your errors, and have your partner look at them. Record your grammar, punctuation, and mechanics errors in the Error Log (Appendix 3) and your spelling errors in the Spelling Log (Appendix 4).

Individual Activity Rewrite your paper again, using the editing feedback you received from other students.

Reflecting on Your Writing

When you have completed your own essay, answer these six questions.

1. What was most difficult about this assignment?

2. What was easiest?

3. What did you learn about comparison and contrast by completing this assignment?

4. What do you think are the strengths of your comparison/contrast essay? Place a wavy line by the parts of your essay that you feel are very good.

5. What are the weaknesses, if any, of your paper? Place an X by the parts of your essay you would like help with. Write any questions you have in the margins.

6. What did you learn from this assignment about your own writing process—about preparing to write, about writing the first draft, about revising, and about editing?

Division/Classification: From Reading to Writing

This chapter includes four reading selections and several writing assignments with guidance in peer evaluation and reflection. It ends with suggestions about how to lead your instructor through your writing in ways that will benefit both of you.

Reading Division/Classification

Here are four essays that follow the guidelines for good division/classification writing. "Rapport: How to Ignite It" by Camille Lavington divides and classifies personality types by communication styles, and "The Ways We Lie" by Stephanie Ericsson divides and classifies the various lies we tell. "Black Music in Our Hands" by Bernice Reagon categorizes different kinds of music she has encountered, while "What Are Friends For?" by Marion Winik discusses different types of friends. As you read, notice how the authors' categories support the points they are making.

RAPPORT: HOW TO IGNITE IT
Camille Lavington

Focusing Your Attention

1. Do you get along easily with others? Do you like different types of people?

2. The essay you are about to read classifies the different personality traits in people. What are your dominant personality traits? What impression do you usually make on people? How do you know you make this particular impression?

Expanding Your Vocabulary

The following words are important to your understanding of this essay. Organize this list into two columns—words you know and words you don't know. Write the definitions of the words you don't know above their words in the essay.

rapport: chemistry between people (title)

reticent: reserved, shy (paragraph 2)

Henry Kissinger: U.S. secretary of state during the Nixon administration (paragraph 2)

out of sync: out of step, out of alignment (paragraph 2)

persona: image, public identity (paragraph 2)

affinity: liking, attraction (paragraph 4)

endowed: gifted (paragraph 4)

remedied: fixed, corrected (paragraph 6)

hyperactive: energetic (paragraph 9)

intrusive: pushy (paragraph 9)

paradoxically: surprisingly, contrary to what was expected (paragraph 9)

reservoir: supply (paragraph 9)

eliciting: bringing forth, drawing out (paragraph 13)

vogue: trend, fad, style (paragraph 13)

osmosis: effortless learning, absorption (paragraph 17)

ESP: intuition, insight (paragraph 17)

cosmic: coming from the universe (paragraph 17)

charismatic: charming (paragraph 17)

nonconformity: difference from the norm (paragraph 17)

prudent: cautious (paragraph 21)

affluent: wealthy (paragraph 22)

monster: huge (paragraph 23)

superiority complex: the feeling that one is more important than other people (paragraph 23)

frivolities: matters of little importance (paragraph 23)

cerebral: intellectual (paragraph 24)

stick-in-the-mud: an old-fashioned or unprogressive person (paragraph 24)

from the heart: based on emotion (paragraph 25)

from the gut: based on intuition or insight rather than reason (paragraph 25)

empathetic: kindly, sensitive to the feelings of others (paragraph 25)

modified: adapted, changed (paragraph 25)

got strokes: was praised or rewarded (paragraph 25)

spontaneous: impulsive (paragraph 26)

all is not hearts and flowers: the situation is not entirely positive (paragraph 26)

psychoanalyze: try to explain the thoughts and emotions of others (paragraph 26)

benchmarks: criteria, milestones, points of reference (paragraph 29)

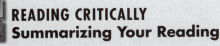

READING CRITICALLY
Summarizing Your Reading

As demonstrated in the Introduction, practice your summary skills on the following essay. Then work with someone in the class, and write a single paragraph that represents both of your summaries.

RAPPORT: HOW TO IGNITE IT
Camille Lavington

It happens in a flash, based entirely on surface cues, but people use first impressions to make sometimes irreversible judgments. 1

So don't be reticent about the talent you've been given. It's your obligation to share it with the world, and your personality is the driving force behind your talent. As Henry Kissinger once said, history is fueled not by impersonal forces, but by personalities. If yours is out of sync, it may need some work. That doesn't mean adopting a phony persona; it simply means adjusting your communicating style in order to relate better to others. 2

Understanding your own personality makes it easier to spot someone with whom you'd like to connect. There are simple signs that signal personality types, and you can recognize them—even in strangers. 3

4   We are all a combination of many personality traits, but most people have a stronger affinity for one. Or you may be one of those rarely gifted individuals who are *evenly* endowed in *every* style.

5   **Introverts** are deep thinkers who prefer time alone to read, or stare at their computer screens, or gaze into outer space. They strive for, and appreciate, excellence. Ironically, introverts often have meaningful friendships. These are their positive qualities. But, as with all personality types, there are negative aspects: Introverts have a tendency to be suspicious and worried. Introverts can also be intellectual snobs who are unaccepting of others and perfectionists to a fault. They may be self-centered and have friends who are jealous of them.

6   Much of introversion is caused by shyness and lack of experience. Of all the personality traits, I think that introversion is the one characteristic that most needs to be remedied. Why? Introversion borders on selfishness. By hanging back during interactions with others, introverts are protecting themselves. A conversation is like a canoe that requires the exertion of both participants to keep moving forward; an introvert isn't engaging his paddle. It's everyone's job to contribute to relationships and to make others comfortable.

7   **Extroverts** aren't perfect, but society tends to reward their behavior. They have many good qualities, including their friendliness and magnetism. Energetic and sparkling, they inspire others. They like people, variety, and action. Extroverts like to chat a lot. They get their energy from other people.

8   You won't see an extrovert going to the movies alone, eating dinner alone, taking a vacation alone. Extroverts are born leaders. It should come as no surprise that most CEOs and politicians are extroverts.

9   Still, extroverts can be hyperactive and intrusive. They need to be the center of attention at all times, and they have a habit of boasting. They're looking for a vote of confidence from the outside, even if they have to solicit it. Paradoxically, this is sometimes because they don't tap into their own reservoir of strength and thus haven't learned their own value.

10   The easiest way to achieve rapport with others is to remember that time together is either a learning or an entertaining experience. With this attitude, you'll always be eager to draw people into any dialogue by inviting them to add a comment or an opinion—rather than draining other people's energy by dominating or shortchanging the conversation.

11   Lock two extroverts in a room, and each will complain that the other is a poor conversationalist. (An extrovert thinks a good conversationalist is someone who is interested in what *he* has to say.)

12   **Sensers** are just-the-facts people, and they get that way by using their objective senses, rather than their intuition, to gather information. A senser relies on his eyes and ears for clues. Practical and bottom-line oriented, sensers are doers who want action and want it now. They are competitive and highly organized, and they set high standards for themselves.

13   Sensers are master manipulators who have a talent for eliciting the response they want from people; many actors, comedians, and salespeople are sensers for just that reason. Sensers prefer to wear comfortable clothing, but peer pressure means so much

to them that they will give in to the current vogue and wear what people they admire are wearing.

On the negative side, sensers can be self-involved, arrogant, and status-seeking. They tend to act first and think later. Also, they can be domineering and lacking in trust.   14

Sometimes you will be thrown off by a senser's easygoing manner because of his sense of humor, but don't waste his time. Get to the point quickly; remember that he's action-oriented and looking for short-term personal gain. If you have no previous knowledge about his temperament, take a look around for clues. A senser decorates his walls and bookshelves with personal trophies and memorabilia that remind him of his conquests.   15

You will lose points if you ever try to upstage a senser. This type, of all the others, wants to be the center of interest, as indicated by all of the personal trophies on his walls.   16

Intuitors make up a scant 10% of the population. So you're dealing with a rare bird. Albert Einstein is the classic intuitor—a genius who didn't speak until he was six years old. Intuitors gather information through a sort of osmosis, absorbing ESP signals and cosmic energy. Creative, imaginative, and original, they are driven by inspiration and a powerful intellect. Intuitors see the big picture in spite of a tenuous grasp of the details. Intuitors can be quite charismatic, although they tend to be unaware of their effect on people. They are also magnets to each other—finding their counterparts in the arts, sciences, wherever. Their nonconformity makes them dress in unusual combinations. In fact, they'll wear anything.   17

On the other hand, intuitors can drive others to madness. At times they're unrealistic and impractical. They're allergic to focusing on details. Fantasy-bound, they can be long on vision and short on action.   18

To approach an intuitor, spark her curiosity. When picking the brain of an intuitor, ask her to problem-solve without following any rules. You want to hear her unedited ideas.   19

If you're trying to impress an intuitor, don't waste time. You'll lose her attention if you give her a lot of background. Instead, respect her right-brain ability to jump to the heart of the matter in a flash.   20

Thinkers are the mainstay of society. They make life better because of their strong work ethic and high standards. Deliberate, prudent, and objective thinkers dwell in the world of rationality and analysis. Thinkers like to sleep on it. Many are effective communicators, possibly because they consider carefully before they speak. They make good jurors, who wait until closing arguments are concluded before weighing the evidence carefully. Their checkbooks are balanced.   21

Thinkers tend to like tailored, conservative clothing. If they're affluent, they have a tie that shows they met the rigid qualifications for entry to a top-ranked school. Teaching is a profession often favored by thinkers.   22

Thinkers can get trapped in their love of analysis, becoming over cautious and indecisive. They can be frustrating in a relationship by being too rigid, impersonal, and unemotional. Some of them walk around with monster superiority complexes, trying at every turn to prove they're smarter than others. Some don't care how they look, because they're trying to send a message: *I have too big a brain to concern myself with frivolities like appearance.* But they're not out to hurt anyone; they forget their own feelings as well as the feelings of others. Thinkers often forget to stop and smell the roses.   23

24   These cerebral types can sound like sticks-in-the-mud, but don't take them lightly. Some of the finest minds in the world fall into this category. Put this trait together with extroversion and you've got one remarkable leader.

25   **Feelers** operate from the heart and the gut. They're warm and always observing interactions among people and interpreting them: *Why didn't she invite me to that meeting? Was that look he gave me a sign of disapproval?* Feelers read between the lines. They are nurturing and empathetic. Their need for an emotional response can have an odd side effect: Whatever childhood behavior got attention from their parents is the one they'll pursue in a modified form as adults—so a feeler child who got strokes for bringing home straight A's will turn into a feeler adult who works overtime at the office.

26   Feelers are not trendsetters; they are more comfortable in the mainstream, following traditional values. They like colorful clothes that reflect their emotions. They are loyal, spontaneous, and persuasive. But all is not hearts and flowers. Feelers overreact and get defensive if things don't go their way. Their need to psychoanalyze everyone gets them into trouble as they over-personalize every interaction, stirring up conflict. Some are guilt-ridden, ruled by thoughts of what they've done wrong.

27   **Judges** aren't any more judgmental than the rest of us. Any personality type can be judgmental.

28   If you are a judge, you like to think you have some control over life. Judges are structured and organized; they want to finish things and move along. They set standards for themselves and for others and follow them. Judges are surprised every time someone fails to live up to his or her agreement, as if that were unusual. Judges set goals and meet them—thriving on the resulting sense of closure.

29   Dealing with a judge is simple: Make a commitment, and live up to it. Set goals, and use benchmarks to measure your performance by objective standards. Fail to meet a judge's expectations of you, and you'll travel a rocky road.

30   **Perceivers** are always receptive to more information or stimulation before acting. They take each day as it comes and don't kick themselves for letting chores slide into tomorrow. Perceivers generally grew up in either an unstructured environment or a very structured one against which they rebel as adults. These people can be very kind to others because they're kind to themselves. They don't become angry because you're late or take offense if you ask them a personal question. They see life as a process. A lot of artistic people fall into this category.

31   Pressure tactics just don't work with perceivers, but perceivers are so easy to be around that they are certainly worth rewarding with a little patience.

32   Once you've discovered what makes the other person tick—which traits are getting in the way of good communication between the two of you—then you have to decide what to do with that information.

Thinking Critically About Content

1. What are the eight different personality types Lavington outlines in her essay?

2. Are these personality traits evenly distributed in you, or is one dominant? Explain your answer.

3. Do you agree with Lavington when she says, "Don't be reticent about the talent you've been given. It's your obligation to share it with the world" (paragraph 2)?

Thinking Critically About Purpose and Audience

4. What do you think Lavington's purpose is in this essay?

5. Who do you think is her primary audience?

6. When did you last make an important judgment based on a first impression of someone? Was your impression fairly accurate?

Thinking Critically About Paragraphs

7. Explain how the topic sentence works in paragraph 7. Does it supply the controlling idea for the entire paragraph? Are the other sentences in this paragraph related to the topic sentence?

8. Why do you think Lavington discusses these personality types in this particular order? What is her rationale for moving from one type to the next?

9. How does Lavington start her essay? Is it effective?

10. Write an alternative conclusion to Lavington's essay.

To keep track of your critical thinking progress, go to Appendix 1.

THE WAYS WE LIE
by Stephanie Ericsson

Focusing Your Attention

1. Do you find that you don't tell the truth in every situation? When do you stretch the truth? Why do you stretch the truth?

2. In the essay you are about to read, the author categorizes the different types of lies we tell every day. These categories will help you realize how often we all lie. How often do you lie or stretch the truth in a typical day? What are the consequences of these lies? Explain your answer.

Expanding Your Vocabulary

The following words are important to your understanding of this essay. Organize this list into two columns—words you know and words you don't know. Write the definitions of the words you don't know above their words in the essay.

haggard: looking unwell or tired (paragraph 2)

merit: worth or value (paragraph 4)

penance: punishment for wrongdoing (paragraph 6)

façades: deceptive outer appearance (paragraph 10)

plethora: an excessive amount (paragraph 11)

recklessly: lacking concern for consequences (paragraph 12)

blatant: openly unashamed (paragraph 14)

deflectors: people who cause deviation (paragraph 16)

culprit: someone or something that is responsible for a negative outcome (paragraph 16)

rabbinical: relating to Rabbis or Jewish teachings (paragraph 18)

renegade: someone who defies set principles (paragraph 19)

obliterated: destroyed (paragraph 22)

invulnerability: incapable of being harmed (paragraph 25)

schizophrenics: people having a mental disorder involving hallucinations (paragraph 30)

catatonia: immobility (paragraph 30)

gamut: the complete range of something (paragraph 31)

READING CRITICALLY
Summarizing Your Reading

Once again, write a summary of the following essay, and exchange it with another person in your class. Then combine your two summaries into one summary that accurately represents the main ideas in this essay.

THE WAYS WE LIE
by Stephanie Ericsson

1   The bank called today and I told them my deposit was in the mail, even though I hadn't written a check yet. It'd been a rough day. The baby I'm pregnant with decided to do aerobics on my lungs for two hours, our three-year-old daughter painted the living-room couch with lipstick, the IRS put me on hold for an hour, and I was late to a business meeting because I was tired.

2   I told my client that traffic had been bad. When my partner came home, his haggard face told me his day hadn't gone any better than mine, so when he asked, "How was your

day?" I said, "Oh, fine," knowing that one more straw might break his back. A friend called and wanted to take me to lunch. I said I was busy. Four lies in the course of a day, none of which I felt the least bit guilty about.

We lie. We all do. We exaggerate, we minimize, we avoid confrontation, we spare people's feelings, we conveniently forget, we keep secrets, we justify lying to the big-guy institutions. Like most people, I indulge in small falsehoods and still think of myself as an honest person. Sure I lie, but it doesn't hurt anything. Or does it?   3

I once tried going a whole week without telling a lie, and it was paralyzing. I discovered that telling the truth all the time is nearly impossible. It means living with some serious consequences: The bank charges me $60 in overdraft fees, my partner keels over when I tell him about my travails, my client fires me for telling her I didn't feel like being on time, and my friend takes it personally when I say I'm not hungry. There must be some merit to lying.   4

But if I justify lying, what makes me any different from slick politicians or the corporate robbers who raided the S&L industry? Saying it's okay to lie one way and not another is hedging. I cannot seem to escape the voice deep inside me that tells me: When someone lies, someone loses.   5

What far-reaching consequences will I, or others, pay as a result of my lie? Will someone's trust be destroyed? Will someone else pay *my* penance because I ducked out? We must consider the *meaning of our actions*. Deception, lies, capital crimes, and misdemeanors all carry meanings. *Webster's* definition of *lie* is specific: 6

1. a false statement or action especially made with the intent to deceive;
2. anything that gives or is meant to give a false impression.

A definition like this implies that there are many, many ways to tell a lie. Here are just a few.   7

The White Lie

A man who won't lie to a woman has very little consideration for her feelings.

—Bergen Evens

The white lie assumes that the truth will cause more damage than a simple, harmless untruth. Telling a friend he looks great when he looks like hell can be based on a decision that the friend needs a compliment more than a frank opinion. But, in effect, it is the liar deciding what is best for the lied to. Ultimately, it is a vote of no confidence. It is an act of subtle arrogance for anyone to decide what is best for someone else.   8

Yet not all circumstances are quite so cut-and-dried. Take, for instance, the sergeant in Vietnam who knew one of his men was killed in action but listed him as missing so that the man's family would receive indefinite compensation instead of the lump-sum pittance the military gives widows and children. His intent was honorable. Yet for 20 years this family kept their hopes alive, unable to move on to a new life.   9

Façade

Et tu, Brute?

—Caesar

We all put up façades to one degree or another. When I put on a suit to go to see a client, I feel as though I am putting on another face, obeying the expectation that serious   10 businesspeople wear suits rather than sweatpants. But I'm a writer. Normally, I get up, get the kids off to school, and sit at my computer in my pajamas until four in the afternoon. When I answer the phone, the caller thinks I'm wearing a suit (though the UPS man knows better).

11   But façades can be destructive because they are used to seduce others into an illusion. For instance, I recently realized that a former friend was a liar. He presented himself with all the right looks and the right words and offered lots of new consciousness theories, fabulous books to read, and fascinating insights. Then I did some business with him, and the time came for him to pay me. He turned out to be all talk and no walk. I heard a plethora of reasonable excuses, including in-depth descriptions of the big break around the corner. In six months of work, I saw less than a hundred bucks. When I confronted him, he raised both eyebrows and tried to convince me that I'd heard him wrong, that he'd made no commitment to me. A simple investigation into his past revealed a crowded graveyard of disenchanted former friends.

Ignoring the Plain Facts

Well, you must understand that Father Porter is only human.

—A Massachusetts Priest

12   In the '60s, the Catholic Church in Massachusetts began hearing complaints that Father James Porter was sexually molesting children. Rather than relieving him of his duties, the ecclesiastical authorities simply moved him from one parish to another between 1960 and 1967, actually providing him with a fresh supply of unsuspecting families and innocent children to abuse. After treatment in 1967 for pedophilia, he went back to work, this time in Minnesota. The new diocese was aware of Father Porter's obsession with children, but they needed priests and recklessly believed treatment had cured him. More children were abused until he was relieved of his duties a year later: By his own admission, Porter may have abused as many as a hundred children.

13   Ignoring the facts may not in and of itself be a form of lying, but consider the context of this situation. If a lie is *a false action done with the intent to deceive,* then the Catholic Church's conscious covering for Porter created irreparable consequences. The church became a co-perpetrator with Porter.

Deflecting

When you have no basis for an argument, abuse the plaintiff.

—Cicero

14   I've discovered that I can keep anyone from seeing the true me by being selectively blatant. I set a precedent of being up-front about intimate issues, but I never bring up the things I truly want to hide; I just let people assume I'm revealing everything. It's an effective way of hiding.

15   Any good liar knows that the way to perpetuate an untruth is to deflect attention from it. When Clarence Thomas exploded with accusations that the Senate hearings were a "high-tech lynching," he simply switched the focus from a highly charged subject to a radioactive subject. Rather than defending himself, he took the offensive and accused the country of racism. It was a brilliant maneuver. Racism is now politically incorrect in official circles—unlike sexual harassment, which still rewards those who can get away with it.

Some of the most skilled deflectors are passive-aggressive people who, when accused of inappropriate behavior, refuse to respond to the accusations. This you-don't-exist stance infuriates the accuser, who, understandably, screams something obscene out of frustration. The trap is sprung and the act of deflection successful because now the passive-aggressive person can indignantly say, "Who can talk to someone as unreasonable as you?" The real issue is forgotten and the sins of the original victim become the focus. Feeling guilty of name-calling, the victim is fully tamed and crawls into a hole, ashamed. I have watched this fighting technique work thousands of times in disputes between men and women, and what I've learned is that the real culprit is not necessarily the one who swears the loudest.

Omission

The cruelest lies are often told in silence.
—R. L. Stevenson

Omission involves telling most of the truth minus one or two key facts whose absence changes the story completely. You break a pair of glasses that are guaranteed under normal use and get a new pair, without mentioning that the first pair broke during a rowdy game of basketball. Who hasn't tried something like that? But what about omission of information that could make a difference in how a person lives his or her life?

For instance, one day I found out that rabbinical legends tell of another woman in the Garden of Eden before Eve. I was stunned. The omission of the Sumerian goddess Lilith from Genesis—as well as her demonization by ancient misogynists as an embodiment of female evil—felt like spiritual robbery. I felt like I'd just found out my mother was really my stepmother. To take seriously the tradition that Adam was created out of the same mud as his equal counterpart, Lilith, redefines all of Judeo-Christian history.

Some renegade Catholic feminists introduced me to a view of Lilith that had been suppressed during the many centuries when this strong goddess was seen only as a spirit of evil. Lilith was a proud goddess who defied Adam's need to control her, attempted negotiations, and, when this failed, said adios and left the Garden of Eden.

This omission of Lilith from the Bible was a patriarchal strategy to keep women weak. Omitting the strong-woman archetype of Lilith from Western religions and starting the story with Eve the Rib has helped keep Christian and Jewish women believing they were the lesser sex for thousands of years.

Stereotypes and Cliches

Where opinion does not exist, the status quo becomes stereotyped, and all originality is discouraged.
—Bertrand Russell

Stereotype and cliché serve a purpose as a form of shorthand. Our need for vast amounts of information in nanoseconds has made the stereotype vital to modern communication. Unfortunately, it often shuts down original thinking, giving those hungry for the truth a candy bar of misinformation instead of a balanced meal. The stereotype explains a situation with just enough truth to seem unquestionable.

All the "isms"—racism, sexism, ageism, et al.—are founded on and fueled by the stereotype and the clichés, which are lies of exaggeration, omission, and ignorance. They are always dangerous. They take a single tree and make it a landscape. They destroy curiosity. They close minds and separate people. The single mother on welfare is assumed to be cheating. Any black male could tell you how much of his identity is obliterated daily by stereotypes. Fat people, ugly people, beautiful people, old people, large-breasted women, short men, the mentally ill, and the homeless all could tell you how much more they are like us than we want to think. I once admitted to a group of people that I had a mouth like a truck driver. Much to my surprise, a man stood up and said. "I'm a truck driver, and I never cuss." Needless to say, I was humbled.

Groupthink

Who is more foolish, the child afraid of the dark or the man afraid of the light?

—Maurice Freehill

23   Irving Janis, in *Victims of Group Think*, defines this sort of lie as a psychological phenomenon within decision-making groups in which loyalty to the group has become more important than any other value, with the result that dissent and the appraisal of alternatives are suppressed. If you've ever worked on a committee or in a corporation, you've encountered groupthink. It requires a combination of other forms of lying-ignoring facts, selective memory, omission, and denial, to name a few.

24   The textbook example of groupthink came on December 7, 1941. From as early as the fall of 1941, the warnings came in, one after another, that Japan was preparing for a massive military operation. The navy command in Hawaii assumed Pearl Harbor was invulnerable—the Japanese weren't stupid enough to attack the United States' most important base. On the other hand, racist stereotypes said the Japanese weren't smart enough to invent a torpedo effective in less than 60 feet of water (the fleet was docked in 30 feet); after all, US technology hadn't been able to do it.

25   On Friday, December 5, normal weekend leave was granted to all the commanders at Pearl Harbor, even though the Japanese consulate in Hawaii was busy burning papers. Within the tight, good-ole-boy cohesiveness of the US command in Hawaii, the myth of invulnerability stayed well entrenched. No one in the group considered the alternatives. The rest is history.

Out-And-Out Lies

The only form of lying that is beyond reproach is lying for its own sake.

—Oscar Wilde

26   Of all the ways to lie, I like this one the best, probably because I get tired of trying to figure out the real meanings behind things. At least I can trust the bald-faced lie. I once asked my five-year-old nephew, "Who broke the fence?" (I had seen him do it.) He answered, "The murderers." Who could argue?

27   At least when this sort of lie is told it can be easily confronted. As the person who is lied to, I know where I stand. The bald-faced lie doesn't toy with my perceptions—it argues with them. It doesn't try to refashion reality; it tries to refute it. *Read my lips.* . . . No sleight of hand. No guessing. If this were the only form of lying, there would be no such things as floating anxiety or the adult-children-of-alcoholics movement.

Dismissal

Pay no attention to that man behind the curtain!
I am the Great Oz!

—The Wizard Of Oz

Dismissal is perhaps the slipperiest of all lies. Dismissing feelings, perceptions, or even the raw facts of a situation ranks as a kind of lie that can do as much damage to a person as any other kind of lie.   28

The roots of many mental disorders can be traced back to the dismissal of reality. Imagine that a person is told from the time she is a tot that her perceptions are inaccurate. *"Mommy, I'm scared."* "No you're not, darling." *"I don't like that man next door. He makes me feel icky."* "Johnny, that's a terrible thing to say. Of course you like him. You go over there right now and be nice to him."   29

I've often mused over the idea that madness is actually a sane reaction to an insane world. Psychologist R. D. Laing supports this hypothesis in *Sanity, Madness and the Family*, an account of his investigation into the families of schizophrenics. The common thread that ran through all of the families he studied was a deliberate, staunch dismissal of the patient's perceptions from a very early age. Each of the patients started out with an accurate grasp of reality, which, through meticulous and methodical dismissal, was demolished until the only reality the patient could trust was catatonia.   30

Dismissal runs the gamut. Mild dismissal can be quite handy for forgiving the foibles of others in our day-to-day lives. Toddlers who have just learned to manipulate their parents' attention sometimes are dismissed out of necessity. Absolute attention from the parents would require so much energy that no one would get to eat dinner. But we must be careful and attentive about how far we take our "necessary" dismissals. Dismissal is a dangerous tool, because it's nothing less than a lie.   31

Delusion

We lie loudest when we lie to ourselves.
—Eric Hoffer

I could write the book on this one. Delusion, a cousin of dismissal, is the tendency to see excuses as facts. It's a powerful lying tool because it filters out information that contradicts what we want to believe. Alcoholics who believe that the problems in their lives are legitimate reasons for drinking rather than results of the drinking offer the classic example of deluded thinking. Delusion uses the mind's ability to see things in myriad ways to support what it wants to be the truth.   32

But delusion is also a survival mechanism we all use. If we were to fully contemplate the consequences of our stockpiles of nuclear weapons or global warming, we could hardly function on a day-to-day level. We don't want to incorporate that much reality into our lives because to do so would be paralyzing.   33

Delusion acts as an adhesive to keep the status quo intact. It shamelessly employs dismissal, omission, and amnesia, among other sorts of lies. Its most cunning defense is that it cannot see itself.   34

The liar's Punishment [. . .] is that he cannot believe anyone else.
—George Bernard Shaw

35   These are only a few of the ways we lie or are lied to. As I said earlier, it's not easy to entirely eliminate lies from our lives. No matter how pious we may try to be, we will still embellish, hedge, and omit to lubricate the daily machinery of living. But there is a world of difference between telling functional lies and living a lie. Martin Buber once said, "The lie is the spirit committing treason against itself." Our acceptance of lies becomes a cultural cancer that eventually shrouds and reorders reality until moral garbage becomes as invisible to us as water is to a fish.

36   How much do we tolerate before we become sick and tired of being sick and tired? When will we stand up and declare our *right* to trust? When do we stop accepting that the real truth is in the fine print? Whose lips do we read this year when we vote for president? When will we stop being so reticent about making judgments? When do we stop turning over our personal power and responsibility to liars?

37   Maybe if I don't tell the bank the check's in the mail I'll be less tolerant of the lies told me every day. A country song I once heard said it all for me: "You've got to stand for something, or you'll fall for anything."

Thinking Critically About Content

1. According to Ericsson, why do we all lie?

2. What are the 10 types of lies the author delineates?

3. Why does Ericsson claim that telling the truth all the time is "almost impossible" (paragraph 4)?

Thinking Critically About Purpose and Audience

4. Why do you think Ericsson wrote this essay?

5. Who would be most interested in this essay?

6. Which of these types of lies do you tell most often? Why do you resort to them?

Thinking Critically About Paragraphs

7. What examples does Ericsson use to explain the category of "Omission" (paragraphs 17–20)? Add one more example to this list.

8. Underline two transitions in paragraphs 8 and 9. Then explain how they make the discussion of white lies smooth and coherent.

9. Choose one paragraph, and decide whether or not it has enough details. Explain your answer.

10. Write an alternate introduction to Ericsson's essay.

To keep track of your critical thinking progress, go to Appendix 1.

BLACK MUSIC IN OUR HANDS
by Bernice Reagon

Focusing Your Attention

1. What are some of your main interests in life? Have any of these interests been part of your life for a long time? How have they changed over time?

2. In the essay you are about to read, the writer divides and classifies music from a number of different perspectives. What role does music play in your life? Has it always played this role? How has it changed in your life over the years?

Expanding Your Vocabulary

The following words are important to your understanding of this essay. Organize this list into two columns—words you know and words you don't know. Which of the words you don't know can you guess from their sentences?

Albany State: college in Albany, Georgia (paragraph 1)

contralto soloist: a woman singer with a very low voice (paragraph 1)

arias: songs in an opera (paragraph 1)

lieder: traditional German songs (paragraph 1)

Nathaniel Dett: 1882–1943, American composer and pianist (paragraph 1)

William Dawson: 1899–1990, African American composer (paragraph 1)

unaccompanied: without musical instruments (paragraph 2)

ornate: complex (paragraph 2)

congregational responses: singing by the people in the pews in reply to someone at the front of the church (paragraph 2)

Civil Rights Movement: push for equal rights for African Americans in the 1950s and 1960s (paragraph 5)

integrative: uniting (paragraph 5)

Albany Movement: a movement started in Albany, Georgia, and led by Reverend Martin Luther King Jr. that hoped to gain more freedom for African Americans but ended in racial violence (paragraph 8)

Freedom Singers: African Americans who sang about civic rights during the Civil Rights Movement (paragraph 12)

Georgia Sea Island Singers: international performing artists who sing about African American culture (paragraph 13)

Newport Festival: summer music festival held in Newport, Rhode Island (paragraph 13)

repertoire: collection of songs that an artist is able to perform (paragraph 13)

casings: coverings (paragraph 16)

sit-in: an act of protest in which demonstrators sit down and refuse to leave the premises (paragraph 17)

Wallace: George Wallace, 1919–1998, the segregationist governor of Alabama (paragraph 17)

Freedom Rides: rides taken by civil rights activists to ensure that public facilities had been desegregated (paragraph 17)

ensemble: a group of musicians who perform together (paragraph 17)

Thelonious Monk: 1917–1982, composer and pianist who created a new type of jazz known as bebop (paragraph 18)

Charlie Mingus: 1922–1979, jazz performer on bass and piano, hailed as a composer and a poet (paragraph 18)

SNCC: Student Nonviolent Coordinating Committee, a group of black and white students that promoted peace between races (paragraph 18)

Coltrane: John Coltrane, 1926–1967, jazz saxophonist who also played the flute (paragraph 18)

Charlie Parker: 1920–1955, a bebop jazz artist who played the alto saxophone (paragraph 18)

Coleman Hawkins: 1901–1969, known as the father of the jazz tenor saxophone (paragraph 18)

compost: mixture (paragraph 20)

READING CRITICALLY
Summarizing Your Reading

As before, practice your summary skills on the following essay. Then work with someone in the class, and write a single paragraph that represents both of your summaries.

BLACK MUSIC IN OUR HANDS
by Bernice Reagon

In the early 1960s, I was in college at Albany State. My major interests were music and biology. In music I was a contralto soloist with the choir, studying Italian arias and German lieder. The black music I sang was of three types: (1) Spirituals sung by the college choir. These were arranged by such people as Nathaniel Dett and William Dawson and had major injections of European musical harmony and composition. (2) Rhythm 'n' Blues, music done by and for Blacks in social settings. This included the music of bands at proms, juke boxes, and football game songs. (3) Church music; gospel was a major part of Black church music by the time I was in college. I was a soloist with the gospel choir.

Prior to the gospel choir, introduced in my church when I was twelve, was many years' experience with unaccompanied music—Black choral singing, hymns, lined out by strong song leaders with full, powerful, richly ornate congregational responses. These hymns were offset by upbeat, clapping call-and-response songs.

I saw people in church sing and pray until they shouted. I knew *that* music was part of a cultural expression that was powerful enough to take people from their conscious selves to a place where the physical and intellectual were being worked in harmony with the spirit. I enjoyed and needed that experience. The music of the church was an integral part of the cultural world into which I was born.

Outside of church, I saw music as good, powerful sounds you made or listened to. Rhythm and blues—you danced to; music of the college choir—you clapped after the number was finished.

The Civil Rights Movement changed my view of music. It was after my first march. I began to sing a song and in the course of singing changed the song so that it made sense for that particular moment. Although I was not consciously aware of it, this was one of my earliest experiences with how my music was supposed to *function*. This music was to be integrative of and consistent with everything I was doing at that time; it was to be tied to activities that went beyond artistic affairs such as concerts, dances, and church meetings.

The next level of awareness came while in jail. I had grown up in a rural area outside the city limits, riding a bus to public school or driving to college. My life had been a pretty consistent, balanced blend of church, school, and proper upbringing. I was aware of a Black educated class that taught me in high school and college of taxi cabs I never rode in and of people who used buses I never boarded. I went to school with their children.

In jail with me were all these people. All ages. In my section were women from about thirteen to eighty years old. Ministers' wives and teachers and teachers' wives who had only nodded at me or clapped at a concert or spoken to my mother. A few people from my classes. A large number of people who rode segregated city buses. One or two women who had been drinking along the two-block stretch of Little Harlem as the march went by. Very quickly, clashes arose: around age, who would have authority, what was proper behavior?

1

2

3

4

5

6

7

8   The Albany Movement was already a singing movement, and we took the songs to jail. There the songs I had sung because they made me feel good or because they said what I thought about a specific issue did something. I would start a song, and everybody would join in. After the song, the differences among us would not be as great. Somehow, making a song required an expression of that which was common to us all. The songs did not feel like the same songs I had sung in college. This music was like an instrument, like holding a tool in your hand.

9   I found that although I was younger than many of the women in my section of the jail, I was asked to take on leadership roles. First as a song leader and then in most other matters concerning the group, especially in discussions or when speaking with prison officials.

10   I fell in love with that kind of music. I saw that to define music as something you listen to, something that pleases you, is very different from defining it as an instrument with which you can drive a point. In both instances, you can have the same song. But using it as an instrument makes it a different kind of music.

11   The next level of awareness occurred during the first mass meeting after my release from jail. I was asked to lead the song that I had changed after the first march. When I opened my mouth and began to sing, there was a force and power within myself I had never heard before. Somehow this music—music I could use as an instrument to do things with, music that was mine to shape and change so that it made the statement I needed to make—released a kind of power and required a level of concentrated energy I did not know I had. I liked the feeling.

12   For several years, I worked with the Movement eventually doing Civil Rights songs with the Freedom Singers. The Freedom Singers used the songs, interspersed with narrative, to convey the story of the Civil Rights Movement's struggles. The songs were more powerful than spoken conversation. They became a major way of making people who were not on the scene feel the intensity of what was happening in the South. Hopefully, they would move the people to take a stand, to organize support groups or participate in various projects.

13   The Georgia Sea Island Singers, whom I first heard at the Newport Festival, were a major link. Bessie Jones, coming from within twenty miles of Albany, Georgia, had a repertoire and song-leading style I recognized from the churches I had grown up in. She, along with John Davis, would talk about songs that Black people had sung as slaves and what those songs meant in terms of their struggle to be free. The songs did not sound like the spirituals I had sung in college choirs; they sounded like the songs I had grown up with in church. There I had been told the songs had to do with worship of Jesus Christ.

14   The next few years I spent focusing on three components: (1) the music I had found in the Civil Rights Movement; (2) songs of the Georgia Sea Island Singers and other traditional groups and the ways in which those songs were linked to the struggles of Black peoples at earlier times; (3) songs of the church that now sounded like those traditional songs and came close to having, for many people, the same kind of freeing power.

15   There was another experience that helped to shape my present-day use of music. After getting out of jail, the mother of the church my father pastored was at the mass meeting. She prayed, a prayer I had heard hundreds of times. I had focused on its sound,

tune, rhythm, chant, whether the moans came at the proper pace and intensity. That morning I heard every word that she said. She did not have to change one word of the prayer she had been praying for much of her Christian life for me to know she was addressing the issues we were facing at that moment. More than her personal prayer, it felt like an analysis of the Albany, Georgia, Black community.

My collection, study, and creation of Black music has been, to a large extent, about freeing the sounds and the words and the messages from casings in which they have been put, about hearing clearly what the music has to say about Black people and their struggle.   16

When I first began to search, I looked for what was then being called folk music, rather than for other Black forms, such as jazz, rhythm and blues, or gospel. It slowly dawned on me that during the Movement we had used all those forms. When we were relaxing in the office, we made up songs using popular rhythm and blues tunes; songs based on rhythm and blues also came out of jails, especially from the sit-in movement and the march to Selma, Alabama. "Oh Wallace, You Never Can Jail Us All" is an example from Selma. "You Better Leave Segregation Alone" came out of the Nashville Freedom Rides and was based on a bit by Little Willie John, "You Better Leave My Kitten Alone." Gospel choirs became the major musical vehicle in the urban center of Birmingham, with the choir led by Carlton Reese. There was also a gospel choir in the Chicago work, as well as an instrumental ensemble led by Ben Branch.   17

Jazz had not been a strong part of my musical life. I began to hear it as I traveled north. Thelonious Monk and Charlie Mingus played on the first SNCC benefit at Carnegie Hall. I heard of and then heard Coltrane. Then I began to pick up the pieces that had been laid by Charlie Parker and Coleman Hawkins and whole lifetimes of music. This music had no words. But, it had power, intensity, and movement under various degrees of pressure; it had vocal texture and color. I could feel that the music knew how it felt to be Black and Angry, Black and Down, Black and Loved, Black and Fighting.   18

I now believe that Black music exists in every place where Black people run, every corner where they live, every level on which they struggle. We have been here a long while, in many situations. It takes all that we have created to sing our song. I believe that Black musicians/artists have a responsibility to be conscious of their world and to let their consciousness be heard in their songs.   19

And we need it all—blues, gospel, ballads, children's games, dance, rhythms, jazz, lovesongs, topical songs—doing what it has always done. We need Black music that functions in relation to the people and community who provide the nurturing compost that makes its creation and continuation possible.   20

Thinking Critically About Content

1. Reagon divides and classifies music into at least three different categories. What are these categories?

2. What are the main differences in these categories?

3. What does Reagon mean when she says, "It takes all that we have created to sing our song" (paragraph 19)?

Thinking Critically About Purpose and Audience

4. What do you think Reagon's purpose is in this essay?

5. What makes this purpose both personal and social?

6. Who do you think is Reagon's main audience?

Thinking Critically About Essays

7. Explain how the topic sentence works in paragraph 5. Does it supply the controlling idea for the entire paragraph?

8. Choose a paragraph from this essay, and explain whether or not it is unified. Be as specific as possible.

9. What do you think "in our hands" means in the title of this essay?

10. What role does music play in your life? Divide and classify its role in your life over the years.

To keep track of your critical thinking progress, go to Appendix 1.

WHAT ARE FRIENDS FOR?
by Marion Winik

Focusing Your Attention

1. Who do you rely on to talk out your problems? To confide in? To tell secrets to? How do these people fit into your life? How do you fit into theirs?

2. In the essay you are about to read, the author divides and classifies the types of friends people generally have. What do you think these types are?

Expanding Your Vocabulary

The following words are important to your understanding of this essay. Organize this list into two columns—words you know and words you don't know. Which of the words you don't know can you guess from their sentences?

half-slip: undergarment worn by women (paragraph 1)

innumerable: too many to count (paragraph 2)

Aquarena Springs: a theme park in San Marcos, Texas, that is now a preservation and education center (paragraph 2)

infallible: unfailing (paragraph 6)

indispensable: absolutely necessary (paragraph 8)

wistful: nostalgic (paragraph 10)

ill-conceived: poorly planned (paragraph 10)

inopportune: inconvenient (paragraph 11)

tonic: boost (paragraph 14)

READING CRITICALLY
Summarizing Your Reading

Once again, write a summary of the following essay, and exchange it with another person in your class. Then combine your two summaries into one summary that accurately represents the main ideas in this essay.

WHAT ARE FRIENDS FOR?
by Marion Winik

I was thinking about how everybody can't be everything to each other, but some people can be something to each other, thank God, from the ones whose shoulders you cry on to the ones whose half-slips you borrow to the nameless ones you chat with in the grocery line. 1

Buddies, for example, are the workhorses of the friendship world, the people out there on the front lines, defending you from loneliness and boredom. They call you up, they listen to your complaints, they celebrate your successes and curse your misfortunes, and you do the same for them in return. They hold out through innumerable crises before concluding that the person you're dating is no good, and even then understand if you ignore their good counsel. They accompany you to a movie with subtitles or to see the diving pig at Aquarena Springs. They feed your cat when you are out of town and pick you up from the airport when you get back. They come over to help you decide what to wear on a date. Even if it is with that creep. 2

What about family members? Most of them are people you just got stuck with, and though you love them, you may not have very much in common. But there is that rare exception, the Relative Friend. It is your cousin, your brother, maybe even your aunt. The two of you share the same views of the other family members. Meg never should have divorced Martin. He was the best thing that ever happened to her. You can confirm each other's memories of things that happened a long time ago. Don't you remember when Uncle Hank and Daddy had that awful fight in the middle of Thanksgiving dinner? Grandma always hated Grandpa's stamp collection; she probably left the windows open during the hurricane on purpose. 3

While so many family relationships are tinged with guilt and obligation, a relationship with a Relative Friend is relatively worry-free. You don't even have to hide your vices from this delightful person. When you slip out Aunt Joan's back door for a cigarette, she is already there. 4

Then there is that special guy at work. Like all the other people at the job site, at first he's just part of the scenery. But gradually he starts to stand out from the crowd. Your friendship is cemented by jokes about co-workers and thoughtful favors around the office. Did you see Ryan's hair? Want half my bagel? Soon you know the names of his turtles, what he did last Friday night, exactly which model CD player he wants for his birthday. His handwriting is as familiar to you as your own. 5

6   Though you invite each other to parties, you somehow don't quite fit into each other's outside lives. For this reason, the friendship may not survive a job change. Company gossip, once an infallible source of entertainment, soon awkwardly accentuates the distance between you. But wait. Like School Friends, Work Friends share certain memories which acquire a nostalgic glow after about a decade.

7   A Faraway Friend is someone you grew up with or went to school with or lived in the same town as until one of you moved away. Without a Faraway Friend, you would never get any mail addressed in handwriting. A Faraway Friend calls late at night, invites you to her wedding, always says she is coming to visit but rarely shows up. An actual visit from a Faraway Friend is a cause for celebration and binges of all kinds. Cigarettes, Chips Ahoy, bottles of tequila.

8   Faraway Friends go through phases of intense communication, then may be out of touch for many months. Either way, the connection is always there. A conversation with your Faraway Friend always helps to put your life in perspective: When you feel you've hit a dead end, come to a confusing fork in the road, or gotten lost in some crackerbox subdivision of your life, the advice of the Faraway Friend—who has the big picture, who is so well acquainted with the route that brought you to this place—is indispensable.

9   Another useful function of the Faraway Friend is to help you remember things from a long time ago, like the name of your seventh-grade history teacher, what was in that really good stir-fry, or exactly what happened that night on the boat with the guys from Florida.

10   Ah, the Former Friend. A sad thing. At best a wistful memory, at worst a dangerous enemy who is in possession of many of your deepest secrets. But what was it that drove you apart? A misunderstanding, a betrayed confidence, an unrepaid loan, an ill-conceived flirtation. A poor choice of spouse can do in a friendship just like that. Going into business together can be a serious mistake. Time, money, distance, cult religions: all noted friendship killers. You quit doing drugs, you're not such good friends with your dealer anymore.

11   And lest we forget, there are the Friends You Love to Hate. They call at inopportune times. They say stupid things. They butt in, they boss you around, they embarrass you in public. They invite themselves over. They take advantage. You've done the best you can, but they need professional help. On top of all this, they love you to death and are convinced they're your best friend on the planet.

12   So why do you continue to be involved with these people? Why do you tolerate them? On the contrary, the real question is, What would you do without them? Without Friends You Love to Hate, there would be nothing to talk about with your other friends. Their problems and their irritating stunts provide a reliable source of conversation for everyone they know. What's more, Friends You Love to Hate make you feel good about yourself, since you are obviously in so much better shape than they are. No matter what these people do, you will never get rid of them. As much as they need you, you need them too.

13   At the other end of the spectrum are Hero Friends. These people are better than the rest of us; that's all there is to it. Their career is something you wanted to be when you grew up—painter, forest ranger, tireless doer of good. They have beautiful homes filled with special handmade things presented to them by villagers in the remote areas they have visited in their extensive travels. Yet they are modest. They never gossip. They are always helping others, especially those who have suffered a death in the family or an illness. You would think people like this would just make you sick, but somehow they don't.

14   A New Friend is a tonic unlike any other. Say you meet her at a party. In your bowling league. At a Japanese conversation class, perhaps. Wherever, whenever, there's that

spark of recognition. The first time you talk, you can't believe how much you have in common. Suddenly, your life story is interesting again, your insights fresh, your opinion valued. Your various shortcomings are as yet completely invisible.

It's almost like falling in love.   15

Thinking Critically About Content

1. How many types of friends does Winik introduce? What are they?
2. On what basis does Winik create these categories?
3. In what ways is a new friend "a tonic" (paragraph 14)?

Thinking Critically About Purpose and Audience

4. Why do you think Winik wrote this essay?
5. Who would be most interested in this essay?
6. How does this essay make you feel about the role of friends in your life?

Thinking Critically About Essays

7. How does Winik organize her essay? Why do you think she puts her categories in this order?
8. How does the author develop each category? Use one paragraph to explain your answer.
9. Explain Winik's title.
10. Write a detailed description of one of your friends. Why is this person a friend of yours?

To keep track of your critical thinking progress, go to Appendix 1.

Writing Division/Classification

This section offers opportunities for you to apply what you have learned in this chapter to your own writing. Provided here are guidelines for writing a division/classification essay and for peer evaluation. Refer to the model division/classification essays in this chapter before you write your own essay. Then pause at the end of the chapter to reflect briefly on what you have learned.

Guidelines for Writing a Division/Classification Essay

1. Decide on your purpose for writing, and make it part of your thesis statement.
2. Divide your topic into categories that don't overlap.
3. Clearly explain each category.
4. Organize your categories logically.
5. Use transitions to move your readers through your essay.

Writing About Your Reading

1. In the first essay, Camille Lavington divides and classifies the personality types she sees in the human race. Using her essay as a reference, explain what category you fit into and why you fit there.

2. Using Stephanie Ericsson's categories, divide the lies you tell in a typical week of your life into categories. Then explain each category.

3. In the third essay, Reagon talks about the changing role of music in her life. Divide and classify one of your interests over the years.

4. Divide and classify your friends into meaningful categories, and write an essay explaining your classification system.

5. What process do you have to go through to come up with an interesting comparison or contrast? How is it different from the process you go through for other rhetorical modes?

Writing About Your World

1. Think of the many occasions in your life that require different types of clothes. For example, you would never wear to a funeral what you wear to the beach. Group the routine events in your life, and explain how various clothes in your wardrobe are appropriate for specific types of events.

2. What jobs will you be qualified for when you finish college? Classify these jobs into a few categories, and explain your interest in each category.

3. What are some rituals in your own life? Do these rituals serve a purpose in your life? Use division and classification to explain three rituals that you follow.

4. We all dream about trips we'd like to take. Sometimes we get to take one of these trips. Others have to remain dreams. What are your ideal trips? Discuss the types of trips you would like to take. What categories do they fall into? Why do you dream about these types of travel?

5. Create your own division/classification assignment (with the help of your instructor), and write a response to it.

Revising

Small Group Activity (5–10 minutes per writer) Working in groups of three or four, read your division/classification essays to each other. Those listening should record their reactions on a copy of the Peer Evaluation Form in Appendix 2A. After your group goes through this process, give your evaluation forms to the appropriate writers so that each writer has two or three peer comment sheets for revising.

Paired Activity (5 minutes per writer) Using the completed Peer Evaluation Forms, work in pairs to decide what you should revise in your essay. If time allows, rewrite some of your sentences, and have your partner look at them.

Individual Activity Rewrite your paper, using the revising feedback you received from other students.

Editing

Paired Activity (5–10 minutes per writer) Swap papers with a classmate, and use the editing portion of your Peer Evaluation Form to identify as many grammar, punctuation, mechanics, and spelling errors as you can. If time allows, correct some of your errors, and have your partner look at them. Record your grammar, punctuation, and mechanics errors in the Error Log (Appendix 3) and your spelling errors in the Spelling Log (Appendix 4).

Individual Activity Rewrite your paper again, using the editing feedback you received from other students.

Reflecting on Your Writing   When you have completed your own essay, answer these six questions.

1. What was most difficult about this assignment?

2. What was easiest?

3. What did you learn about division and classification by completing this assignment?

4. What do you think are the strengths of your division/classification essay? Place a wavy line by the parts of your essay that you feel are very good.

5. What are the weaknesses, if any, of your paper? Place an X by the parts of your essay you would like help with. Write any questions you have in the margins.

6. What did you learn from this assignment about your own writing process—about preparing to write, about writing the first draft, about revising, and about editing?

Definition: From Reading to Writing

This chapter includes four reading selections and several writing assignments. It then offers guidance in peer evaluation and reflection, ending with suggestions about how to lead your instructor through your writing in ways that will benefit both of you.

Reading Definition

The four essays here show how definition works in an essay. "The Fire Inside" by Gary Mack provides a clear definition of motivation as it works in human beings. The second essay, "What Is Poverty?" by Jo Goodwin Parker, defines poverty from the author's personal experience. "What Is Intelligence, Anyway?" by Isaac Asimov defines intelligence with a humorous touch, and "Spanglish Spoken Here" by Janice Castro explains how English and Spanish words and phrases are combined in many American communities on a daily basis. As you read, notice how the writers make their points through well-chosen examples and details.

THE FIRE INSIDE
by Gary Mack

Focusing Your Attention

1. Do you think there are different types of motivation? What are they?
2. The essay you are about to read defines *motivation*. What is the clearest goal in your life right now? What moves you toward that goal?

Expanding Your Vocabulary

The following word is important to your understanding of this essay. Highlight it in the essay before you begin to read. Then refer to this definition when you get to this word in the essay.

elite: a group of people considered by some to be superior (paragraph 11)

READING CRITICALLY
Reacting Critically to your Reading

For this reading, practice generating your reactions by recording the author's ideas on the left side of a piece of paper and your own reactions on the right. These notes will also help you understand the essay on an analytical level. Share your notes with someone in the class.

THE FIRE INSIDE
by Gary Mack

Each of us has a fire in our hearts for something. It's our goal in life to find it and keep it lit.

—Mary Lou Retton

All I want out of life is that when I walk down the street folks will say, "There goes the greatest hitter who ever lived."

—Ted Williams

1   He remembers gazing into the night sky as a boy, long, long ago. Each time he saw a falling star, he made a wish. "Please," he said, "let me be the hitter I want to be." As he grew older, his love for hitting a baseball didn't fade as many childhood infatuations do. The art form became his focus, his passion, his singular goal. "A man has to have goals, for a day, for a lifetime," he said upon reflection. "Mine was to have people say, 'There goes Ted Williams, the greatest hitter who ever lived.'"

2   On July 13, 1999, major league baseball staged its annual midsummer classic at Fenway Park in Boston. It was a glorious evening, perfect for stargazing. As part of the pregame festivities, the National and American League All-Star teams were introduced to the sellout crowd. So were the legends of the game. One by one, the announcer presented the members of baseball's All-Century team.

3   Near the end of the roll call, a golf cart appeared in the old ballpark. Along with millions of other TV viewers, I watched as it slowly paraded around the field, its heroic passenger smiling, waving, greeted with warm cheers.

4   Cameras flashed like winking stars, and when the announcer welcomed him and honored him, his voice was close to reverence. "That's Ted Williams! The greatest hitter who ever lived."

5   Motivation is a popular word, especially in sports. It comes from a Latin word meaning "to move." Athletes can move in one of two ways, either toward seeking pleasure (rewards) or toward avoiding pain (punishment). Motivation can be the desire to succeed or the fear of failure. I believe the best and healthiest motivation is the one that pushed Ted Williams, the last major leaguer to hit over .400 in one season, to reach his goal and live his dream.

6   An athlete's success is said to depend upon four factors—physical ability, physical training, mental training, and desire or drive. The desire to succeed needs to be stronger than the fear of failure.

7   "You hear a lot of athletes who say they are motivated by a fear of failure," pitcher David Cone said. "I couldn't disagree more. To me, it's an opportunity. This is what we live and play for. There's no place I'd rather be than right here, right now, pitching big games down the stretch for the Yankees."

8   Muhammad Ali illustrates one of my favorite stories about motivation. When he was growing up in Louisville, he got a job sacking groceries. He didn't make much money, but he saved enough to buy a secondhand bicycle. He loved that blue bicycle. He was proud of it. He had worked hard for it and earned it. One day someone stole his bike. He was heartbroken. "I walked all over Louisville that summer, looking for that bicycle," Ali said, picking up the narrative. "I walked and looked, looked and walked. Never found it to this day. But every time I got into the ring, I looked across at the other fighter, and I told myself, 'Hey, that's the guy who stole my bicycle!' "

9   Athletes find motivation in different ways. Roger Clemens said he thrived on the doubts that others had of him. The pitcher went into the 1997 season intent on proving the Red Sox had made a mistake by letting him go.

10   The most successful athletes are self-motivated. "The most important thing is to love your sport," said Peggy Fleming, the former Olympic figure-skating champion. "Never do it to please someone else; it has to be yours. That is all that will justify the hard work needed to achieve success."

11   At a workshop with elite teenage athletes, I asked one young man to relate his most enjoyable sports experience. He recalled being 10 or 11 years old. He talked about how much fun he had shooting hoops. As the teen relived the memory, his father's eyes welled with tears. The young man who wanted to quit his high school team was still playing basketball for his father's sake. It was his dad's dream, not his own.

12   What we associate with pleasure we pursue. What we associate with pain we avoid. Playing sports as a kid should be an enjoyable, positive, and rewarding experience. But too often, impressionable youngsters are embarrassed by a coach, or they worry about pleasing their parents. Participating in sports then becomes a painful, even punishing experience. As a coach, I would want my kids to have fun. I would want them to be eager and excited. I would want them to feel they are improving and focusing on the process rather than the outcome.

13   Motivation gets you moving in a direction. Being on a mission provides the emotion. Clemens was on a mission after he left the Red Sox. Arnold Schwarzenegger also had a mission. His vision created what he calls "want power." Schwarzenegger said, "My wanting to be Mr. Universe came about because I saw myself so clearly, being up there on the stage and winning."

14   Carl Lewis had an ambitious mission and a powerful vision, too. "I want to be remembered as a person who felt there was no limitation to what the human body and mind can do, and be the inspiration to lead people, and do things they never hoped to do."

15   At spring training, Alex Rodriguez designed T-shirts for himself and his Seattle Mariners teammates. The printed message read, "We're On A Mission, Sir."

16   How about you? Does a fire burn inside you? Do you have a mission? What is it? What motivates you? If it is fear of failure, let that emotion go. The best motivation is "want" power, that prideful desire to achieve.

Thinking Critically About Content

1. How does the author define motivation?

2. How are motivation and athletes related?

3. According to Mack, what four factors regulate an athlete's success?

Thinking Critically About Purpose and Audience

4. Why do you think Mack wrote this essay?

5. Who do you think is his primary audience?

6. How do you find motivation when you are in a competitive situation?

Thinking Critically About Paragraphs

7. The author repeats the phrase "want power" twice (paragraphs 12 and 15)? What is this type of power? Why does the author repeat these words in the essay?

8. How is paragraph 5 organized? Why do you think Mack puts these details in this particular order?

9. Choose one paragraph, and explain its tone or mood.

10. Write a summary of this essay for your English class.

To keep track of your critical thinking progress, go to Appendix 1.

WHAT IS POVERTY?
by Jo Goodwin Parker

Focusing Your Attention

1. How do you generally feel about people who are less fortunate than you? Why do you feel this way?

2. In the essay you are about to read, the author defines poverty from her own experience. How would you define poverty? On what do you base your definition?

Expanding Your Vocabulary

The following words are important to your understanding of this essay. Highlight them throughout the essay before you begin to read. Then refer to this list as you get to these words in the essay.

stench: stink, foul odor (paragraph 1)

privy: toilet (paragraph 2)

grits: cornmeal mush (paragraph 4)

oleo: margarine (paragraph 4)

devour: eat (paragraph 5)

antihistamines: medications for colds and allergies (paragraph 5)

repossessed: taken away for failing to make installment payments (paragraph 8)

READING CRITICALLY
Reacting Critically as you Read

Once again, practice generating your reactions to your reading by recording the author's ideas on the left side of a piece of paper and your own reactions on the right. This activity will help you understand this essay at a deeper level than reading without annotating it. Share your notes with someone in the class.

WHAT IS POVERTY?
by Jo Goodwin Parker

1   You ask me what is poverty? Listen to me. Here I am, dirty, smelly, and with no "proper" underwear on and with the stench of my rotting teeth near you. I will tell you. Listen to me. Listen without pity. I cannot use your pity. Listen with understanding. Put yourself in my dirty, worn out, ill-fitting shoes, and hear me.

2   Poverty is getting up every morning from a dirt-and-illness-stained mattress. The sheets have long since been used for diapers. Poverty is living in a smell that never leaves. This is a smell of urine, sour milk, and spoiling food sometimes joined with the strong smell of long-cooked onions. Onions are cheap. If you have smelled this smell, you did not know how it came. It is the smell of the outdoor privy. It is the smell of young children who cannot walk the long dark way in the night. It is the smell of the milk which has gone sour because the refrigerator long has not worked, and it costs money to get it fixed. It is the smell of rotting garbage. I could bury it, but where is the shovel? Shovels cost money.

3   Poverty is being tired. I have always been tired. They told me at the hospital when the last baby came that I had chronic anemia caused from poor diet, a bad case of worms, and that I needed a corrective operation. I listened politely—the poor are always polite. The poor always listen. They don't say that there is no money for iron pills or better food or worm medicine. The idea of an operation is frightening and costs so much that, if I had dared, I would have laughed. Who takes care of my children? Recovery from an operation takes a long time. I have three children. When I left them with "Granny" the last time I had a job, I came home to find the baby covered with fly specks and a diaper that had not been changed since I left. When the dried diaper came off, bits of my baby's flesh came

with it. My other child was playing with a sharp bit of broken glass, and my oldest was playing alone at the edge of a lake. I made twenty-two dollars a week, and a good nursery school costs twenty dollars a week for three children. I quit my job.

Poverty is dirt. You can say in your clean clothes coming from your clean house, "Anybody can be clean." Let me explain about housekeeping with no money. For breakfast I give my children grits with no oleo or cornbread without eggs and oleo. This does not use up many dishes. What dishes there are, I wash in cold water and with no soap. Even the cheapest soap has to be saved for the baby's diapers. Look at my hands, so cracked and red. Once I saved for months to buy a jar of Vaseline for my hands and the baby's diaper rash. When I had saved enough, I went to buy it and the price had gone up two cents. The baby and I suffered on. I have to decide every day if I can bear to put my cracked sore hands into the cold water and strong soap. But you ask, why not hot water? Fuel costs money. If you have a wood fire it costs money. If you burn electricity, it costs money. Hot water is a luxury. I do not have luxuries. I know you will be surprised when I tell you how young I am. I look so much older. My back has been bent over the wash tubs every day for so long I cannot remember when I ever did anything else. Every night I wash every stitch my school age child has on and just hope her clothes will be dry by morning.

Poverty is staying up all night on cold nights to watch the fire, knowing one spark on the newspaper covering the walls means your sleeping child dies in flames. In summer, poverty is watching gnats and flies devour your baby's tears when he cries. The screens are torn, and you pay so little rent you know they will never be fixed. Poverty means insects in your food, in your nose, in your eyes, and crawling over you when you sleep. Poverty is hoping it never rains because diapers won't dry when it rains and soon you are using newspapers. Poverty is seeing your children forever with runny noses. Paper handkerchiefs cost money, and all your rags you need for other things. Even more costly are antihistamines. Poverty is cooking without food and cleaning without soap.

Poverty is asking for help. Have you ever had to ask for help, knowing your children will suffer unless you get it? Think about asking for a loan from a relative, if this is the only way you can imagine asking for help. I will tell you how it feels. You find out where the office is that you are supposed to visit. You circle that block four or five times. Thinking of your children, you go in. Everyone is busy. Finally, someone comes out, and you tell her that you need help. That never is the person you need to see. You go see another person, and after spilling the whole shame of your poverty all over the desk between you, you find that this isn't the right office after all—you must repeat the whole process, and it never is any easier at the next place.

You have asked for help, and after all it has a cost. You are again told to wait. You are told why, but you don't really hear because of the red cloud of shame and the rising cloud of despair.

Poverty is remembering. It is remembering quitting school in junior high because "nice" children had been so cruel about my clothes and my smell. The attendance officer came. My mother told him I was pregnant. I wasn't, but she thought I could get a job and help out. I had jobs off and on, but never long enough to learn anything. Mostly, I remember being married. I was so young then. I am still young. For a time, we had all the things you have. There was a little house in another town, hot water and everything.

Then my husband lost his job. There was unemployment insurance for a while and what few jobs I could get. Soon, all our nice things were repossessed and we moved back here. I was pregnant then. This house didn't look so bad when we first moved in. Every week it gets worse. Nothing is ever fixed. We now had no money. There were a few odd jobs for my husband, but everything went for food then, as it does now. I don't know how we lived through three years and three babies, but we did. I'll tell you something: After the last baby died, I destroyed my marriage. It had been a good one, but could you keep on bringing children in this dirt? Did you ever think how much it costs for any kind of birth control? I knew my husband was leaving the day he left, but there were no goodbyes between us. I hope he has been able to climb out of this mess somewhere. He never could hope with us to drag him down.

9   That's when I asked for help. When I got it, you know how much it was? It was, and is, seventy-eight dollars a month for the four of us; that is all I ever can get. Now you know why there is no soap, no needles and thread, no hot water, no aspirin, no worm medicine, no hand cream, no shampoo. None of these things forever and ever and ever. So that you can see clearly, I pay twenty dollars a month rent, and most of the rest goes for food. For grits and cornmeal, and rice and milk and beans. I try my best to use only the minimum electricity. If I use more, there is that much less for food.

10   Poverty is looking into a black future. Your children won't play with my boys. They will turn to other boys who steal to get what they want. I can already see them behind the bars of their prison instead of behind the bars of my poverty. Or will they turn to the freedom of alcohol or drugs and find themselves enslaved. And my daughter? At best, there is for her a life like mine.

11   But you say to me, there are schools. Yes, there are schools. My children have no extra books, no magazines, no extra pencils, or crayons, or paper and most important of all, they do not have health. They have worms, they have infections, they have pink-eye all summer. They do not sleep well on the floor or with me in my one bed. They do not suffer from hunger, my seventy-eight dollars keeps us alive, but they do suffer from malnutrition. Oh yes, I do remember what I was taught about health in school. It doesn't do much good. In some places there is a surplus commodities program. Not here. The county said it cost too much. There is a school lunch program. But I have two children who will already be damaged by the time they get to school.

12   But, you say to me, there are health clinics. Yes, there are health clinics, and they are in the town. I live out here eight miles from town. I can walk that far (even if it is 16 miles both ways), but can my little children? My neighbor will take me when he goes; but he expects to get paid, one way or another. I bet you know my neighbor. He is that large man who spends his time at the gas station, the barbershop, and the corner store complaining about the government spending money on the immoral mothers of illegitimate children.

13   Poverty is an acid that drips on pride until all pride is worn away. Poverty is a chisel that chips on honor until honor is worn away. Some of you say that you would do something in my situation, and maybe you would, for the first week or the first month, but for year after year after year?

14   Even the poor can dream—a dream of a time when there is money. Money for the right kinds of foods, for worm medicine, for iron pills, for toothbrushes, for hand cream, for hammer and nails and a bit of screening, for a shovel, for a bit of paint, for some

sheeting, for needles and thread. Money to pay for a trip to town. And, oh, money for hot water and money for soap. A dream of when asking for help does not eat away the last bit of pride. When the office you visit is as nice as the offices of other governmental agencies, when there are enough workers to help you quickly, when workers do not quit in defeat and despair. When you have to tell your story to only one person and that person can send you for other help and you don't have to prove your poverty over and over again.

I have come out of my despair to tell you this. Remember I did not come from   15
another place or another time. Others like me are all around you. Look at us with an angry heart; anger will help you help me. Anger that will let you tell of me. The poor are always silent. Can you be silent too?

Thinking Critically About Content

1. Parker develops her definition of poverty with a series of examples from her own life. Which of these examples communicates most clearly to you what poverty is? Explain your answer.

2. Explain the meaning of Parker's final paragraph. What is the main message of this paragraph?

3. Do you think the level of poverty that Parker describes is still a major part of our society? Give evidence for your answer.

Thinking Critically About Purpose and Audience

4. Why do you think Parker wrote this essay?

5. Who do you think is Parker's audience in this essay? Explain your answer.

6. Does this essay make you feel more or less pity for those who live below the poverty line? Explain your answer.

Thinking Critically About Paragraphs

7. What do you think Parker is saying in her first paragraph? Why do you think she starts her essay this way?

8. Parker's style is very curt and to the point in this essay. Instead of transitions, she uses parallel lists and pronouns to give her paragraphs coherence. Look specifically at paragraph 11. Underline the words and phrases that are in list form. Then explain the feeling these lists create in the paragraph.

9. Many of Parker's paragraphs start with a definition of poverty, "Poverty is. . . ." What effect does this repetition have on the essay as a whole?

10. Paragraph 13 is a collection of metaphors that explain poverty. Metaphors are comparisons expressed without using *like* or *as* with words that cannot be taken literally. Make sure you understand the two metaphors Parker uses in the first two sentences. Then rewrite this paragraph in your own words.

To keep track of your critical thinking progress, go to Appendix 1.

WHAT IS INTELLIGENCE, ANYWAY?
by Isaac Asimov

Focusing Your Attention

1. Do you ever feel smart in some subjects and not so smart in others? What do you think is the reason for these differences?

2. The essay you are about to read uses examples to explain different types of intelligence we all have. Do you think people can be intelligent in one area and not in another? How could this happen? Do you think these "intelligences" could be altered?

Expanding Your Vocabulary

The following words are important to your understanding of this essay. Highlight them throughout the essay before you begin to read. Then refer to this list as you come across these words in the essay.

aptitude: natural ability (paragraph 1)

KP: kitchen police or workers in the military (paragraph 1)

complacent: smug and satisfied (paragraph 2)

bents: angles (paragraph 2)

oracles: people with great wisdom (paragraph 3)

academician: someone connected to education (paragraph 4)

intricate: complicated or detailed (paragraph 4)

foist: impose something unnecessary (paragraph 4)

arbiter: person who settles a dispute (paragraph 4)

raucously: harshly or loudly (paragraph 6)

READING CRITICALLY
Reacting Critically to Your Reading

As you have throughout this chapter, practice generating your reactions to your reading by recording the author's ideas on the left side of a piece of paper and your own reactions on the right. These notes will also help you understand the essay on an analytical level. Share your notes with someone in the class.

WHAT IS INTELLIGENCE, ANYWAY?
by Isaac Asimov

What is intelligence, anyway? When I was in the Army, I received a kind of apti-   1
tude test that all soldiers took and, against a normal of 100, scored 160. No one at
the base had ever seen a figure like that, and for two hours they made a big fuss over
me. (It didn't mean anything. The next day I was still a buck private with KP as my
highest duty.)

All of my life I've been registering scores like that, so that I have the complacent   2
feeling that I'm highly intelligent, and I expect other people think so too. Actually,
though, don't such scores simply mean that I am very good at answering the type of academic questions that are considered worthy of answers by the people who make up the
intelligence tests, people with intellectual bents similar to mine?

For instance, I had an auto repairman once, who, on these intelligence tests,   3
could not possibly have scored more than 80, by my estimate. I always took it for
granted that I was far more intelligent than he was. Yet, when anything went wrong
with my car, I hastened to him with it, watched him anxiously as he explored its vitals,
and listened to his pronouncements as though they were divine oracles—and he
always fixed my car.

Well, then, suppose my auto repairman devised questions for an intelligence test.   4
Or suppose a carpenter did, or a farmer, or, indeed, almost anyone but an academician.
By every one of those tests, I'd prove myself a moron. And I'd be a moron too. In a
world where I could not use my academic training and my verbal talents but had to do
something intricate or hard, working with my hands, I would do poorly. My intelligence, then, is not absolute but is a function of the society I live in and of the fact that
a small subsection of that society has managed to foist itself on the rest as an arbiter of
such matters.

Consider my auto repairman, again. He had a habit of telling me jokes whenever he   5
saw me. One time he raised his head from under the automobile hood to say, "Doc, a deaf-
and-dumb guy went into a hardware store to ask for some nails. He put two fingers together on the counter and made hammering motions with the other hand. The clerk
brought him a hammer. He shook his head and pointed to the two fingers he was hammering. The clerk brought him nails. He picked out the sizes he wanted and left. Well,
doc, the next guy who came in was a blind man. He wanted scissors. How do you suppose
he asked for them?"

Indulgently, I lifted my right hand and made scissoring motions with my first two   6
fingers. Whereupon my auto repairman laughed raucously and said, "Why, you dumb
jerk, he used his *voice* and asked for them." Then he said, smugly, "I've been trying that on
all my customers today." "Did you catch many?" I asked. "Quite a few," he said, "but
I knew for sure I'd catch you." "Why is that?" I asked. "Because you're so goddamned
educated, doc, I knew you couldn't be very smart."

And I have an uneasy feeling he had something there.   7

Thinking Critically About Content

1. What is the main idea of this essay?

2. What does Asimov mean when he says his intelligence "is not absolute but is a function of the society I live in" (paragraph 4)?

3. Think of a synonym for "smart" in paragraph 6. What is Asimov implying about intelligence in this paragraph.

Thinking Critically About Purpose and Audience

4. What do you think Asimov's purpose is in this essay?

5. Who do you think is his primary audience?

6. What would Asimov's audience say education and intelligence have in common?

Thinking Critically About Essays

7. How does Asimov use examples in this definition essay?

8. What would Asimov say is his actual definition of *intelligence?*

9. Does this essay imply there are different types of intelligence? Explain your answer with details from the essay.

10. Write a paragraph defining *intelligence* from the auto repairman's point of view.

To keep track of your critical thinking progress, go to Appendix 1.

SPANGLISH SPOKEN HERE
by Janice Castro

Focusing Your Attention

1. Have you ever made up words? What were the sources of these creations?

2. The essay you are about to read discusses the various ways we have combined English and Spanish in the United States over the years. Do you live in an area that draws from more than one language? What signs of multiple languages do you see in your immediate environment?

Expanding Your Vocabulary

The following words are important to your understanding of this essay. Highlight them throughout the essay before you begin to read. Then refer to this list as you get to these words in the essay.

bemused: confused or bewildered (paragraph 1)

linguistic currency: valued language (paragraph 2)

syntax: the arrangement of words into sentences (paragraph 3)

languorous: enjoyable inactivity (paragraph 5)

hybrids: things made from a combination of two other things (paragraph 6)

gaffes: embarrassing blunders (paragraph 10)

luxuriant: rich or thick (paragraph 10)

READING CRITICALLY
Reacting Critically to Your Reading

Once again, practice generating your reactions to your reading by recording the author's ideas on the left side of a piece of paper and your own reactions on the right. This activity will help you understand this essay at a deeper level than reading without annotating it. Share your notes with someone in the class.

SPANGLISH SPOKEN HERE
by Janice Castro

In Manhattan a first-grader greets her visiting grandparents, happily exclaiming, "Come here, sientate!" Her bemused grandfather, who does not speak Spanish, nevertheless knows she is asking him to sit down. A Miami personnel officer understands what a job applicant means when he says, "Quiero un part time." Nor do drivers miss a beat reading a billboard alongside a Los Angeles street advertising CERVEZA-SIX-PACK! 1

This free-form blend of Spanish and English, known as Spanglish, is common linguistic currency wherever concentrations of Hispanic Americans are found in the U.S. In Los Angeles, where 55 percent of the city's three million inhabitants speak Spanish, Spanglish is as much a part of daily life as sunglasses. Unlike the broken-English efforts of earlier immigrants from Europe, Asia, and other regions, Spanglish has become a widely accepted conversational mode used casually—even playfully—by Spanish-speaking immigrants and native-born Americans alike. 2

Consisting of one part Hispanicized English, one part Americanized Spanish, and more than a little fractured syntax, Spanglish is a bit like a Robin Williams comedy routine: a crackling line of cross-cultural patter straight from the melting pot. Often it enters Anglo homes and families through the children, who pick it up at school or at play with their young Hispanic contemporaries. In other cases, it comes from watching TV; many an Anglo child watching *Sesame Street* has learned *uno dos tres* almost as quickly as *one two three*. 3

Spanglish takes a variety of forms, from the Southern California Anglos who bid farewell with the utterly silly "*hasta la* bye-bye" to the Cuban American drivers in Miami who *parquean their carros*. Some Spanglish sentences are mostly Spanish, with a quick detour for an English word or two. A Latino friend may cut short a conversation by glancing at his watch and excusing himself with the explanation that he must "*ir al supermarket*." 4

5   Many of the English words transplanted in this way are simply handier than their Spanish counterparts. No matter how distasteful the subject, for example, it is still easier to say "income tax" than *impuesto sobre la renta*. At the same time, many Spanish-speaking immigrants have adopted such terms as VCR, microwave, and dishwasher for what they view as largely American phenomena. Still other English words convey a cultural context that is not implicit in the Spanish. A friend who invites you to *lonche* most likely has in mind the brisk American custom of "doing lunch" rather than the languorous afternoon break traditionally implied by *almuerzo*.

6   Mainstream Americans exposed to similar hybrids of German, Chinese, or Hindi might be mystified. But even Anglos who speak little or no Spanish are somewhat familiar with Spanglish. Living among them, for one thing, are 19 million Hispanics. In addition, more American high school and university students sign up for Spanish than for any other foreign language.

7   Only in the past ten years, though, has Spanglish begun to turn into a national slang. Its popularity has grown with the explosive increases in U.S. immigration from Latin American countries. English has increasingly collided with Spanish in retail stores, offices and classrooms, in pop music and on street corners. Anglos whose ancestors picked up such Spanish words as *rancho, bronco, tornado,* and *incommunicado,* for instance, now freely use such Spanish words as *gracias, bueno, amigo,* and *por favor.*

8   Among Latinos, Spanglish conversations often flow easily from Spanish into several sentences of English and back.

9   Spanglish is a sort of code for Latinos: the speakers know Spanish, but their hybrid language reflects the American culture in which they live. Many lean to shorter, clipped phrases in place of the longer, more graceful expressions their parents used. Says Leonel de la Cuesta, an assistant professor of modern languages at Florida International University in Miami:" In the U.S., time is money, and that is showing up in Spanglish as an economy of language." Conversational examples: *taipiar* (type) and *winshi-wiper* (windshield wiper) replace *escribir a maquina* and *limpiaparabrisas.*

10   Major advertisers, eager to tap the estimated $134 billion in spending power wielded by Spanish-speaking Americans, have ventured into Spanglish to promote their products. In some cases, attempts to sprinkle Spanish through commercials have produced embarrassing gaffes. A Braniff airlines ad that sought to tell Spanish-speaking audiences they could settle back *en* (in) luxuriant *cuero* (leather) seats, for example, inadvertently said they could fly without clothes (*encuero*). A fractured translation of the Miller Lite slogan told readers the beer was "Filling, and less delicious." Similar blunders are often made by Anglos trying to impress Spanish-speaking pals. But if Latinos are amused by mangled Spanglish, they also recognize these goofs as a sort of friendly acceptance. As they might put it, *no problema.*

Thinking Critically About Content

1. Write a definition of *Spanglish* in your own words.

2. How does Spanglish usually enter Anglo homes?

3. What does Castro think is the main reason this hybrid language started to catch on in American society?

Thinking Critically About Purpose and Audience

4. Why do you think Castro wrote this essay?
5. Who do you think is her primary audience?
6. What do you suspect the primary audience for this essay thinks of Spanglish and its use in society today?

Thinking Critically About Essays

7. Castro uses a few comparisons to make her point about language. One is "linguistic currency," an implied comparison equating language use with money. Find one other comparison in this essay.
8. Give some examples from your own experience of words and/or phrases from different languages. Are these examples common where you live?
9. In your opinion, is the last sentence of the essay effective: "As they might put it, *no problema*"?
10. Choose one paragraph, and write a paragraph analyzing its mood and tone.

To keep track of your critical thinking progress, go to Appendix 1.

Writing Definition

This section offers opportunities for you to apply what you have learned in this chapter to your own writing. It provides guidelines for writing a definition essay and for peer evaluation. Loop back into the chapter as necessary when you need to consult a good example of definition. Then pause at the end of the chapter to reflect briefly on what you have learned.

Writing About Your Reading

1. In the first essay, Gary Mack defines *motivation*. Write your own definition of *motivation* or of another aspect of life, such as *pleasure*, *recreation*, or *athletics*.
2. Using Jo Goodwin Parker's method of development through examples, define *wealth*.
3. In the third essay, Isaac Asimov defines *intelligence*. Write your own definition of another state of mind, such as *joy*, *fear*, *loneliness*, or *stress*.
4. Using Castro's method of development through example, define for your class a made-up word of your own.
5. Now that you have studied different approaches to the process of definition, what makes a definition effective or useful for you? Apply what you have studied about definition to your answer.

Writing About Your World

1. What does education mean to you? Define *education* in a detailed essay.
2. The concept of "family" has undergone a number of changes over the past few years. How would you define this term in our current society?

3. Define *relaxation* or *stress*, depending on your mood today.

4. Define one of the following abstract terms: *fear, love, inferiority, wonder, pride, self-control, discipline, anger, freedom, violence, assertiveness, courtesy, kindness.*

5. Create your own definition assignment (with the help of your instructor), and write a response to it.

Revising

Small Group Activity (5–10 minutes per writer) Working in groups of three or four, read your definition essays to each other. The listeners should record their reactions on a copy of the Peer Evaluation Form in Appendix 2A. After your group goes through this process, give your evaluation forms to the appropriate writers so that each writer has two or three peer comment sheets for revising.

Paired Activity (5 minutes per writer) Using the completed Peer Evaluation Forms, work in pairs to decide what you should revise in your essay. If time allows, rewrite some of your sentences, and have your partner look at them.

Individual Activity Rewrite your paper, using the revising feedback you received from other students.

Editing

Paired Activity (5–10 minutes per writer) Swap papers with a classmate, and use the editing portion of your Peer Evaluation Form to identify as many grammar, punctuation, mechanics, and spelling errors as you can. If time allows, correct some of your errors, and have your partner look at them. Record your grammar, punctuation, and mechanics errors in the Error Log (Appendix 3) and your spelling errors in the Spelling Log (Appendix 4).

Individual Activity Rewrite your paper again, using the editing feedback you received from other students.

Reflecting on Your Writing

When you have completed your own essay, answer these six questions.

1. What was most difficult about this assignment?

2. What was easiest?

3. What did you learn about definition by completing this assignment?

4. What do you think are the strengths of your definition essay? Place a wavy line by the parts of your essay that you feel are very good.

5. What are the weaknesses, if any, of your paper? Place an X by the parts of your essay you would like help with. Write any questions you have in the margins.

6. What did you learn from this assignment about your own writing process—about preparing to write, about writing the first draft, about revising, and about editing?

Cause and Effect: From Reading to Writing

This chapter includes four reading selections and several writing assignments. It offers guidance in peer evaluation and reflection, ending with suggestions about how to lead your instructor through your writing in ways that will benefit both of you.

Reading Cause/Effect

Here are four essays that follow the guidelines for writing a good cause/effect essay. In "Does Game Violence Make Teens Aggressive?," Kristin Kalning discusses the connection between violent video games and real violence, and in "Life Sentences," Corky Clifton analyzes the role of writing in his life as a prisoner. Then "Shedding the Weight of My Dad's Obsession" by Linda Lee Andujar deals with the lifelong burden of an insensitive father, and "Happiness Is Catching: Why Emotions Are Contagious" by Stacey Colino analyzes the role of moods in our daily lives. As you read, notice how the writers make their points through thoughtful, detailed reasoning.

DOES GAME VIOLENCE MAKE TEENS AGGRESSIVE?
by Kristin Kalning

Focusing Your Attention

1. Do you play violent video games and/or watch violent movies? If so, how do you feel after observing this type of violence?

2. The essay you are about to read openly discusses the relationship between game violence and real violence. What do you think this relationship is? How do you think we might control this relationship?

137

Expanding Your Vocabulary

The following words are important to your understanding of this essay. As you read, circle any words you don't know beyond this list. Then break into groups, and help each other figure out the meanings of these unknown words.

inhibition: self-consciousness (paragraph 1)

MRIs: Magnetic resonance imaging, a medical imaging technique used in radiology to visualize the functions of specific body parts (paragraph 4)

gravitate: move (paragraph 13)

epidemic: major outbreak (paragraph 14)

READING CRITICALLY
Making Connections in Your Reading

As you learned in the Introduction, practice recognizing causes and effects by listing those that appear in the following essay. Put them in two columns on a separate sheet of paper. These lists will help you understand the essay on an analytical level. Compare your notes with those of a classmate.

DOES GAME VIOLENCE MAKE TEENS AGGRESSIVE?
by Kristin Kalning

1   Can video games make kids more violent? A new study employing state-of-the-art brain-scanning technology says that the answer may be yes. Researchers at the Indiana University School of Medicine say that brain scans of kids who played a violent video game showed an increase in emotional arousal—and a corresponding decrease of activity in brain areas involved in self-control, inhibition and attention. Does this mean that your teenager will feel an uncontrollable urge to go on a shooting rampage after playing "Call of Duty?"

2   Vince Mathews, the principal investigator on the study, hesitates to make that leap. But he says he does think that the study should encourage parents to look more closely at the types of games their kids are playing. "Based on our results, I think parents should be aware of the relationship between violent video-game playing and brain function."

3   Mathews and his colleagues chose two action games to include in their research—one violent the other not. The first game was the high-octane but non-violent racing

game "Need for Speed: Underground." The other was the ultra-violent first-person shooter "Medal of Honor: Frontline."

The team divided a group of 44 adolescents into two groups, and randomly assigned the kids to play one of the two games. Immediately after the play sessions, the children were given MRIs of their brains. The scans showed a negative effect on the brains of the teens who played "Medal of Honor" for 30 minutes. That same effect was not present in the kids who played "Need for Speed." The only difference? Violent content.   4

What's not clear is whether the activity picked up by the MRIs indicates a lingering—or worse, permanent—effect on the kids' brains. And it's also not known what effect longer play times might have. The scope of this study was 30 minutes of play, and one brain scan per kid, although further research is in the works.   5

OK. But what about violent TV shows? Or violent films? Has anyone ever done a brain scan of kids that have just watched a violent movie? Someone has. John P. Murray, a psychology professor at Kansas State University, conducted a very similar experiment, employing the same technology used in Mathews' study. His findings are similar. Kids in his study experienced increased emotional arousal when watching short clips from the boxing movie "Rocky IV."   6

So, why is everyone picking on video games? Probably because there's a much smaller body of research on video games. They just haven't been around as long as TV and movies, so the potential effects on children are a bigger unknown. That's a scary thing for a parent.   7

Larry Ley, the director and coordinator of research for the Center for Successful Parenting, which funded Mathews' study, says the purpose of the research was to help parents make informed decisions. "There's enough data that clearly indicates that [game violence] is a problem," he says. "And it's not just a problem for kids with behavior disorders."   8

But not everyone is convinced that this latest research adds much to the debate—particularly the game development community. One such naysayer is Doug Lowenstein, president of the Entertainment Software Association. "We've seen other studies in this field that have made dramatic claims but turn out to be less persuasive when objectively analyzed."   9

The ESA has a whole section of its Web site dedicated to the topic of video game violence, which would suggest that they get asked about it—a lot. And they've got plenty of answers at the ready for the critics who want to lay school shootings or teen aggression at the feet of the game industry. Several studies cited by the ESA point to games' potential benefits for developing decision-making skills or bettering reaction times.   10

Ley, however, argues such studies aren't credible because they were produced by "hired guns" funded by the multi-billion-dollar game industry. "We're not trying to sell [parents] anything," he says. "We don't have a product. The video game industry does."   11

Increasingly parents are more accepting of video game violence, chalking it up to being a part of growing up. "I was dead-set against violent video games," says Kelley Windfield, a Sammamish, Wa.-based mother of two. "But my husband told me I had to start loosening up."   12

Laura Best, a mother of three from Clovis, Calif., says she looks for age-appropriate games for her 14 year-old son, Kyle. And although he doesn't play a lot of games,   13

14   he does tend to gravitate towards shooters like "Medal of Honor." But she isn't concerned that Kyle will become aggressive as a result. "That's like saying a soccer game or a football game will make a kid more aggressive," she says. "It's about self-control, and you've got to learn it."

Ley says he believes further research, for which the Center for Successful Parenting is trying to arrange, will prove a cause-and-effect relationship between game violence and off-screen aggression. But for now, he says, the study released last week gives his organization the ammunition it needs to prove that parents need to be more aware of how kids are using their free time. "Let's quit using various Xboxes as babysitters instead of doing healthful activities," says Ley, citing the growing epidemic of childhood obesity in the United States. And who, really, can argue with that?

© 2010 msnbc.com Reprints
http://www.msnbc.msn.com/id/16099971/

Thinking Critically About Content

1. According to the study conducted by Vince Mathews and his colleagues, what is the relationship between violence and video games?

2. According to this essay, what do similar studies show about the effects of violent movies on viewers?

3. According to the Entertainment Software Association, what are two benefits of playing video games?

Thinking Critically About Purpose and Audience

4. What do you think is Kaining's purpose in this essay?

5. Who is her primary audience?

6. Why do you think parents are becoming more accepting of video games?

Thinking Critically About Paragraphs

7. What questions about the relationship between violence and video games remain unanswered? Why do you think the author brings up these issues? Explain your answer.

8. What games did the researchers use in their study? How many participants did they study? How long did they study these games? What is the value of furnishing these details in this essay?

9. What other consequences, besides violence, does Larry Ley attribute to the video game industry? Is this an effective ending to this essay?

10. Write a paragraph about the role of video games or violent movies in your life. Do you want to change the part they play in your life?.

To keep track of your critical thinking progress, go to Appendix 1.

LIFE SENTENCES
by Corky Clifton

Focusing Your Attention

1. Think of a time when you acted without carefully analyzing the situation. What were the results?

2. In the essay you are about to read, the writer analyzes his reasons for risking his life to escape from prison. Think of the most difficult decision you have ever had to make. In what way did you analyze the situation and circumstances before you made the decision? Did you think about it for a long time? Discuss it with others? Write about it?

Expanding Your Vocabulary

The following words are important to your understanding of this essay. As you read, circle any words you don't know beyond this list. Then break into groups, and help each other figure out the meanings of these unknown words.

disciplinary reports: reports of misconduct (paragraph 4)

D.A.: district attorney, prosecutor for the government (paragraph 4)

inflict: commit (paragraph 5)

READING CRITICALLY
Making Connections to Your Reading

As you did with the previous essay, list the causes and effects in the following essay on a separate sheet of paper. Then draw lines from specific causes to the related effects. This process will give you some good insights into the author's approach to his topic and his methods of developing his ideas. Compare your notes with those of one of your classmates.

LIFE SENTENCES
by Corky Clifton

Why did I escape? I suppose it was for the same reason that men have fought wars and died for throughout history. I wanted to be free.   1

For 27 years, I have submitted to discipline, the rules, the harsh conditions, the torment of my children growing from babies into men—without ever seeing them. I've   2

Corky Clifton, in an article by Wilbert Rideau and Ron Wikberg from *The Angolite: The Prison News Magazine*, June 1989. Reprinted by permission of Louisiana State Penitentiary, Angola, Louisiana.

never had a visit from any of my family during these 27 years because, being from Ohio, no one could afford the trip here to Louisiana.

3   I once thought, as most people do, that all you had to do in order to get out of prison was just be good and they'll let you out someday. One does not have to be in the prison system very long to learn what a joke that is.

4   If Jesus Christ himself was in here with a life sentence, he couldn't get out unless he had money to put in the right places. I've always been a pretty stubborn person, so even though I was told how the political and Pardon Board system works, I freely submitted to all the prison rules and discipline. After 12 years with a perfect record—no disciplinary reports— I applied to the Pardon Board and was denied any consideration for relief. So I waited 10 more years and applied again, still with an excellent prison record. This time they wouldn't even hear my case. In 1983, I applied to the board for the third time and the Pardon Board cut my time to 50 years. However, the judge and D.A., retired, simply called the governor's legal staff and told them they don't want me to be free—so, end of case. When I applied for my pardon in 1983, the D.A. published an article in the newspaper saying I was a very dangerous man that would kill anyone who got into my way. He said a lot of things which were all designed to turn public opinion against me and justify his reason for protesting my release.

5   In spite of having to endure the torment of prison life all these years without hope, I was still determined to better myself, no longer with any hope that a nice record would get me my freedom but because the years of discipline and hardships had molded my personality to the extent that I no longer desired to do anything criminal. I could not even inflict revenge on my enemies within prison.

6   I taught myself how to repair watches, and for more than 20 years I repaired watches for other prisoners as well as guards. I also taught myself how to paint pictures. At the 1988 Angola Arts & Crafts Festival, I won a second place for one of my watercolors. Aside from all my other accomplishments within prison, I have only two disciplinary reports in 27 years. I proved my honesty and sincerity many times over. Every time I made a friend through correspondence, one of the first things they wanted to know is how come I'm still in prison. I'm always tempted to use up several legal pads trying to explain about the corrupt legal and political system here in Louisiana. But who's gonna believe a man can be kept in here all his life just because some big shot out there doesn't want him out? Well, I am one example of it, and there are hundreds more lifers in here, many of them I know personally, who are in here for no other reason than because some big shot out there doesn't want them to go free. The only way you can get around that is *money*—in the right places.

7   Since the sheriff, the D.A., and/or the judge can dictate who can get out and who can't, then what's the purpose of a pardon board? Why the waste of taxpayers' money? I spent many years in here struggling for freedom. There are many people here in prison, as well as outside, who believe I should be free, but the judge and D.A. say they intend to see that I never go free, as long as I live. How am I supposed to handle that?

8   I'm not Charles Manson or some other mass murderer. I didn't torture or mutilate some child. When I was 23 years old, I killed a man in a robbery. That's bad enough. But the point is, hundreds of prisoners in here for the same and even worse crimes have been pardoned throughout all the years I've been here. The majority of them served only half or less time than I have.

9   Of course, it's no mystery to me why I'm still in prison. The judge and D.A. are keeping me here. But I say that's unfair—should, in fact, be illegal. They prosecuted and sentenced me

27 years ago, and that should be the end of their involvement in my case. They justify keeping me in here by claiming I am still the same dangerous man I was 27 years ago. If this were true, then I would like for someone to explain why, when I escaped a few weeks ago, I did not steal a car, knock someone in the head, or break into one of the many houses I passed.

On the night of April 15, when I finally made up my mind to escape, I knew the odds   10 were against me. I was 52 years old and had already suffered two heart attacks. In those final few days before April 15, I fought many emotional battles with myself. I had a lot to lose, and I'd be letting down a lot of good people who'd put their trust in me. But desperation is pretty hard to win a rational argument with. My time was running out. Had run out, really, because I was certainly in no condition to run through that jungle in the Tunica Hills. But even against all odds, I went for it anyway.

I struggled through those hills, mountains really, for five days and six nights, sleep-   11 ing on the ground, with no food and very little water. I ended up in Mississippi. I saw a lot of people, and I even talked to a few.

After a couple days I knew it would be impossible for me to get away unless I stole a   12 car or knocked someone in the head. Not far from Woodville, Mississippi, I came across a house trailer. I sat in the bushes watching the trailer from about 50 yards away. I watched a woman drive up and unlock the door and go in alone. A few minutes later, she came out and washed her car. I could have knocked her in the head, or even killed her, took her car, and been long gone. But I couldn't bring myself to do that.

I discovered that in reality I could no longer commit the crimes that I once did. So here   13 I stood in those bushes, watching that house trailer, that car, and that lady—my ticket to freedom—and discover I can't pay the price. I can't think of any words that could truly describe the dejection and hopelessness I felt at that moment. There was no way I could continue on as I had those five days past. There was just no strength left in my legs to go on. Resigned to my fate, I walked several hundred yards to the highway and gave myself up.

So now I am left with only two ways left to escape my torment. Just sit here for God   14 knows how many more years and wait on a natural death. Or I can avoid all those sense- less years of misery and take my own life now.

Having to sit in this cell now for several weeks with nothing—even being denied my   15 cigarettes—I have thought a lot about suicide, and it seems to be the most humane way out of a prison I no longer care to struggle in. Suicide or endless torment. Which would you choose?

Thinking Critically About Content

1. What is Clifton analyzing in this essay? How does his title help focus his analysis?
2. Explain two causes and two effects of Clifton's escape from prison.
3. Why do you think Clifton ends this essay with a question? Is this an effective conclusion?

Thinking Critically About Purpose and Audience

4. Why do you think Clifton wrote this essay?
5. Who do you think Clifton's audience is in this essay? Explain your answer.
6. Did the fact that this excerpt was written by a convicted criminal have any effect on you? Explain your answer.

Thinking Critically About Paragraphs

7. In paragraph 2 of his essay, the author mentions the "torment" of not being able to see his children growing up, yet he doesn't mention the crime he committed until paragraph 8. Why do you think he presents his material in this order?

8. Which of Clifton's paragraphs deal with the causes of his escape? Which deal with the effects? Do you think this is a good balance for Clifton's purpose? Explain your answer.

9. How does Clifton organize the details in paragraph 12? Why do you think he chose this method of organization?

10. If you were the district attorney who prosecuted Corky Clifton, how would you respond to Clifton's analysis? Write your response to him in the form of a letter.

To keep track of your critical thinking progress, go to Appendix 1.

SHEDDING THE WEIGHT OF MY DAD'S OBSESSION
by Linda Lee Andujar

Focusing Your Attention

1. Do you have a personal problem that plagues you constantly? What is this problem?

2. The essay you are about to read explains how the author finally shed an emotional burden she carried since her childhood. How do you deal with emotional problems? Where did you learn your "survival skills"? What do you do to find security and safety when you are upset about something?

Expanding Your Vocabulary

The following words are important to your understanding of this essay. As you read, circle any words you don't know beyond this list. Then break into groups, and help each other figure out the meanings of these unknown words.

Bluebird: entry-level organization for future Girl Scouts (paragraph 1)

clambered: climbed awkwardly (paragraph 4)

timber: quality of life (paragraph 5)

authoritarian regimens: strict regulations (paragraph 5)

incarceration: imprisonment (paragraph 7)

skirmish: battle (paragraph 8)

amphetamines: stimulants that lessen appetite (paragraph 9)

diuretics: drugs that increase the production of urine (paragraph 9)

metabolism: bodily process that changes food into energy (paragraph 11)

READING CRITICALLY
Making Connections in Your Reading

Once again, practice recognizing causes and effects by listing them in the following essay. Put them in two columns on a separate sheet of paper. These lists will help you understand the essay on an analytical level. Compare your notes with those of a classmate.

SHEDDING THE WEIGHT OF MY DAD'S OBSESSION
by Linda Lee Andujar

Instead of selling the Camp Fire candy, I ate it. Eight boxes of it. Each Bluebird in our fourth-grade troop was assigned 12 boxes of chocolate candy to sell for a dollar a box. I sold four boxes to my family and then ran out of ideas for selling the rest. 1

As the days passed and the stack of candy remained in a corner of my room, the temptation to eat it overwhelmed my conscience. Two months after we'd been given the goodies, the troop leader announced that the drive was over and we were to bring in our sales money, along with any unsold candy, to the next Tuesday meeting. I rushed home in a panic and counted $4 in my sales money envelope and 12 boxes of candy gone. 2

I thought of the piggy bank filled with silver dollars that my father kept on a shelf in his closet. It was a collection that he added to but never spent. I tried to push this financial resource out of my mind, but Tuesday was approaching, and I still had no money. 3

By Monday afternoon I had no choice. I tiptoed into my parents' bedroom, pulled the vanity chair from Mother's dressing table and carried it to the walk-in closet. There was the piggy bank smiling down at me from the high shelf. After stacking boxes on the chair, I reached up and laid hands on the bank. When I had counted out eight silver dollars, I returned the pig to its place and clambered down. For days I felt bad about my theft, but what I felt even guiltier about was eating all those treats. 4

Throughout my childhood, my parents weighed me every day, and Daddy posted the numbers on my bedroom door. He never called me fat, but I came to learn every synonym. He discussed every health aspect of obesity endlessly. The daily tone and timber of our household was affected by Dad's increasingly authoritarian regimens. 5

I remember one Friday night, months after the candy caper. I heard the garage door rumble shut, and I knew that Daddy was home. He came in the back door, kissed Mother and asked what my weight was for the day. Mother admitted that I was still a pound over the goal he had set. "Get a pillow and a book, Linda," he said. 6

He firmly ushered me to the bathroom, then shut and locked the door behind me. As the door was closing, I caught a glimpse of Mother and my sister looking on as though 7 they were witnessing an execution. For the next two days, the only time I was allowed out was for meals. It was late Sunday evening when I was finally released from my cell, supposedly taught a lesson by my incarceration.

8   The bathroom episode was one skirmish in a long war that had begun when, unlike my older sister, I failed to shed the "baby fat" many children are born with. Although I was cheerful, affectionate, and good-natured, none of these qualities interested my father. He had one slender child—he meant to have two. It was simply a matter of my self-discipline.

9   My slightly chubby figure had become a target for my physician father's frustration as he struggled to establish his medical practice. Dad told me constantly that if I was a pound overweight, I would be teased at school and nobody would like me. I stayed away from the other kids, fearing harsh words that never came. When I was 16, Daddy came up with the ultimate punishment: any day that I weighed more than 118 pounds (the weight my father had deemed ideal for my 5-foot, 4-inch frame) I'd have to pay him. In an attempt to shield me from this latest tactic, my exhausted, loving mother secretly took me to an internist friend of the family who prescribed what he described as "diet pills"—amphetamines and diuretics. Although the pills caused unpleasant side effects like light-headedness, taking them landed me a slim figure and, two years later, an engineer husband.

10   I quit the hated amphetamines at 27 and accepted my divorce as a result of my weight gain. I became a single, working mother devoted to raising my son and daughter. Over time, I realized that people liked my smile and my laugh and, contrary to my father's predictions, didn't shun me because of my size.

11   Many years ago, at my annual physical, I mentioned to my doctor that I couldn't eat the same quantity of food that normal people eat without getting bigger. He kindly reassured me that people do indeed have different metabolisms, some more efficient than others. This discussion ultimately helped me to accept my size and shed the emotional burden carried over from my childhood.

12   My sister and her husband have a daughter who was pudgy as a child. They asked me what they should do about her weight "problem." My reply, "Don't make it an issue. Let her find her own weight level." To their great credit, they did.

Thinking Critically About Content

1. What is Andujar analyzing in this essay?

2. The author is very honest and open about the causes and effects of her weight problem. What is the most fundamental cause and the ultimate effect?

3. What does Andujar seem upset about when she says, "Although I was cheerful, affectionate, and good-natured, none of these qualities interested my father" (paragraph 8)?

Thinking Critically About Purpose and Audience

4. What do you think Andujar's purpose is in this essay?

5. Who do you think is her primary audience?

6. Explain the essay's title.

Thinking Critically About Essays

7. Andujar opens her essay with the story about the Camp Fire candy. Do you think this is an effective beginning? Explain your answer.

8. Paragraph 5 gives us a hint of what the real problem is in Andujar's life. How does the writer organize her details in that paragraph?

9. What is the topic sentence of paragraph 9? Do all the sentences in that paragraph support this topic sentence? Explain your answer.

10. Write a paragraph about the role of a particular relative in your life. Are you very emotionally attached to this person? How did you become so close?

To keep track of your critical thinking progress, go to Appendix 1.

HAPPINESS IS CATCHING: WHY EMOTIONS ARE CONTAGIOUS
by Stacey Colino

Focusing Your Attention

1. Are you easily influenced by other people's moods? How do you know this?

2. In the essay you are about to read, Stacey Colino explains how we "catch" the feelings of others. Think of someone who generally makes you happy and someone who usually makes you sad. What is the difference between these two people? How do they each approach life? How do they each relate to you?

Expanding Your Vocabulary

The following words are important to your understanding of this essay. As you read, circle any words you don't know beyond this list. Then break into groups, and help each other figure out the meanings of these unknown words.

elation: joy, happiness (paragraph 1)

euphoria: extreme happiness (paragraph 1)

inoculate against: become immune to, resist (paragraph 1)

milliseconds: thousandths of a second (paragraph 2)

synchronize: coordinate (paragraph 2)

extroverts: outgoing people (paragraph 4)

engulfed: completely surrounded, overwhelmed (paragraph 5)

introverts: shy, quiet people (paragraph 5)

susceptible to: easily influenced by (paragraph 8)

mimicry: copying (paragraph 9)

READING CRITICALLY
Making Connections in Your Reading

As you did for the previous essays, list the causes and effects in the following essay on a separate sheet of paper. Then draw lines from specific causes to the related effects. This process will give you some good insights into the author's approach to her topic and her methods of developing her ideas. Compare your notes with those of one of your classmate's.

HAPPINESS IS CATCHING:
WHY EMOTIONS ARE CONTAGIOUS
by Stacey Colino

1   Researchers have found that emotions, both good and bad, are nearly as contagious as colds and flus. You can catch elation, euphoria, sadness, and more from friends, family, colleagues, even strangers. And once you understand how to protect yourself, you can inoculate yourself against the bad.

2   Mood "infection" happens in milliseconds, says Elaine Hatfield, Ph.D., a professor of psychology at the University of Hawaii in Honolulu and coauthor of *Emotional Contagion* (Cambridge University Press, 1994). And it stems from a primitive instinct: During conversation, we naturally tend to mimic and synchronize our facial expressions, movements, and speech rhythms to match the other person's. "Through this, we come to feel what the person is feeling," explains Dr. Hatfield. In other words, it puts us in touch with their feelings and affects our behavior.

3   Not surprisingly, spouses are especially likely to catch each other's moods, but so are parents, children, and good friends. In fact, a recent study at the University of Texas Medical Branch at Galveston found that depression was highly contagious among college roommates. "The same thing can occur with a spouse or co-worker, where one person is moderately depressed," says study author Thomas E. Joiner Jr., Ph.D., assistant professor of psychiatry and behavioral sciences.

4   Dr. Hatfield's research shows that extroverts and emotionally expressive people tend to transmit their feelings more powerfully. There's also a breed of people who, consciously or not, may want or need you to feel what they feel; they're the ones who live by the adage "misery loves company." They manipulate other people's moods—perhaps without even realizing it—to gain the upper hand or to feel better about themselves. "They express emotion to get a response—perhaps attention or sympathy," says Ross Buck, Ph.D., professor of communication sciences and psychology at the University of Connecticut.

5   On the other hand, some personality types are more likely to be engulfed by others' moods. Introverts are vulnerable because they're easily aroused. So are highly sensitive

Stacey Colino, "Happiness Is Catching: Why Emotions Are Contagious," *Family Circle,* March 12, 1996. Reprinted by permission of the author.

individuals who react physically to emotionally charged situations—their hearts flutter before giving a speech, for example.

If anyone knows how quickly moods spread, it's Ginny Graves, 33, a San Francisco writer. Last year, when she was pregnant with her first child, her mood took a nosedive every time she saw a particular friend. 6

"Basically nothing good was going on in her life—she didn't like her job, and she was obsessed with her weight," recalls Ginny. "I tried to bolster her up, but whenever I talked to her, I'd feel tense and tired." Afterward, Ginny was left with a case of the moody blues that lingered a day or so. 7

Indeed, there's some evidence that women may be particularly susceptible to catching moods, perhaps because we're better able to read other people's emotions and body language, according to psychologist Judith Hall, Ph.D., professor of psychology at Northeastern University in Boston. 8

Since women perceive facial expressions so readily, we may be more likely to mimic them—and wind up sharing the feeling. Just how mimicry leads to catching a mood is not known, notes John T. Cacioppo, Ph.D., professor of psychology at Ohio State University and coauthor of *Emotional Contagion*. One theory holds that when you frown or smile, the muscular movements in your face alter blood flow to the brain, which in turn affects mood; another theory maintains that the sensations associated with specific facial expressions trigger emotional memories—and hence the feelings—linked with those particular expressions. 9

With any luck, we catch the happy moods—infectious laughter at a dinner party or a colleague's enthusiasm for a project, for instance. Some psychologists suspect, however, that negative emotions—especially depression and anxiety—may be the most infectious of all. "For women, stress and depression are like emotional germs—they jump from one person to the next," notes Ellen McGrath, Ph.D., a psychologist in Laguna Beach, California, and author of *When Feeling Bad Is Good* (Bantam, 1994). 10

Being susceptible to other people's moods does make for a rich emotional life. But let's face it: When you catch a happy mood, you don't want to change it. Downbeat emotions are harder to deal with. And who wants her life to be ruled by other people's bad moods? 11

Fortunately, there are ways to protect yourself from unpleasant emotions, while letting yourself catch the good ones. For starters, pay attention to how you feel around different people, suggests Dr. McGrath. Then label your emotions—noting, for example, whether you feel optimistic around your best friend or gloomy after seeing your aunt. Then ask yourself if you're feeling what you do because you actually feel that way or because you've caught a mood from the other person. Just recognizing that an emotion belongs to someone else, not you, can be enough to short-circuit its transmission. 12

Once you know how people affect you, you can be more selective about whom you spend time with. Instead of going on an all-day outing with family members who bring you down, for instance, try spending shorter periods of time with them. Another solution is to give yourself a time-out: It could be as simple as a restroom break during an intense dinner. 13

14   Putting up emotional barriers is not the answer, though. If the channels are open, both positive and negative influences flow in. Shutting out the bad precludes you from catching joyful moods, too. Instead, it's better to monitor the floodgates—and to come to your own rescue when you feel yourself catching other people's negativity. And if you get swept up in another person's excitement, sit back and enjoy the ride.

Thinking Critically About Content

1. What is Colino analyzing in this essay? How does her title help focus her analysis?
2. Name two causes and two effects of people's moods.
3. How does Colino suggest that you can protect yourself from unpleasant emotions?

Thinking Critically About Purpose and Audience

4. Why do you think Colino wrote this essay?
5. Considering that this essay was originally published in a magazine called *Family Circle*, who do you think Colino's intended audience is? Explain your answer.
6. Are you susceptible to other people's moods? Why or why not?

Thinking Critically About Essays

7. The author of this essay quotes many authorities in the field of psychology. Are these quotations convincing to you? Explain your answer.
8. Which of Colino's paragraphs deal primarily with causes? With effects? Do you think this is a good balance? Explain your answer.
9. Find five transitions in Colino's essay that work well, and explain why they are effective.
10. Discuss the emotional climate in the place where you live. Are you able to separate your emotions from those of the people you live with? Are you affected by the emotions of roommates, friends, family? How might you manage emotional swings after reading this essay?

To keep track of your critical thinking progress, go to Appendix 1.

Writing Cause/Effect

This final section provides opportunities for you to apply what you have learned in this chapter to your own writing. It furnishes the guidelines for writing a cause/effect essay and a checklist for peer evaluation. Consult the essays in this chapter for examples of good cause/effect writing. Finally, pause at the end of the chapter to reflect briefly on what you have learned.

Guidelines for Writing a Cause/Effect Essay

1. Write a thesis statement that explains what you are analyzing.
2. Choose facts, details, and reasons to support your thesis statement.
3. Do not mistake coincidence for cause or effect.
4. Search for the real causes and effects connected with your subject.
5. Organize your essay so that your readers can easily follow your analysis.

Writing About Your Reading

1. Many significant studies have established the connection between TV watching and violent behavior. What other reasons might there be for an increase in aggression in our society? Explain your answer.

2. In "Life Sentences," Corky Clifton explains that he is desperate to escape from prison. He can no longer stand "the torment." Have you ever wanted to escape from certain people or a specific situation in your life? How do you escape when you want to?

3. Are you currently dealing with any personal dilemmas? What are they? Does one bother you more than the others? Write an essay analyzing the causes and effects of this particular dilemma.

4. In "Happiness Is Catching," Stacey Colino talks about how contagious moods are. Do you think you might have been responsible for putting someone in a good or bad mood? What were the circumstances? How did someone "catch" your mood? Write an essay analyzing the causes and effects of the situation.

5. How would looking closely at causes and effects help you live a better life? How would the process of discovering causes and effects help you think through your decisions and problems more logically? Explain your answer.

Writing About Your World

1. Write an essay about an important event that altered your attitude toward an authority figure in your life (a parent, a religious leader, a teacher, a club sponsor, a supervisor or boss). What brought about the change? What were the results of the change?

2. Choose a major problem in society today, and propose a solution to it. Explain its causes as necessary.

3. We all deal with change differently, but it is generally difficult to accept change in our lives. Think of a significant change in your life, and write about

its causes and effects. What was the incident? What were the circumstances connected with the incident?

4. Write an essay that analyzes the causes of a current social problem—homelessness, drugs, environmental concerns—including the reasons for its existence.

5. Create your own cause/effect assignment (with the help of your instructor), and write a response to it.

Revising

Small Group Activity (5–10 minutes per writer) Working in groups of three or four, read your cause/effect essays to each other. Those listening should record their reactions on a copy of the Peer Evaluation Form in Appendix 2A. After your group goes through this process, give your evaluation forms to the appropriate writers so that each writer has two or three peer comment sheets for revising.

Paired Activity (5 minutes per writer) Using the completed Peer Evaluation Forms, work in pairs to decide what you should revise in your essay. If time allows, rewrite some of your sentences, and have your partner look at them.

Individual Activity Rewrite your paper, using the revising feedback you received from other students.

Editing

Paired Activity (5–10 minutes per writer) Swap papers with a classmate, and use the editing portion of your Peer Evaluation Form to identify as many grammar, punctuation, mechanics, and spelling errors as you can. If time allows, correct some of your errors, and have your partner look at them. Record your grammar, punctuation, and mechanics errors in the Error Log (Appendix 3) and your spelling errors in the Spelling Log (Appendix 4).

Individual Activity Rewrite your paper again, using the editing feedback you received from other students.

Reflecting on Your Writing   When you have completed your own essay, answer these six questions.

1. What was most difficult about this assignment?

2. What was easiest?

3. What did you learn about cause and effect by completing this assignment?

4. What do you think are the strengths of your cause/effect essay? Place a wavy line by the parts of your essay that you feel are very good.

5. What are the weaknesses, if any, of your paper? Place an X by the parts of your essay you would like help with. Write any questions you have in the margins.

6. What did you learn from this assignment about your own writing process—about preparing to write, about writing the first draft, about revising, and about editing?

Argument: From Reading to Writing

This chapter includes six reading selections and several writing assignments. It offers guidance in peer evaluation and reflection, ending with suggestions about how to lead your instructor through your writing in ways that will benefit both of you.

Reading Arguments

Here are six examples of good argument essays. The first is an essay by Jeff Chu called "Who Gets the Break?," which discusses the issue of whether or not illegal immigrants should receive in-state college tuition. The next essay, "Wrong Call for Regulating Sexting" by Warner Todd Huston, tries to persuade readers that we must take action at home to stop the "crass" attitudes of our teens. The last four essays are on two different topics. The first is social networking: "Social Networking Benefits Validated," by Karen Goldberg Goff, and "Social Depression, Loneliness, and Depression," by Stella Lau. The second topic is loitering and gang violence: "Anti-Loitering Laws Can Reduce Gang Violence" by Richard Willard and "Anti-Loitering Laws Are Ineffective and Biased" by David Cole. As you read, notice how the writers make their claims through thoughtful, detailed reasoning.

WHO GETS THE BREAK?
by Jeff Chu

Focusing Your Attention

1. Think of all the ways you use your education in a typical day. What percentage of your day draws on your learning in school?

2. You are about to read an essay that represents the controversy around the issue of funding a college education for illegal immigrants. What do you think are the relevant issues? Why would American citizens care about these issues?

Expanding Your Vocabulary

The following words are important to your understanding of this essay. To help you add them to your vocabulary, write out a synonym and an example from your own experience for each new word.

furor: an outbreak of public anger or excitement (paragraph 2)

subsidize: support financially (paragraph 2)

repeal: revoke or annul (paragraph 6)

pragmatism: a practical approach (paragraph 6)

READING CRITICALLY
Recognizing Facts and Opinions in Your Reading

As demonstrated in the Introduction, separate the facts and opinions in the following essay by highlighting them in two different colors. Then put an X by any points that you disagree with or want to challenge. These notes will give you insights into the topic and guide you to a deeper level of understanding. Compare your notes with someone else's in the class.

WHO GETS THE BREAK?
by Jeff Chu

1   "Pamela" would like you to know that she loves art; that she would have gotten honors at her graduation from Marlborough High School in Marlborough, Massachusetts last month, except for a slip on her Algebra II final; that she would go to the Massachusetts College of Art this fall, but her restaurant-worker parents can't pay the nearly $18,000 tuition; and that the tuition would cost just $6,400 if state legislators approved a bill to allow students like her, an illegal immigrant, to pay in-state rates at Massachusetts' public colleges and universities.

2   Pamela, who arrived with her family from Chile in 2000 and does not wish to reveal her real name, is one of an estimated 50,000 to 65,000 illegal immigrants who got diplomas from U.S. high schools this spring. They graduated into a furor over in-state tuition,

one of the fiercest debates over immigration policy today. Illegal aliens can qualify for in-state tuition rates in nine states, including Texas, Kansas, and California. But a lawsuit challenging Kansas' law and the failure of legislatures to approve similar policies in 18 other states this year reflect widespread unease about such benefits. Proponents in most of those 18 states plan to try again next session. Massachusetts' bill is still alive, but Governor Mitt Romney has said he will veto it. Pamela remains hopeful: "All I want is an opportunity to become somebody." Should the state subsidize her efforts?

Surprisingly, money is not the big issue. In Texas, which in 2001 became the first state to grant such tuition benefits, fewer than 8,000 un documented immigrants—out of a public college population of more than 1 million—got reduced rates last year. Mark Krikorian of the Center for Immigration Studies, a think tank that favors tighter immigration rules, says it is more a matter of principle: "Extending in-state tuition is a way of legitimizing their presence. It is back-door amnesty."   3

Education is a tricky battleground. There's an emotion to it that makes it different from day laborers hanging out in front of the Home Depot," says Krikorian. In North Carolina an in-state-tuition bill died in committee in May after talk radio helped stir a fervor "one hundred times bigger than Terri Schiavo," in the words of Kevin Miller, a host at WPTF in Raleigh. Many listeners were worried that expanded in-state rates would not only suck up taxpayer dollars but would also make it harder for the kids to get into top state schools like the University of North Carolina at Chapel Hill. Opponents also fear that extending one privilege would open the door to granting other benefits now reserved for legal residents. "The other side is afraid this is the beginning of something more," says Josh Bernstein, of the national immigration Law Center.   4

Both sides blame the Federal Government for embroiling states in this debate. In 1982 the Supreme Court ruled that states must educate illegal immigrants through the 12th grade. But what then? A 1996 federal law prohibits state-level "residency-based" benefits for illegal immigrants unless they are available to all U.S. citizens—in other words, to out-of-state residents too. So states crafted rules that aren't based on residency. To qualify for in-state rates at public colleges in Kansas, for example, you must spend three years in the state's high schools. University of Missouri–Kansas City law professor Kris Kobach, counsel for 24 out-of-state students challenging the law, says this still violates the federal statute as well as the Constitution's equal-protection clause by "discriminating against U.S. citizens." Says plaintiff Heidi Hydeman, an Iowan who paid out-of-state fees (now $12,691 a year vs. $4,737 in-state) to attend K.U.: "It's just not fair."   5

Congress could clear this legal thicket by approving the proposed Dream Act, which would repeal the federal residency-rule ban and grant temporary legal status to undocumented graduates of U.S. high schools. But despite bipartisan support, the bill has failed to get to the floor in the past two sessions of Congress. "The Federal Government hasn't shown much interest in sending [illegal immigrants] home," says Sue Storm, sponsor of the Kansas bill. "It's in all our best interests for them to be educated." Opponents didn't buy that brand of pragmatism. "It's so politically correct to say, 'Oh, these poor people have dreams!' Well, we all have dreams," says Lorrie Hall, founder of the Massachusetts Coalition for Immigration Reform. "They are taking places from Americans—and we have to subsidize them."   6

7   Whatever happens in Massachusetts, Pamela wants to stay in the country she sees as her home. She isn't sure what she will do if she doesn't go to college. She can't work legally, though she might do some babysitting. But her long-term plan is clear. "I'd like to become an American citizen," she says. That would be one way to solve the tuition problem.

Thinking Critically About Content

1. What is Chu's main point in this essay?
2. Explain the "Dream Act" (paragraph 6) in your own words.
3. Are you convinced that "money is not the big issue" (paragraph 3)? Explain your answer.

Thinking Critically About Purpose and Audience

4. What do you think is Chu's purpose in writing this essay?
5. Who would be most interested in this essay?
6. An essential ingredient in writing an effective argument is to pull the readers into the situation. How does Chu accomplish this? Explain your answer.

Thinking Critically About Paragraphs

7. Chu begins and ends this essay with a story about a real illegal immigrant who has been to American high school. Is this an effective beginning and ending? Explain your answer.
8. What does the author mean when he says "Education is a tricky battleground" (paragraph 4)? How does Chu organize his details to support this topic sentence?
9. Does Chu represent two different sides of the argument on this topic? List his points in two columns. Which side is most convincing to you? Explain your answer.
10. As a United States citizen, write a personal response to "Pamela."

To keep track of your critical thinking progress, go to Appendix 1.

WRONG CALL FOR REGULATING SEXTING
by Warner Todd Huston

Focusing Your Attention

1. At what age or in what situation do you think children understand the dangers of the Internet?
2. In the essay you are about to read, the writer discusses the dangers connected with sending to others nude or revealing pictures electronically. What do you think some of these issues are?

Expanding Your Vocabulary

The following words are important to your understanding of this essay. To help you add them to your vocabulary, write out a synonym and an example from your own experience for each new word.

circumspect: discrete (paragraph 2)

salacious: sexy (paragraph 2)

surged: moved quickly (paragraph 2)

epithets: labels (paragraph 3)

ribbing: teasing (paragraph 3)

sexting: to send sexy pictures through text messaging (paragraph 4)

low-born: unimportant (paragraph 4)

intrusive: interfering (paragraph 4)

agitating: making a fuss (paragraph 6)

onus: responsibility (paragraph 6)

crass: ridiculous (paragraph 9)

raunchy: sexually inappropriate (paragraph 11)

non-chalant: relaxed (paragraph 11)

precipitated: caused (paragraph 11)

instilled: taught (paragraph 11)

propriety: respectability (paragraph 11)

taunting: teasing (paragraph 12)

promulgated: spread (paragraph 15)

epidemic: outbreak (paragraph 21)

coarsening: to make rude (paragraph 22)

READING CRITICALLY
Recognizing Facts and Opinions in Your Reading

As in the previous essay, separate the facts and opinions in the following essay by highlighting them in two different colors. Then put an X by any points that you disagree with or want to challenge. These notes will give you insights into the topic and guide you to a deeper level of understanding. Compare your notes with someone else's in the class.

WRONG CALL FOR REGULATING SEXTING
by Warner Todd Huston

1   No one wants to see a beautiful 18-year-old girl commit suicide. No one wants to make any worse the pain that surviving family members feel. No one wants to make light of the situation that causes a child or young person to chose suicide either. But high emotion makes for bad laws, and this is no exception.

2   Last year, Jessica Logan imagined that she was sending a nude cell-phone photo of herself only to her new boyfriend. But he was not as circumspect as she might have hoped, passing the salacious picture to his friends and they to theirs, until it surged through some seven Cincinnati high schools.

3   It wasn't long before Jessica was the butt of jokes and the target of epithets like "slut" and "porn queen." The ribbing shook her so hard that she hanged herself in her bedroom last July.

4   And now, parents Albert and Cynthia Logan want new laws passed to somehow stop "sexting" of nude or half nude photos from one teen's cell-phone to another. Unfortunately, such laws are just a bad idea. They will do nothing to stop the low-born practice, while only piling more strangling regulations on the business community as well as giving government and police officials even more intrusive powers into our individual lives.

5   There is nothing wrong with trying to convince kids that emailing nude photos of themselves is not a good idea, of course, and the Logan's are undertaking that effort. But the there-ought-to-be-a-law mentality is not effective here, as it isn't in most cases on such emotional issues.

6   Absurdly, the Logans are agitating to place more onus on schools for stopping this new age problem of "cyberbullying" and "sexting."

7   "Schools need to understand our kids are targeting each other and technology is being used as a weapon," Aftab said. "None of them (the schools) know what to do. Many of them . . . think it's not their problem. They want to close their eyes and put fingers in their ears, saying it's a home issue."

8   Sorry, parents, but if your children are sending nude cell-phone photos of themselves to each other, the solution is not to force schools to get involved. The solution is to take away the darn cell-phone!

9   Sadly, what we have here is not a lack of laws, but a crass culture. A national study by the National Campaign to Prevent Teen and Unplanned Pregnancy revealed that one in five teen girls or 22 percent say they have electronically sent or posted nude or semi-nude images online of themselves.

10   Salacious attitudes are instilled in kids by raunchy entertainment, coarse advertising. and the non-chalant attitude of parents to these influences. It needs to be pointed out that this sad suicide was precipitated in the first place by the girl sending the nude photo to a boyfriend she only had been dating for two months. Sadly, this young girl was not instilled with an attitude of propriety in her behavior. Just as sadly, she is not alone. Too many of our children never seem to be told what behavior is unacceptable in our country today.

11   There is a reason, though, that this poor child was so hard hit by the taunting she was confronted with. We lack a sense of shame in our culture and when it hits it is like

a ton of bricks that many don't quite understand. Young Jessica suddenly found herself with a bad reputation, deserved or no, because of her own actions. "I watched her get kicked out of maybe three or four parties over the summer just for having 'a reputation,' " said Steven Arnett, a friend of hers who graduated last year from Moeller High School.

12 This is a sad, sad object lesson for other kids imagining there are no consequences for sending salacious photos of themselves all across the Internet. There ARE consequences to your actions. This must be learned by our youth, but it is a lesson that is missing from society today.

13 Unfortunately, just the wrong sort of lesson is being promulgated by teachers, lawmakers, and these parents with this incident. "It is a form of bullying, and that is something we cannot tolerate. The difficulty is stopping it. . . . That's why we stress with our kids that the moment you push 'send,' the damage is done," said Sycamore Superintendent Adrienne James. All the onus put on "the bullying" and none put on the person that sent the nude photo to begin with is simply not a complete lesson. The better lesson is to focus equally on both the sender and the bullies, not just the bullies. The wrap up is typical of the wrong-headed emphasis we too often place on the situations that confront us in our modern society.

14 Albert and Cynthia Logan have gone public with Jessie's story, hoping to change vague state laws that don't hold anyone accountable for sexting. They also want to warn kids about what can happen when nude cell-phone photos are shared.

15 "We want a bill passed," Cynthia Logan said.

16 "It's a national epidemic. Nobody is doing anything—no schools, no police officers, no adults, no attorneys, no one."

17 It isn't the laws that are the problem. It's the overindulgence of kids' "self-esteem," a complete lack of moral instruction, a coarsening of our society, and a corresponding assumption by too many parents that everyone else should be responsible for their own children's behavior.

18 Again, it is horrendous that this beautiful young woman took her own life over this embarrassment. But it is the lack of imagining that actions have consequences, that embarrassment is a result, that reputations can be destroyed with casual actions little thought out, that all too often is a lesson learned too late.

19 It isn't only the Logans' fault. There is little doubt that they loved their daughter. But this incident is indicative of some major errors in our society that need to be fixed. If it isn't, these heart-wrenching incidents will grow until the total breakdown of society is complete, and no "law" will stop it.

Thinking Critically About Content

1. What does Huston see as the relationship between kids' attitudes today and "raunchy entertainment" (paragraph 10)?

2. Why does the author think a law for controlling sexting is "wrong-headed" (paragraph 13)?

3. What does the author mean by the statement "What we have here is not a lack of laws, but a crass culture" (paragraph 9)?

Thinking Critically About Purpose and Audience

4. What do you think Huston's purpose is in this essay?

5. Who do you think would be most interested in this essay?

6. What effect do you think this essay would have on parents?

Thinking Critically About Essays

7. Describe in a complete sentence the writer's argument.

8. Why do you think Huston cites statistics about sexting (paragraph 9) to support his argument?

9. Do you think the story about Jessica Logan is an effective way to start this essay? Explain your answer.

10. This essay argues against the Logans' solution to the growing sexting problem, but doesn't offer any concrete alternatives. Write a paragraph with some clear, realistic suggestions for solving this new problem in our society.

To keep track of your critical thinking progress, go to Appendix 1.

ARGUING A POSITION

Focusing Your Attention

1. What role does social networking play in your life? Is it important to you? What percentage of your day do you spend on social network sites?

2. In the two essays you will be reading, one writer tries to persuade the readers that social networking has important advantages for its users while the other essay tells readers that social networking is dangerous in many ways. Although you have not yet read the essays, which one do you think you will agree with?

READING CRITICALLY
Recognizing Facts and Opinions in Your Reading

Once again, highlight the facts and opinions in both of the following essays, put an X by ideas you disagree with, and form your own opinions about the issues surrounding social networking. Be prepared to defend your thoughts with details from the essays and examples from your own experience.

SOCIAL NETWORKING BENEFITS VALIDATED
by Karen Goldberg Goff

Expanding Your Vocabulary

The following words are important to your understanding of this essay. To help you add them to your vocabulary, write out a synonym and an example from your own experience for each new word.

gaming: playing video games (paragraph 1)

self-directed: independent (paragraph 4)

micro-expert: minor expert (paragraph 6)

autonomy: independence; self-sufficiency (paragraph 6)

tweens: children whose age falls between adolescents and teens (paragraph 7)

untrustworthy: not able to be trusted (paragraph 11)

SOCIAL NETWORKING BENEFITS VALIDATED
by Karen Goldberg Goff

1 Texting, blogs, Facebook, gaming, and instant messages might seem, to some, to be just more reasons to stare at a computer screen. Thinking like that is so 2008, any middle schooler will tell you. Now a study that looked at the online habits of 800 teenagers backs them up.

2 Researchers in the study, titled the Digital Youth Project and conducted primarily at the University of Southern California and the University of California at Berkeley, found that in our increasingly technological world, the constant communication that social networking provides is encouraging useful skills. The study looked at more than 5,000 hours of online observation and found that the digital world is creating new opportunities for young people to grapple with social norms, explore interests, develop technical skills, and work on new forms of self-expression.

3 "There are myths about kids spending time online—that it is dangerous or making them lazy," says Mizuko Ito, lead author of the study, which will be the basis of a forthcoming book, "Hanging Out, Messing Around, Geeking Out: Living and Learning With New Media." "But we found that spending time online is essential for young people to pick up the social and technical skills they need to be competent citizens in the digital age."

4 Co-author Lisa Tripp, now an assistant professor at Florida State University, says technology, including YouTube, iPods, and podcasting, creates avenues for extending

one's circle of friends, boosts self-directed learning, and fosters independence. "Certain technical skills in the coming years are not going to be just about consuming media," she says. "It is also going to be about producing media. It is not just about writing a blog, but also how to leave comments that say something. Learning to communicate like this is contributing to the general circulation of culture." That means anything from a video clip to a profile page is going to reflect the self-expression skills one has, so teens might as well practice what will say who they are.

5   Social networking also contributes greatly to teens' extended friendships and interests, Ms. Tripp says. While the majority of teens use sites such as MySpace and Facebook to "hang out" with people they already know in real life, a smaller portion uses them to find like-minded people. Before social networking, the one kid in school who was, say, a fan of Godzilla or progressive politics might find himself isolated. These days, that youngster has peers everywhere.

6   "This kind of communication has let teens expand their social circle by common interests," Ms. Tripp says. "They can publicize and distribute their work to online audiences and become sort of a micro-expert in that area." The study found that young people's learning with digital media often is more self-directed, with a freedom and autonomy that is less apparent than in a classroom. The researchers said youths usually respect one another's authority online, and they often are more motivated to learn from one another than from adults.

7   Parents, however, still have an important role to play when it comes to tweens, teens, and social networking, the researchers say. They need to accept that technology is a necessary and important part of the culture for young people and, other experts say, be aware of with whom the teens are communicating. Monica Vila, founder of theonlinemom.com, an online resource for digital-age parenting, says parents need to set parameters just as they would "at any other playground." "This kind of study puts a lot of facts behind the value of social networking," Ms. Vila says.

8   It is up to parents to monitor what is being expressed, she says. She recommends that parents "have a presence" in their child's online social network. That doesn't necessarily mean "friending," communicating, and commenting, but it does mean having a password or knowing who your child's online friends are. One Fairfax County mother of a middle schooler, who asked that her name not be used to protect her daughter's privacy, says she was skeptical at first when her daughter wanted a Facebook page. "I was hesitant for all the reasons we hear about, such as how it could bring in unwelcome visitors," the woman says, "but eventually I realized that this is the main medium for kids keeping in touch. It has gone from email to IM to texting to Facebook in such a quick progression. [Social networking] is like the modern-day equivalent of the lunch table. If you are not on Facebook, then you are not in the loop." The woman says she stays in the loop because she knows her daughter's password, and her daughter knows her mom can access her page whenever she wants—and can see who is there and what they are posting.

9   A few rules: no putting your exact whereabouts on your status update, and be aware of who is tagging you in a photo because if that photo contains unflattering behavior, it could come back to haunt you. Also, the mom has a Facebook page of her own, although she is not yet among her daughter's 100-plus friends. "I have become accepting that there are more positives than negatives from social networking," the woman says, noting that

she is pleased to see the connection of her daughter's network through various circles such as school and sports. "It is allowing a lot of dialogue among people who may not otherwise have a chance for a lot of dialogue." Those are all good rules and observations, Ms. Vila says.

"I like to catch parents before this whole process starts," she says. "That way you can set the ground rules early and [not] be trying to catch up. If your kids know that you have a presence in their online community, you are acting like a chaperone. If they won't friend you, you should at least have their password." 10

"It is not that kids are untrustworthy," Ms. Vila says. "It is that they often lack processing skills. Parents need to explain that images may be damaging. They may not be able to think past the next day, let alone what will happen when they are looking for a job six years later." Studies such as the Digital Youth Project and the report "Enhancing Child Safety and Online Technologies," issued recently by Harvard University's Berkman Center for Internet and Society, show that social networking has earned a place in American culture from which there is no turning back, Ms. Vila says. 11

"A few years ago, parents were saying, 'I don't want any of that stuff coming into my house,' even about video games," she says. "Then they realized, 'I have no choice; it is all around me.'" Now studies are saying technology is going to encourage skills for jobs we didn't know existed. At the very least, social networking is encouraging technology skills, and that is going to be essential to the digital economy. 12

[http://www.washingtontimes.com/news/2009/jan/28/social-networking-benefits-validated/print/]

SOCIAL DEPRESSION, LONELINESS, AND DEPRESSION
by Stella Lau

Expanding Your Vocabulary

The following words are important to your understanding of this essay. To help you add them to your vocabulary, write out a synonym and an example from your own experience for each new word.

social integration: social involvement (paragraph 1)

correlation: relationship; correspondence (paragraph 5)

impediment: hindrance (paragraph 7)

disembodied: separated (paragraph 8)

"Man cannot live without attachment to some object which transcends and survives him . . . he is too little . . . we have no other object than ourselves we cannot avoid the thought that our efforts will finally end in nothingness, since we ourselves disappear" (*Suicide*). —Emile Durkheim

SOCIAL DEPRESSION, LONELINESS, AND DEPRESSION
by Stella Lau

1   Sociologist Emile Durkheim (April 15, 1858—November 15, 1917) is one of the originators of modern sociology. The quote above from his famous book *Suicide* explains the cause of depression due to social isolation and loneliness. This theory says that too little integration with society or a community leads to suicide. There are no goals set outside the self, and people feel that life is meaningless; there is nothing greater than themselves to live for. For example, Durkheim compared widowed people with children and widowed people without children. He found that widowed people with children are more protected against suicide than their counterparts because they have something greater than themselves to live for, their children. When you have something you're obligated to outside yourself (i.e., a network of friends or family), you're more protected from depression and suicide. Social integration provides goals and meanings for people to live for. For someone who is depressed, there is little to no meaning left in life. Everyday activities, such as eating and exercising seem meaningless. They are constantly mourning their own dead inner selves.

2   Social isolation, loneliness, and depression are all interrelated. Studies have shown that the more time spent on the Internet leads to social isolation and loneliness, which in turn leads to depression. Even though online communities and instant messaging allow a person to stay connected with friends and family as well as expanding their social network, the more time spent socializing online is time spent away from socializing in the real world.

Online Communities

3   In a survey I conducted with 500 people, ages ranging from 18–25, the results showed that 46 percent of the subjects <u>routinely spend</u> three or more hours <u>per day</u> browsing through people's pages on the various online communities. This study shows that people spend hours in a virtual world where the people of the pages they are browsing through may not even know of them. Just reading about other people and their lives already takes time away from actual socializing with friends. By browsing these pages, people become so absorbed into a virtual world that they become disconnected from reality.

4   They feel like they are getting to know someone without actually knowing them. The friends on one's "friends list" may not even be friends. They could be acquaintances or people you just met. However, many people consider these as "friends" and do not even see or talk to them after adding them. People try to gather the most friends on their list to look popular. The physical contact and presence of being with a friend thus fades and one slowly becomes disconnected from reality.

5   As the chart below shows (taken from a Stanford Study), there is a correlation between the number of hours on online social networks and one's social isolation. The more hours spent leads to an increase social isolation in all three categories: usage of the phone, time spent with family, and social events.

Instant Messaging

6   Instant messaging also causes social isolation and disembodiment because you are simply having conversations that are not real. You start losing social skills in the real world as you master your social skills chatting behind a computer screen.

Online communities correlate to instant messaging and further add to the impedi- 7
ment of one's social life. Since you can browse other people's pages and find out their interests, it makes it easy to find people with similar interests as you. You can then message
them, ask for the screen names, and start chatting online. From there, you start building a
virtual friendship with the other, comfortable to talk to a complete stranger because you
are protected by the space between your computer and the stranger's computer.

As this process repeats itself (finding people with common interests as you), people find 8
this more convenient than finding someone in the real world with such interests as you.
People then become comfortable to this process and are likely to socialize in the virtual world
rather than with real people. In addition, people can easily alter their identity behind the computer screen. When put in real social situations, a person who has been accustomed to the
online social life will not know how to behave and act around other people and will likely find
it difficult to socialize with others. This, in turn, will lead to social awkwardness and furthers
the desire to comfortably socialize on the Internet. As this social awkwardness strengthens in
the real world, people more and more desire the comfort and ease of chatting online that they
soon become disembodied from reality, and therefore, isolate themselves from the world.

Thinking Critically About Content

1. What is the main argument of each essay?

2. According to the Digital Youth Project, what four types of skills did the
   researchers find young people developed through social networking sites?

3. How does Stella Lau introduce her main point about the dangers of social networking? Is this an effective approach to her argument? Explain your answer.

Thinking Critically About Purpose and Audience

4. What type of audience do you think would be most interested in the topic of
   these two essays? Explain your answer.

5. What tone do the authors use in these essays?

6. Which essay do you agree with more? Did you agree with that position before
   you read the essays? If you changed your mind as a result of reading one of these
   essays, which part of the essay made you change your mind? Explain your answer.

Thinking Critically About Paragraphs

7. Discuss the authors' methods of organizing their ideas. How are their methods of organization different in these essays? How are they the same?

8. Compare the conclusions in these two essays. Do these conclusions each
   reflect the main points of their essays?

9. Which paragraph is most convincing to you in each essay? What makes each
   one so convincing?

10. Write a paragraph explaining one of the ideas or facts that both essays agree on.

To keep track of your critical thinking progress, go to Appendix 1.

ARGUING A POSITION

Focusing Your Attention

1. If you were asked to take a position for or against a topic of great importance to you or to society, what are some of the topics you would consider?

2. In the two essays that you will be reading, one writer claims that if we control loitering, we can control gang activity. The other writer claims loitering is not related to gang activity. Before you read these essays, try to predict some of the arguments each author will make.

READING CRITICALLY
Recognizing Facts and Opinions in Your Reading

As you have done throughout the chapter, highlight the facts and opinions in both of the following essays, put an X by ideas you disagree with, and form your own opinions about the issue of loitering and gang violence. Be prepared to defend your thoughts with details from the essays and examples from your own experience.

ANTI-LOITERING LAWS CAN REDUCE GANG VIOLENCE
by Richard Willard

Expanding Your Vocabulary

The following words are important to your understanding of this essay. To help you add them to your vocabulary, write out a synonym and an example from your own experience for each new word.

anti-loitering: forbidding people to hang around in a public place without an obvious reason (title)

innovative: clever, original (paragraph 1)

curfew: time by which individuals must be off the public streets (paragraph 1)

statutes: laws (paragraph 1)

court injunctions: orders issued by the courts (paragraph 1)

deterrence: avoidance (paragraph 1)

sanctions: punishments (paragraph 1)

constrained: limited (paragraph 1)

discretion: personal judgment (paragraph 1)

gang-loitering ordinances: laws against gangs hanging around public places without reason (paragraph 2)

implemented: used, enforced (paragraph 2)

pervasiveness: extent (paragraph 2)

engenders: produces, causes (paragraph 3)

panhandling: begging for money (paragraph 5)

vending: the selling of merchandise (paragraph 5)

commons: open public areas such as parks and squares (paragraph 6)

prevalent: widespread (paragraph 7)

skewed: distorted (paragraph 7)

augment: increase (paragraph 10)

condemnation: blame (paragraph 10)

suppression: control (paragraph 11)

abatement: decrease (paragraph 11)

ANTI-LOITERING LAWS CAN REDUCE GANG VIOLENCE
by Richard Willard

1   Chicago is not alone in seeking to resist the devastating effects of gang violence. Having witnessed the failure of more traditional policing methods, many other threatened localities—from Los Angeles to Washington, D.C.—have reacted by passing a variety of innovative laws, which range from curfew measures to anti-loitering statutes to court injunctions against specific gang members. All of these measures emphasize prevention and deterrence strategies over increased criminal sanctions. In order to meet the particular challenges of increased gang violence, communities have also strongly supported constrained expansions of police discretion to help communities reassert their own law-abiding norms.

2   Residents of high-crime communities are much more likely to support gang-loitering ordinances, curfews, and other order-maintenance policies, which they perceive to be appropriately moderate yet effective devices for reducing crime. Communities have implemented these policies in various ways, tailored to their particular needs and depending on the pervasiveness of the problem.

Maintaining Order

3   Just as community disorder engenders increasing disorder and crime, reinforcement of [existing] community law-abiding norms engenders increasing social order and

Richard Willard, "Anti-Loitering Laws Can Reduce Gang Violence," *Supreme Court Debates* (Washington, DC: Congressional Digest Corp. February 1999). Reprinted by permission of the publisher.

prevents more serious crime. Modern policing theory has undergone a "quiet revolution" to learn that, in cooperation with community efforts, enforcing community public order norms is one of the most effective means of combating all levels of crime. By focusing on order maintenance and prevention, advocating a more visible presence in policed areas, and basing its legitimacy on the consent of policed populations, police can most effectively prevent the occurrence of more serious crime.

4   New York City's experience confirms this. Today, that city has much less crime than it did five years ago. From 1993 to 1996, the murder rate dropped by 40 percent, robberies dropped by 30 percent, and burglary dropped by more than 25 percent, more than double the national average.

5   These drops are not the result of increased police resources, but rather more effectively applied resources. While New York has not increased its law enforcement expenditures substantially more than other cities, since 1993 the city began to focus intensively on "public order" offenses, including vandalism, aggressive panhandling, public drunkenness, unlicensed vending, public urination, and prostitution. This focus on order maintenance is credited for much of the crime reduction.

6   Anti-loitering ordinances implement community-driven order maintenance policing citywide—appropriate to the extreme pervasiveness of Chicago's gang problem—but on a neighborhood scale. Preservation of neighborhood commons is essential to ensuring healthy and vital cities.

Ineffective Strategies

7   Gang loitering works to increase disorder. Order-maintenance policing strikes a reasonable intermediate balance between harsh criminal penalties and inaction. Conventional suppression strategies are ineffective in gang-threatened communities. Where gang activity is prevalent, individuals are more likely to act in an aggressive manner in order to conform to gang norms of behavior. When numerous youths act according to these skewed norms, more are likely to turn to crime: Widespread adoption of aggressive mannerisms sends skewed signals about public attitudes toward gang membership and creates barriers to mainstream law-abiding society, which strongly disfavors aggression.

8   Accordingly, policies that "raise the price" of gang activity can sometimes function at cross-purposes. If juveniles value willingness to break the law, delinquency may be seen as "status-enhancing." As penalties grow more severe, lawbreaking gives increasing status. More severe punishments may also provoke unintended racist accusation, if community minorities view harsher penalties as unfairly applied to their particular groups. Thus, any strategy dependent on harsh penalties may in fact be "at war with itself."

Why Anti-Loitering Laws Work

9   Strategies that instead attack public signals to juveniles' peers about the value of gang criminality are more effective. Gang anti-loitering laws do this, for example, by "authorizing police to disperse known gang members when they congregate in public places" or by "directly prohibiting individuals from displaying gang allegiance through distinctive gestures or clothing." By preventing gangs from flaunting their authority, such laws establish community authority while combating the perception that gangs have high status. As that perception weakens, so does the pressure to join gangs that youths might otherwise perceive.

Such strategies also positively influence law-abiding adults. Gang-loitering laws augment law-abiders' confidence so that they can oppose gangs. When public deterrence predominates, individuals are much less likely to perceive that criminality is widespread and much more likely to see private precautions as worthwhile. When the community as a whole is again able to express its condemnation, gang influence quickly wanes. 10

The most successful anti-gang programs combine effective gang suppression programs with targeted community aid efforts: increased social services, job placement, and crisis intervention. Civil gang abatement, together with other government and community-based efforts, has reduced crime and visibly improved the neighborhood's quality of life. 11

Chicago has also implemented alternative community aid programs. Since 1992, for example, the Gang Violence Reduction Project has targeted Little Village to serve as a model gang violence reduction program. 12

The program coordinates increased levels of social services—the carrot—in conjunction with focused suppression strategies—the stick. The result has been a lower level of serious gang violence among the targeted gangs than among comparable gangs in the area. The project also noted improvement in residents' perceptions of gang crime and police effectiveness in dealing with it. Chicago's anti-loitering ordinance is the necessary "stick" of an effective gang violence reduction equation. 13

ANTI-LOITERING LAWS ARE INEFFECTIVE AND BIASED
by David Cole

Expanding Your Vocabulary

The following words are important to your understanding of this essay. To help you add them to your vocabulary, write out a synonym and an example from your own experience for each new word.

anti-loitering: forbidding people to hang around in a public place without an obvious reason (title)

starkly: boldly (paragraph 1)

ordinance: law (paragraph 1)

due process: the requirement that laws treat all individuals fairly (paragraph 1)

discretion: personal judgment (paragraph 3)

empirical: theoretical (paragraph 4)

aldermen: members of the town council or governing board (paragraph 4)

apartheid regime: political system in which people of different races were separated (paragraph 4)

disparities: differences (paragraph 4)

invalidated: canceled (paragraph 5)

unfettered: free, unlimited (paragraph 6)

mores: moral attitudes (paragraph 6)

strictures: restraints and limits (paragraph 6)

discriminatory: biased, unfair (paragraph 6)

legitimacy: acceptance as lawful (paragraph 6)

cynicism: doubt, distrust (paragraph 6)

alienation: sense of not belonging (paragraph 6)

Kerner Commission: task force established by President Lyndon Johnson to investigate the causes of race riots (paragraph 7)

street sweeps: stopping and searching everyone on the street as if they are guilty of a crime (paragraph 7)

antithetical: opposing (paragraph 7)

carte blanche: complete freedom (paragraph 7)

impeding: blocking, obstructing (paragraph 7)

ANTI-LOITERING LAWS ARE INEFFECTIVE AND BIASED
by David Cole

1   Do "quality of life" policing and "community" policing, the law enforcement watchwords of the nineties, require the abandonment or dilution of civil rights and civil liberties? On December 9, 1998, the Supreme Court heard arguments in a case that starkly poses that question. At issue is a sweeping Chicago ordinance that makes it a crime for gang members or anyone associated with them merely to stand in public "with no apparent purpose." Chicago calls the offense "gang loitering," but it might more candidly be termed "standing while black." Sixty-six of the more than 45,000 Chicago citizens arrested for this offense in the three years that the law was on the books challenged its constitutionality, and in 1997 the Illinois Supreme Court unanimously ruled that it violated due process.

2   But the Supreme Court agreed to review that decision, and lined up in defense of the ordinance is not only the city of Chicago but also the United States, the attorneys general of 31 states, the National District Attorneys Association, the International Association of Chiefs of Police, the U.S. Conference of Mayors, and, perhaps most interesting, a pair of otherwise liberal University of Chicago law professors representing several Chicago neighborhood groups.

Disputing the Arguments for Loitering Laws

3   The ordinance's advocates argue that it played a critical role in making Chicago's high-crime neighborhoods safe and therefore served the interests of the minority poor

David Cole, "Anti-Loitering Laws are Ineffective and Biased." Reprinted with permission from the January 4, 1999 issue of *The Nation*. For subscription information, call 1-800-333-8536. Portions of each week's *The Nation* magazine can be accessed at http://www.thenation.com.

who live there. They suggest that strict constitutional standards need to be loosened in order to give police the discretion to engage in the day-to-day encounters of "quality of life" or "community" policing. Most astounding, they argue that criminal laws no longer must be clear in places where minority groups have a voice in the political process and can protect themselves. These arguments resonate with one commonly heard these days, particularly but not exclusively in [former] Mayor Rudolph Giuliani's New York City—namely, that heavy-handed police efforts directed at the inner city benefit minority residents by making their neighborhoods safer places in which to grow up, work, and live.

The arguments fail. First, as an empirical matter it is far from clear that the minority community in Chicago supported the law or that minority communities generally favor "quality of life" policing efforts that send so many of their residents to jail. The majority of Chicago's African-American aldermen voted against the ordinance; one representative, predicting that the law would be targeted at young black men, compared it to South Africa's apartheid regime. And voter turnout rates are so low in the inner city that it is difficult to say whether any elected official speaks for that community. The notion that minorities no longer need the protection of constitutional law simply ignores the racial disparities evident at every stage of the criminal justice system.

4

It is also not clear that the antigang law actually benefited anyone, much less Chicago's minority communities. Chicago did experience a falling crime rate while the law was in effect, but so did the rest of the nation. And the crime rate continued to fall after the ordinance was invalidated. So it is far from proven that arresting tens of thousands for standing in public had any positive effects.

5

Law Enforcement Must Build Trust

Most important, giving the police unfettered discretion to sweep the city streets of "undesirable" youth probably undermines safety by incurring distrust among those community members whose trust the police need most. The law's most powerful tool is its legitimacy. The more people believe the law is legitimate, the more likely they are to internalize its mores, obey its strictures, and cooperate with police. When laws are enforced in discriminatory ways, they lose their legitimacy. Cynicism and alienation about the criminal law are nowhere higher than among minorities and the urban poor, and laws like Chicago's only feed the alienation by inviting selective enforcement.

6

Indeed, law enforcement authorities and experts have long understood the importance of maintaining the community's faith and trust. Thirty years ago, the Kerner Commission reported that such support "will not be present when a substantial segment of the community feels threatened by the police and regards the police as an occupying force." The father of "quality of life" policing, George Kelling, has argued that street sweeps are antithetical to its goals precisely because they foster enmity, not community. And Attorney General Janet Reno has written that effective crime control requires "a greater sense of community and trust between law enforcement and the minority community." Yet her Justice Department, the City of Chicago, and the majority of our nation's state attorneys general fail to understand that you don't build trust by unleashing the police on minority communities with carte blanche to arrest anyone standing in public without an apparent purpose. Civil rights and civil liberties, far from impeding law enforcement, are critical to preserving its legitimacy.

7

Thinking Critically About Content

1. Make a list of the reasons, evidence, and statistics each writer uses to convince the reader of his position.

2. Explain how both writers use the anti-loitering laws in Chicago to argue different positions.

3. Which essay contains the most convincing evidence in your opinion? Why is it so convincing to you?

Thinking Critically About Purpose and Audience

4. What do you think the writers' purposes are in these essays?

5. What type of audience would be most interested in the subject of these two essays? Explain your answer.

6. If you changed your mind as a result of reading one of these essays, what in the essay caused the change?

Thinking Critically About Essays

7. State each writer's point of view in a single sentence.

8. How do both writers organize their essays? Make a rough outline of each essay to demonstrate your answer.

9. Which points do the two writers agree on? Which points do they disagree on? Explain your answer.

10. Write your own argument about the relationship between loitering and gang activity.

To keep track of your critical thinking progress, go to Appendix 1.

Writing Arguments

This section provides opportunities for you to apply what you have learned in this chapter to your writing. To this end, it furnishes a summary of the guidelines for writing an argument essay. Refer to the essays in this chapter for good examples of arguments. Finally, pause at the end of the chapter to reflect briefly on what you have learned.

Writing About Your Reading

1. "Who Gets the Break?" discusses the complex issues surrounding state subsidies for illegal immigrants in higher education. Choose another controversial subject related to higher education, and discuss its complexities in a way similar to Chu.

2. In "Wrong Call for Regulating Sexting," Huston tries to convince his readers that sexting is the result of a moral breakdown in our culture. Argue for or

Guidelines for Writing an Argument Essay

1. State your opinion on your topic in your thesis statement.
2. Find out as much as you can about your audience before you write.
3. Choose evidence that supports your thesis statement.
4. Anticipate opposing points of view.
5. Find some common ground.
6. Maintain a reasonable tone.
7. Organize your essay so that it presents your position as effectively as possible.

against Huston's stand on this issue. What do you think are the main causes of this new epidemic?

3. The two essays on social networking discuss the pros and cons of this new source of communication. Using the evidence in these two selections, write an essay explaining your position on this topic.

4. The next pro and con essays deal mainly with loitering as it relates to gang activity. Think of another strategy for fighting gang activity, and attempt to convince a group in authority to try your solution to the problem. Gather as much evidence as you can before you begin to write.

5. How can being able to develop good arguments and persuade people of your point of view help you in life? How might this ability give you the edge over other people on the job market?

Writing About Your World

1. Choose an ad and discuss its effectiveness. How does it appeal to its viewers? What line of reasoning does it follow? What would the ad say if it could talk directly to you?

2. We all have strong opinions on controversial issues. A newspaper or newscast might remind you of some of these subjects. Choose a current controversial issue, and, presenting your evidence in an essay, try to convince your class-mates that your opinion is right.

3. Write a letter to a potential employer for the job of your dreams, arguing that you are the best candidate for the job. Try to convince the employer not only that you are the perfect person for the job but also that you can take the position into new directions. Follow the format for a well-developed argument essay.

4. Persuade the leader of an organization that your position on an important topic affecting the organization is the best choice. To find a topic, think of your

own work experience, or talk to someone who has work experience. Organize your evidence as effectively as possible.

5. Create your own argument/persuasion assignment (with the help of your instructor), and write a response to it.

Revising

Small Group Activity (5–10 minutes per writer) Working in groups of three or four, read your argument essays to each other. Those listening should record their reactions on a copy of the Peer Evaluation Form in Appendix 2A. After your group goes through this process, give your evaluation forms to the appropriate writers so that each writer has two or three peer comment sheets for revising.

Paired Activity (5 minutes per writer) Using the completed Peer Evaluation Forms, work in pairs to decide what you should revise in your essay. If time allows, rewrite some of your sentences, and have your partner look at them.

Individual Activity Rewrite your paper, using the revising feedback you received from other students.

Editing

Paired Activity (5–10 minutes per writer) Swap papers with a classmate, and use the editing portion of your Peer Evaluation Form to identify as many grammar, punctuation, mechanics, and spelling errors as you can. If time allows, correct some of your errors, and have your partner look at them. Record your grammar, punctuation, and mechanics errors in the Error Log (Appendix 3) and your spelling errors in the Spelling Log (Appendix 4).

Individual Activity Rewrite your paper again, using the editing feedback you received from other students.

Reflecting on Your Writing When you have completed your own essay, answer these six questions.

1. What was most difficult about this assignment?

2. What was easiest?

3. What did you learn about arguing by completing this assignment?

4. What do you think are the strengths of your argument? Place a wavy line by the parts of your essay that you feel are very good.

5. What are the weaknesses, if any, of your paper? Place an X by the parts of your essay you would like help with. Write any questions you have in the margins.

6. What did you learn from this assignment about your own writing process—about preparing to write, about writing the first draft, about revising, and about editing?

Appendix 1: Critical Thinking Log

Circle the critical thinking questions you missed after each essay you read.
Have your instructor explain the pattern of errors.

Reading	Content	Purpose and Audience		Essays		Number Correct
Describing						
Amy Tan	1 2 3	4 5 6		7 8 9	10	
Alice Walker	1 2 3	4 5 6		7 8 9	10	
Mario Suarez	1 2 3	4 5 6		7 8 9	10	
Linda Hogan	1 2 3	4 5 6		7 8 9	10	
Narrating						
Sandra Cisneros	1 2 3	4 5 6		7 8 9	10	
Michael Arredondo	1 2 3	4 5 6		7 8 9	10	
Lynda Berry	1 2 3	4 5 6		7 8 9	10	
Stan Higgins	1 2 3	4 5 6		7 8 9	10	
Illustrating						
Chang-Rae Lee	1 2 3	4 5 6		7 8 9	10	
Brent Staples	1 2 3	4 5 6		7 8 9	10	
Richard Rodriguez	1 2 3	4 5 6		7 8 9	10	
France Borel	1 2 3	4 5 6		7 8 9	10	
Analyzing a Process						
Julia Bourland	1 2 3	4 5 6		7 8 9	10	
Russell Freedman	1 2 3	4 5 6		7 8 9	10	
Brian O'Connell	1 2 3	4 5 6		7 8 9	10	
David Levy	1 2 3	4 5 6		7 8 9	10	
Comparing and Contrasting						
Ernesto Galarza	1 2 3	4 5 6		7 8 9	10	
David Brooks	1 2 3	4 5 6		7 8 9	10	
Yi-Fu Tuan	1 2 3	4 5 6		7 8 9	10	
Tony Cohan	1 2 3	4 5 6		7 8 9	10	
Dividing and Classifying						
Camille Lavington	1 2 3	4 5 6		7 8 9	10	
Stephanie Ericsson	1 2 3	4 5 6		7 8 9	10	
Bernice Reagon	1 2 3	4 5 6		7 8 9	10	
Marion Winik	1 2 3	4 5 6		7 8 9	10	
Defining						
Gary Mack	1 2 3	4 5 6		7 8 9	10	
Jo Goodwin Parker	1 2 3	4 5 6		7 8 9	10	
Isaac Asimov	1 2 3	4 5 6		7 8 9	10	
Janice Castro	1 2 3	4 5 6		7 8 9	10	

Analyzing Causes and Effects										
Kristin Kalning	1	2	3	4	5	6	7	8	9	10
Corky Clifton	1	2	3	4	5	6	7	8	9	10
Linda Lee Andujar	1	2	3	4	5	6	7	8	9	10
Stacey Colino	1	2	3	4	5	6	7	8	9	10
Arguing										
Jeff Chu	1	2	3	4	5	6	7	8	9	10
Warner Todd Huston	1	2	3	4	5	6	7	8	9	10
Social Networking	1	2	3	4	5	6	7	8	9	10
Anti-Loitering Laws	1	2	3	4	5	6	7	8	9	10

The legend below will help you identify your strengths and weaknesses in critical thinking.

Legend for Critical Thinking Log	
Questions	**Skill**
1–2	Literal and interpretive understanding
3–6	Critical thinking and analysis
7–9	Analyzing sentences
10	Writing paragraphs

Appendix 2A: Revising

Peer Evaluation Form A

Use the following questions to evaluate your partner's essay in a particular rhetorical mode. Then, continue your evaluation with the standard revision items on the following pages. Direct your comments to your partner. Explain your answers as thoroughly as possible to help your partner revise.

WRITER: _____   PEER: _____

Describing

1. Is the dominant impression clearly communicated?
2. Does the essay use objective and subjective descriptions when needed?
3. Does the essay draw on all five senses?
4. Does the essay show rather than tell?

Narrating

1. What is the essay's main point? If you're not sure, show the writer how he or she can make the main point clearer.
2. Does the writer use the five Ws and one H to construct the essay? Where does the essay need more information?
3. Does the writer develop the essay with vivid details? Where can more details be added?
4. Does the writer build excitement with careful pacing?

Illustrating

1. What is the essay's main point? If you're not sure, show the writer how he or she can make the main point clearer.
2. Did the writer choose examples that are relevant to the main point? If not, which examples need to be changed?
3. Does the writer choose examples the reader can identify with? If not, which examples need to be changed?
4. Does the writer use a sufficient number of examples to make his or her point? Where can more examples be added?

Analyzing a Process

1. Does the writer state in the thesis statement what the reader should be able to do or understand by the end of the essay? If not, what information does the thesis statement need to be clearer?
2. Does the writer know his or her audience?
3. Does the remainder of the essay explain the rest of the process? If not, what seems to be missing?
4. Does the writer end the process essay by considering the process as a whole?

Comparing and Contrasting

1. Does the writer state the point he or she is trying to make in the thesis statement?
2. Does the writer choose items to compare and contrast that will make his or her point most effectively? What details need to be added to make the comparison more effective?
3. Does the writer use as many specific details and examples as possible to expand the comparison?
4. Is the comparison developed in a balanced way?

Dividing and Classifying

1. What is the overall purpose for the essay, and is it stated in the thesis statement? If not, where does the essay need clarification?
2. Did the writer divide the general topic into categories that don't overlap?
3. Did the writer clearly explain each category?
4. Does each topic fit into a category?

Defining

1. Did the writer choose a word or idea carefully and give readers a working definition of it in the thesis statement?
2. Does the writer define his or her term or idea by synonym, category, or negation? Is this approach effective? Why or why not?
3. Does the writer use examples to expand on his or her definition of the term or idea? Where does the definition need more information?
4. Does the writer use other rhetorical strategies—such as description, comparison, or process analysis—to support the definition?

Analyzing Causes and Effects

1. Does the thesis statement make a clear statement about what is being analyzed? If not, what information does it need to be clearer?
2. Did the writer choose facts and details to support the topic sentence? What details need to be added?
3. Does the writer confuse coincidence with causes or effects?
4. Does the writer include the real causes and effects for his or her topic? What details are unnecessary?

Arguing

1. Does the writer state his or her opinion on the subject matter in the thesis statement? What information is missing?
2. Who is the intended audience for this essay? Does the writer adequately persuade this audience? why or why not?
3. Does the writer choose appropriate evidence to support the thesis statement? What evidence is needed? What evidence is unnecessary?
4. Does the writer anticipate the opposing points of view?
5. Does the writer find some common ground?
6. Does the writer maintain a reasonable tone?

Peer Evaluation Form B

After applying the specialized questions in Peer Evaluation Form A to your partner's essay, use the following questions to help you complete the revision process. Direct your comments to your partner. Explain your answers as thoroughly as possible to help your partner revise.

WRITER: _____   PEER: _____

Thesis Statement

1. Does the thesis statement contain the essay's controlling idea and an opinion about that idea?
2. Does the thesis appear as the last sentence of the introduction?

Basic Elements

3. Does the essay have all the basic elements? Is each one effective?

Development

4. Does each paragraph support the thesis statement?
5. Does each paragraph contain enough specific details to develop its topic sentence?

Unity

6. Do all the essay's topic sentences relate directly to the thesis statement?
7. Do the details in each paragraph support its topic sentence?

Organization

8. Is the essay organized logically?
9. Is each body paragraph organized logically?

Coherence

10. Are transitions used effectively so that paragraphs move smoothly and logically from one to the next?
11. Do the sentences move smoothly and logically from one to the next?

Appendix 2B: Editing

Peer Evaluation Form

Use the following questions to help find editing errors in your partner's essay. Mark the errors directly on your partner's paper using the editing symbols on the inside back cover.

WRITER: _____   Peer: _____

Sentences

1. Does each sentence have a subject and a verb?

   Mark any fragments you find with **frag.**

   Put a slash (/) between any fused sentences and comma splices.

2. Do all subjects and verbs agree?

   Mark any subject-verb agreement errors you find with **sv.**

3. Do all pronouns agree with their nouns?

   Mark any pronoun errors you find with **pro agr.**

4. Are all modifiers as close as possible to the words they modify?

   Mark any modifier errors you find with **ad** (adjective or adverb problem), **mm** (misplaced modifier), or **dm** (dangling modifier).

Punctuation and Mechanics

5. Are sentences punctuated correctly?

   Mark any punctuation errors you find with the appropriate symbol under Unit 5 of the editing symbols (inside back cover).

6. Are words capitalized properly?

   Mark any capitalization errors you find with **lc** (lowercase) or **cap** (capital).

Word Choice and Spelling

7. Are words used correctly?

   Mark any words that are used incorrectly with **wc** (word choice) or **ww** (wrong word).

8. Are words spelled correctly?

   Mark any misspelled words you find with **sp.**

Appendix 3: Error Log

List any grammar, punctuation, and mechanics errors you make in your writing on the following chart. Then, to the right of this label, record (1) the actual error from your writing, (2) the rule for correcting this error, and (3) your correction.

Error		
	Example	I went to the new seafood restaurant and I ordered the shrimp.
Comma	**Rule**	Always use a comma before *and, but, for, nor, or, so,* and *yet* when joining two independent clauses.
	Correction	I went to the new seafood restaurant, and I ordered the shrimp.
Error	**Example**	
	Rule	
	Correction	
Error	**Example**	
	Rule	
	Correction	
Error	**Example**	
	Rule	
	Correction	
Error	**Example**	
	Rule	
	Correction	
Error	**Example**	
	Rule	
	Correction	
Error	**Example**	
	Rule	
	Correction	
Error	**Example**	
	Rule	
	Correction	
Error	**Example**	
	Rule	
	Correction	

Appendix 4: Spelling Log

On this chart, record any words you misspell, and write the correct spelling in the space next to the misspelled word. In the right column, write a note to yourself to help you remember the correct spelling. (See the first line for an example.) Refer to this chart as often as necessary to avoid misspelling the same words again.

Misspelled Word	Correct Spelling	Definition/Notes
there	their	there = place; their = pronoun; they're = "they are"

INDEX